Developing
Resilient
Organizations

Developing Resilient Organizations

How to create an adaptive, high-performance and engaged organization

Doug Strycharczyk and Charles Elvin

KoganPage

LONDON PHILADELPHIA NEW DELHI

First published in Great Britain and the United States in 2014 by Kogan Page Limited

2nd Floor, 45 Gee Street	1518 Walnut Street, Suite 1100	4737/23 Ansari Road
London EC1V 3RS	Philadelphia PA 19102	Daryaganj
United Kingdom	USA	New Delhi 110002
		India

www.koganpage.com

© Doug Strycharczyk and Charles Elvin, 2014

The right of Doug Strycharczyk and Charles Elvin to be identified as the authors of this work has been asserted by them in accordance with the Copyright, Designs and Patents Act 1988.

ISBN   978 0 7494 7009 8
E-ISBN 978 0 7494 7010 4

British Library Cataloguing-in-Publication Data

A CIP record for this book is available from the British Library.

Library of Congress Cataloging-in-Publication Data

Strycharczyk, Doug.
  Developing resilient organizations : how to create an adaptive, high-performance and engaged organization / Doug Strycharczyk, Charles Elvin. – 1st Edition.
     pages cm
     ISBN 978-0-7494-7009-8 (paperback) – ISBN 978-0-7494-7010-4 (ebk)   1. Organizational change.
     2. Employees – Training of. 3. Leadership. 4. Personnel management. I. Elvin, Charles.
     II. Title.
     HD58.8.S7947 2014
     658.3–dc23

                                                                                    2014016506

Typeset by Amnet
Print production managed by Jellyfish
Printed and bound by CPI Group (UK) Ltd, Croydon, CR0 4YY

CONTENTS

PART TWO   Practitioner perspectives 131

ABOUT THE AUTHORS

Editors and key authors

Doug Strycharczyk

Doug is CEO for AQR International, now recognized as one of the most innovative test publishers in the world. Doug has a background in organizational development (OD) and people development with global blue chip organizations. AQR publishes very accessible, reliable and valid measures and development programmes for mental toughness, leadership, personality and team working. The focus of AQR's and Doug's activity is on improving performance, well being and positive behaviours.

Working closely with Professor Peter Clough, he is recognized as a leading authority on the application of mental toughness in just about every sector of society and the economy. He is in demand as a speaker at conferences and seminars all over the world.

He has authored *Developing Mental Toughness* (Kogan Page, 2012) with Professor Clough and co-authored a chapter in *Coaching in Education* (Karnac, 2011).

Doug holds a first class honours degree in Economics. He is a Fellow of the Chartered Institute of Personnel Development and a member of the Institute for Leadership and Management. E-mail Doug at doug@aqr.co.uk.

Charles Elvin

Charles Elvin is the CEO of the Institute of Leadership and Management. The Institute of Leadership and Management is the United Kingdom's leading qualifications body for leadership, management and coaching development and a professional body supporting thousands of managers and leaders at every stage of their career. The Institute's wide-ranging research, which is free to access and use, has over the past years highlighted the essential importance of trust for leaders and managers to be successful. The Institute is part of the City and Guilds group of companies dedicated to effective education and its application into work. E-mail Charles at Charles.ELVIN@i-l-m.com.

Contributors

Jo Carruthers

Jo is Director of Academi Wales and has over 15 years' experience in leadership and organization development across both the public and private sectors. Working with boards, executive teams, senior leaders and public-appointed officials Jo is an experienced trainer and facilitator, holding a range of postgraduate qualifications and professional memberships in development and learning. Having trained at Harvard in the areas of leadership and management, Jo is an accredited 360°, mental toughness and emotional intelligence feedback coach. Jo can be contacted at jo.carruthers@wales.gsi.gov.uk.

Murray Clark

Murray is Principal Lecturer in Organization Theory and Research Methodology and the leader of the DBA programme at Sheffield Business School, Sheffield Hallam University. Prior to his academic career, after completing a PhD in Organizational Behaviour at Manchester Business School he was a manager for British Coal and is a qualified mining engineer. He is co-editor of *Business and Management Research Methodologies* (Sage Library in Business and Management, 2006), a co-contributor to *Research Methods for Managers* (Sage, 2010) and co-author of *The Dilemmas of Leadership* (Routledge, 2006). His research interests and other publications have centred mainly on the areas of trust and leadership. Murray can be contacted at m.c.clark@shu.ac.uk.

Professor Peter Clough

Peter is the Chair in Applied Psychology at the Manchester Metropolitan University. Formerly Head of Psychology, Associate Dean (Learning and Teaching) and Reader at the University of Hull, Peter is both a Chartered Sport Psychologist and a Chartered Occupational Psychologist. He is mainly focused on the application of psychology to performance enhancement. More specifically, he researches the area of mental toughness. The work started in the sports domain, but is now extensively used in both business and education. He is contactable at P.Clough@mmu.ac.uk.

Richard Cresswell

Richard is a Fellow of the Institute of Leadership and Management. His employment history includes working in the NHS as a nurse, a clinical manager and vocational training manager. Upon leaving the NHS he became a sole trader delivering environmental, quality and health and safety consultancy. In 2001 he co-founded Learning For Business Ltd. As Managing Director, alongside strategic partners such as Citrix Online and the Institute of Leadership and Management, he delivers UK-regulated qualifications and provides consultancy services both in the United Kingdom and overseas. Key interests include enabling change plus organizational sustainability through ethics. Contact Richard at r.cresswell@learningforbusiness .co.uk.

Andrew Cuthbert

Andrew is a young entrepreneur in the technology space. His background focuses mainly on education and healthcare but his background has spanned the birth of 'social media'. He has an active involvement in the provision of enterprise-level development services supported by his team of technologists. Andrew regularly contributes to his blog at **www.andrewcuthbert .co.uk** and can be contacted at andrew@andrewcuthbert.co.uk.

Dr Fiona Earle

Fiona is a Chartered Occupational Psychologist and Psychology Lecturer at the University of Hull working in the field of Work and Well-being. Fiona specializes in stress, workload and fatigue. With significant consultancy experience, she has expertise in the design of assessment centres, development of bespoke psychometric instruments and management development. E-mail Fiona at F.Earle@hull.ac.uk.

Dr Keith Earle

Keith is a Chartered Sport and Exercise Psychologist working as a senior lecturer at the University of Hull. He is both an active researcher and an applied sport psychologist, working with athletes from a wide range of sports. Keith is the co-developer with Professor Peter Clough of the mental toughness model. Contact Keith at K.Earle@hull.ac.uk.

Rob Noble

Rob is Chief Executive of The Leadership Trust Foundation. He joined the organization in February 2011, after a period with Goldman Sachs in London running equity operations teams. Previously he completed 18 years' service in the British Army where he gained significant operational experience leading tours of duty in Northern Ireland, Sierra Leone, Iraq and Afghanistan. While in the Army Rob specialized in strategic planning and training. Rob has a strong belief that leadership should be seen at all levels of an organization and that unlocking hidden potential is key. Rob is a governor of the Robert Owen Vocational School. Rob can be contacted at RobNoble@leadership.org.uk.

Dr John Perry

John is a Senior Lecturer in Sport and Exercise Psychology at Leeds Trinity University. John is a Chartered Psychologist and an accredited Sport and Exercise Scientist. His published research includes the development of a new model of sportspersonship, examining coping in sport, statistical methods in psychology and mental toughness. John can be contacted at J.Perry@leedstrinity.ac.uk.

Sue Pinder

Sue was awarded an OBE for services to further education. In addition to serving as Principal of two colleges in Scotland, she made a lasting contribution to the development of the college sector in a number of sector leadership roles including Chair of Scotland's Colleges' Principals' Forum. Other senior appointments have included Founding Director of Learning at the Scottish University for Industry. Her passion for helping people to grow and develop now finds expression through her work in management development. E-mail Sue at susan.pinder@tesco.net.

Raymond Robertson

Raymond began his professional life as a teacher prior to moving into politics. In this latter role, he served variously as MP, Chair of the Scottish Conservative and Unionist Party and UK Government Minister. He is a founding director of Halogen Communications Ltd, a leading-edge political and public relations consultancy with offices in Edinburgh and Washington DC. E-mail Raymond at raymond@halogencom.com.

Jo Shuttlewood

Jo is the lead coach and founder of Perform-In-Business. Jo, with her experienced team of psychologically-trained coaches, delivers authentic leadership programmes and coaching for leaders and their teams. Her work centres around mental toughness, emotional intelligence and Time To Think practices. She is a Time To Think facilitator, helping leaders save time through the practice of efficient, crisp thinking. Jo can be contacted at jo@performib.com.

Zoe Sweet

Zoe is the Director of Organizational Development at Academi Wales, responsible for the delivery of the Academi Wales portfolio of learning and development interventions in leadership, management and organizational development. Zoe is currently researching a PhD in mental toughness and resilience in public service leadership and has published and presented at the British Academy of Management and Organizational Development Network Europe academic conferences. Zoe is a qualified mental toughness, emotional intelligence and leadership psychometrics assessor. Zoe can be contacted at zoe.sweet@wales.gsi.gov.uk.

Dr Craig Thomson

Craig has worked in school, further and higher education in the United Kingdom and internationally. Publications have included analysis of the college sector in Scotland and the role of mental toughness in improving college student performance. His doctoral research covered the use of ICT in learning in small businesses. He worked as principal of two colleges in Scotland prior to moving into the private sector where his business interests included tourism and hospitality and management development. E-mail Craig at craig@at-the-shore.co.uk.

Professor Sharon Turnbull

Sharon is Associate Head of Research at The Leadership Trust in Ross-on-Wye, United Kingdom. She is also Visiting Professor at the University of Gloucestershire Business School and the University of Worcester Business School, as well as being a Senior Research Fellow at Lancaster University Management School. She has published widely on leadership and organizational change. She is contactable at sharonturnbull4@gmail.com.

ACKNOWLEDGEMENTS

Our work in this area for the past 15 years has brought us into contact with many inspirational and supportive people. Sometimes they are clients, sometimes collaborators and sometimes they have challenged our thinking.

They are the people who we thank most warmly. Many are contributors to this book and so their names are revealed. They deserve special thanks for giving their time and their ideas so generously. We don't intend to name others. The list is now too long and there is a risk that we might omit someone we should have included.

In terms of getting this job done Doug wishes to take the opportunity to thank his colleague Monika Czwerenko. This is the third book on which she has provided support and is becoming quite expert at this. Her tenacity and commitment to bringing together this piece of work from very busy people is quite exceptional. As is the drive she brings to AQR.

We also wish to thank our editor, Liz Gooster, who has been both remarkably patient and very supportive.

Finally, Doug offers his dedication to his colleague Claudine Rowlands who has supported and encouraged him in creating a special business. AQR is 25 years old this year. We intend it to be a resilient organization well into the 21st century and beyond.

Charles wishes to take this opportunity to thank his wife Alex and his two boys Samuel and Dominic for their continued support of his work in researching and promoting the importance of effective management and high-quality leadership.

Also published by Kogan Page

Developing Mental Toughness: Improving performance, wellbeing and positive behaviour in others

by Peter Clough and Doug Strycharczyk

Mental toughness is about how effectively individuals respond to stress, pressure and challenge. Understanding this concept is essential to improving performance for both the individual and organization, and this groundbreaking book explains mental toughness clearly and effectively. Tracing its development from sports psychology into the world of business, health and education, *Developing Mental Toughness* is the first book to look at mental toughness and its application at the organizational level.

Written for anyone coaching individuals and teams for improved performance, *Developing Mental Toughness* contains practical guidance on delivering techniques that will radically improve people's abilities to harness the effects of stress and pressure.

Learn how to:

- assess mental toughness in individuals and organizations
- improve your own ability to deal with stress
- build a range of techniques required to recognize, use and develop mental toughness

Full of sample exercises and case studies, this book also features the Mental Toughness Questionnaire – a unique self-assessment tool to determine your mental toughness score.

ISBN: 978 0 7494 6377 9

Introduction
What is the purpose of this book?

What can a healthy and successful organization at the start of the 21st century do to give themselves the best chance of still being healthy and successful at the start of 22nd century? What are the components of organizational resilience? What do leaders need to think about, address and act on?

Learned lessons from the past have always been important and valuable and certainly change has happened before... many times. However, relying on previous experience is unlikely to be enough. Changes in societies, attitudes, technologies, our understanding of leadership and our understanding of human psychology mean that the challenges organizations face will probably be unlike any challenges they have faced before.

This book is split into two parts. Part One provides a picture of the 21st century and its challenges, concerning the issues of individual and organizational resilience and for leadership in particular. They are connected.

Part Two provides a collection of views and essays on subjects that the authors, all significant contributors in their fields of expertise, see as vital for organizations to address in order to achieve success and survival in an environment which is ever-changing and contains more unknowns than ever before.

These are by no means comprehensive. We see issues and opportunities emerge almost daily. They are designed to illustrate the need for thinking about the future. They can also be read independently but we think they are better understood within the context of the book's title.

Nor are all the views expressed here supported by all the contributing authors and editors. They are not. But it is important to be open to all of these ideas and thoughts. They illustrate the point that there are different futures possible for the same or similar organizations.

If there is one unifying theme it is the need for a special kind of resilience that we are beginning to know as mental toughness. This represents a proactive expression of resilience. Described more fully in Professor Peter Clough's chapter, it is the difference between gritting your teeth in the face of adversity and change and welcoming change and embracing all the opportunities that this brings with it no matter how uncomfortable the journey. If individuals need to be mentally tough then, equally, so do organizations in how they address both opportunities and challenges.

Similarly, themes such as trust have emerged as vital for organizations to ensure they are not only thinking about but actively addressing. All the themes in the book interrelate and connect even though they have been written about separately.

Ultimately, this book is intended to provide a diverse set of perspectives and case studies, all of which seek to challenge readers to ask the same questions of their organization: what do you think lies ahead for your organization, how are you going to think about it and what will you need to do differently to survive?

The role of all leaders of organizations is to steer their people and their organization into the future. That necessarily means trying to predict the future. We aren't here to predict everyone's future. We can't do that. We are here to provoke thinking about your future.

If, on reading this book, you agree with some or all of it, or disagree with it all, we have achieved a big part of our goal. And if you are so inclined, we would be delighted to hear your thoughts, ideas and responses to those expressed here. We have created a dedicated LinkedIn group so that anyone who is interested in contributing to this exciting theme of developing resilient organizations can 'link in' with other like minds.

You can access the group by scanning the QR code below.

PART ONE
Change in the 21st century

A general overview
Developing resilient organizations –
why should it concern us?

DOUG STRYCHARCZYK

In the beginning...

At the beginning of the 21st century there was generally a feeling of contentment around the world. True, there were still wars and conflicts going on and some perennial problems such as poverty were still around – much remained to be done to create a fairer world. But it could be argued that most economies and societies seemed to be developing nicely or had reason to be moderately optimistic.

In fact, now long forgotten, the issue that most concerned almost everyone was something that came to be called the 'Millennium Bug'. For some reason only known to the geeky, it was believed that every piece of electronic equipment would stop working at midnight on 31 December 1999. It created a temporary industry that occupied hundreds of thousands of IT experts around the world.

To the disappointment of the IT community and to everyone else's relief, nothing untoward happened on that date. Computers, cooker timers, watches continued to work pretty much as they had the day before. Many concluded that it was a false alarm – everything continued to work perfectly well. No one even had to reboot anything. Some in the IT industry will claim that it was their diligence and preparation that eliminated the problem and that's why nothing untoward happened.

There was even a feeling that, at last, leaders in all walks of life had learned how to manage economies, societies and businesses in such a way that we were unlikely to know crisis or recession again. Politicians, economists and business leaders were being credited with an increasing mastery of the world in which we lived, worked and played.

Within a few years this view had changed quite dramatically. By 2008 much of the so-called 'developed world' had plunged rapidly into recession. Not just any recession but one that was to become one of the worst for a century. For the next few years, dealing with the fallout from this became the main preoccupation of global leaders. The blame for this recession was, probably quite rightly, placed at the feet of the global financial community, which had adopted inappropriate, sometimes unethical and mostly unsustainable practices.

It has become normal to describe this period from 2008 onwards as a recession. When economists talk about a recession, they often describe it in terms of contractions of the gross GDP of an economy over a period of time. That might describe what is happening. It doesn't explain why contractions are happening. That is the more interesting question. History tells us that economists are often also talking about the economy going through a period of transition or change. A recession can be an indication that something no longer works well, that something has stopped working or that circumstances are now different and it is time to adapt. The change is usually significant and generally represents something that might be fundamental, important and which has to happen quickly.

In fact, change happens all the time and usually most types of change happen steadily and incrementally. It is often imperceptible and most people, societies and organizations take it in their stride. Even when it is sudden and dramatic, eg when a piece of new technology like the iPad is developed, it can be welcomed with open arms and adopted with astonishing speed without any significant detrimental impact.

The 2008 financial crisis signalled a need for change and it is true that a response to the challenge was an urgent requirement. However, with it came a host of consequences that meant it had a significant and negative impact on the lives of many. Most of the populations in developed countries found their standards of living dropping when for most of the previous 20–30 years these had risen steadily year on year. The ability to create enterprises and re-build economies was hampered by a shortage of capital and a reluctance to invest on the part of many of those who did have capital. One of the curious facts about the 2008 financial crisis is that many big businesses actually built strong cash reserves during this period as they 'battened down the hatches'.

The impact of these changes on most people was severe – most simply didn't know how to deal with them. There were whole generations who only knew about recession and its impact from reading about it in books. So, for the immediate period post-2008, politicians, economists, bankers and business leaders were preoccupied with repairing global financial systems so they would eventually work again.

Important as this was, it wasn't the only aspect of change that had been underway. Some of these other aspects are equally significant and will have a long-term and dramatic impact on the lives of every person on the planet. The global financial crisis appears to have hidden from sight, at least temporarily, a series of other fundamental changes which will impact on the way society works.

These changes are taking place in our workplaces as well as around the world. They impact on the way organizations work and the way people will work in the future. Both are interrelated. People are changing, business is changing, the way we see responsibility and accountability is changing and the way the different peoples of the world interact is changing.

The challenge with this is that change usually has to be managed or handled in some way so that most people can benefit. To do that there are two requirements.

- First, it is essential to notice change, to be aware of its direction and to understand it.
- Second is to understand the consequences of change, which will also often mean looking over the horizon and trying to anticipate further change.

There is probably also a third requirement. Change for most people is, by its nature, often uncomfortable, requiring people, organizations and societies to change the way they see things and the way they behave. There is a need to embrace and to welcome change. It is going to happen anyway. The net effect is almost always positive. It is this notion that underpins what this book is about.

There are two types of organization that emerge: the survivors who have managed to cope in some way with what has happened and those who thrive. The latter have learned to deal with what is happening and see opportunity in the chaos and mayhem where the former mainly see threat.

We, the authors and editors, spend a good deal of our time working with leaders in just about every sector of global society and in the course of our work we travel widely. Our observations are global observations.

In a recession, not everyone suffers. Even in the midst of recession we see that some players are holding their heads above water and some are thriving. Not everyone is desolate and on the brink of disaster. Those in secure, reasonably well-paid jobs can enjoy a recession as their comparative position improves over those who either become unemployed or who have jobs which are not so good and often have had pay frozen for many years. Moreover, this is true even for organizations that operate within the same sector. Many firms and organizations fail in the very same sectors where others have survived.

In the United Kingdom, several household names in the retail world have disappeared from the high street (or the internet if that was where they did their business). At the same time some of their competitors selling the same types of goods and services have gone from strength to strength. In retail, UK business John Lewis has prospered throughout the period of recession while many retailers have gone to the wall. John Lewis is by no means a 'bargain retailer': it is not succeeding by cutting prices, it appears to be succeeding with a better offer than its competitors and with much better levels of customer service. Interestingly, John Lewis is a partnership. All staff are partners in the business. Charles will present a view that the level of trust which underpins this employment relationship is a significant factor in their success.

On another part of the UK high street, grocery retail, we do see a 'budget' factor. The growth of inexpensive food retailers such as Lidl, Netto and Aldi has been at the expense of the traditional giants on the high street. Their promise has been one of good quality at the lowest prices.

So the global financial crisis has provided a challenge and a threat to all organizations. But why do some continue to do well and others don't? It can't just be that the recession has affected some more dramatically than others (although that may be a factor in some situations). It might also be the case that not every economy and society is responding in the same way to what is happening in the wider world.

It is not the recession that determines whether we sink or swim, it is our response to it that matters. As we'll see, this is precisely why mental toughness is a key factor in organizational success. Those that respond positively and adapt to the world as it changes will survive. This is 'organizational Darwinism'.

It continues to surprise (and disappoint) that so many leaders of organizations in the private and public sectors can be very parochial. An astonishing number of these seem unaware of what is happening across the world and hold views that are dangerously out of date. Before we hear howls of indignation, we have to add that there are many leaders who do notice change and how it affects their organizations. Some are extremely alert, seem to be constantly evaluating what is happening around them and are ready to change and develop as circumstances dictate. These are the business leaders whose organizations will emerge thriving when the recession ends.

But they appear to be in the minority.

We will dwell for a moment longer on the subject of recessions. They are not unusual. In fact any backward glance at the last 250 years will reveal that recessions happen fairly frequently. Many economists argue that they are cyclical. Sometimes they are comparatively mild. Sometimes they are severe, plunging whole countries into depression.

Recessions nearly always represent a period of what Joseph Schumpeter called 'creative destruction'. To summarize his work in a few sentences, Schumpeter (1947) theorized that economies develop and grow through business cycles that at some point result in a period of creative destruction. The provocation for this is innovation (ie change) and the agent for innovation, he suggested, is entrepreneurialism. He wrote about two types of entrepreneur: the wild thinker who comes up with new ideas and the large corporation that has the resources to invest in research and development.

Schumpeter suggested that capitalism has within it the seeds of a process where old ways are ousted and replaced with new ways of doing things. He further hypothesized that one of the benefits of capitalism is that education would no longer be only available to a privileged group but would instead become available to everyone who wants it. In turn, this would lead to a much larger group of people having the intellectual capability to challenge the status quo. He argued that this, together with a shortage of fulfilling work for this bigger intellectual group, would lead to a form of discontent, and that one potential outcome would be the 'demise' of full-on capitalism and its replacement by a 'democratic' or 'liberal' capitalism where a new set of values emerges.

This is not new thinking. His most famous work was published in 1942! We'll look at his ideas at several points in this book. What Schumpeter did was show us one way of looking at what is happening around us and forecasting the future. He wrote in the context of his time.

Ultimately Schumpeter presents us with the Darwinian picture offered earlier. The world evolves and changes and, like the species that interested Darwin (2011), those that survive are those who best adapt to change. There has to be some imperative for change, which often comes from innovation. As in business and commerce, it is not actually fitness or size or strength that matters. It is the ability of species to adapt to what is happening around them that determines how they survive and develop.

Coming back to recession and periods of change, there is another interesting observation that can be made. All recessions come to an end at some time. They always have and probably always will. Almost as if by magic, there emerge organizations and businesses who are busy getting on with the business of business and who set about creating jobs, wealth etc.

Sometimes these organizations and businesses will always have been there. They will already have been well suited to adapt – perhaps they are more efficient than their rivals, perhaps they have a better sense of what their market needs. Sometimes they will be new, rising from the ashes, adopting more modern methods and new technologies without a need to remove the old.

Sure enough, during a period of upheaval you will hear the squeals and cries from those that are suffering and whose lives and positions are being threatened and damaged. You won't hear those noises coming from those who are making headway though. They will simply be getting on with it. Magically they emerge and become the next generation of successful enterprises. But of course there is no magic involved.

So what is this book about?

It is not about the 2008 global financial crisis. That had a specific set of issues that received an extraordinary amount of attention.

We believe that there is a series of interrelated changes occurring in global society that represent a much more fundamental set of changes to which everyone must adapt or 'perish'. Some are definable, some are debatable and some have their roots in the past. But they are all happening now.

The purpose of the book is not to identify everything that may be bringing about change and may bring about change in the future. The aim of the book is to provoke thinking about how we can make organizations resilient. It is necessarily forward-looking and speculative. But that's what all managers and leaders should be anyway.

Most management books, quite usefully, look back at what has happened before to review and to identify what can be learned from past events. These don't have to be mistakes, they can be successes too. This approach creates a lot of learning, some of which is useful and some of which is of debatable value. It is important to understand that these analyses are not necessarily independent or objective. Their process is potentially limited by the way evidence is collected, the type of evidence that is gathered and the way it is analysed.

There is value in a systematic, analytical approach. There is also room for insight and intuition. But it is still difficult to gather evidence about the future let alone the present.

A significant portion of the book presents a more detailed discussion of some of the factors that are becoming increasingly important but are as yet still rarely discussed. The book also contains case studies from a range of organizations that have lifted their heads and looked over the horizon. They have begun to put in place processes, actions and development activities that address what they believe lies ahead. Most are global organizations, which gives them an advantage in that they are more likely to be naturally aware of the 'big picture'. But most organizations are not global in their activities, their approaches and in their thinking – and perhaps now need to be.

There is an interesting and consistent element in all of the approaches described in the case studies. Where leaders cannot forecast what lies ahead, they all seem to understand the need to develop a particular quality in their workforces and their organizations: an attitude towards the future and the unknown that is positive about *whatever* lies ahead. These organizations welcome the unknown and the opportunity to push back boundaries. They also see setbacks and problems as ordinary occurrences which, although can be inconvenient and sometimes damaging, have simply to be dealt with. They won't stop them.

Jim Collins in *Good to Great* (2001) identifies pretty much the same thing. He looks very specifically at organizations that have achieved sustained success over a long period of time. Certainly long enough to have known the downs as well as the ups of commercial life. In *Good to Great* he notes that 'The Good to Great companies faced as much adversity as the comparison companies, but they responded to that adversity differently. They hit the realities of their situation head on. As a result, they emerged from adversity even stronger.' He goes on to add that 'a key psychology for leading from good to great is... retain absolute faith that you can and will prevail in the end regardless of the difficulties, AND, at the same time confront the brutal facts of your current reality, whatever they might be.'

There is an important message here. There is no walk of life that doesn't involve facing difficulty at some time. If you are not to be overwhelmed by it and go under, there is little option but to confront it. And mindset is important here. Facing up to adversity and difficulty doesn't have to be threatening. Adversity can and usually is an opportunity. Great companies can even welcome adversity!

Of course mindset belongs to the people in an organization. Elsewhere in his book, Collins identifies getting the right people on board as the priority. He notes that the most successful organizations make sure they have the right people on board, with the right 'character traits and innate capabilities', before they attend to what they need to do (vision, strategy, execution and so on).

Later we will see that what Collins called character traits and innate capabilities is what we call mental toughness and that this is fundamentally important to being able to deal effectively and positively with change and challenge.

A word about the authors and editors

Doug is an economist by training. He has maintained a significant interest in economics throughout his working life and it shapes most of his interests. One of the things that most intrigues him is the creation and distribution of wealth in its widest sense. When we look to the future we are told that the global population will grow from the present estimated 7.2 billion to around 9.6 billion by 2050 (UN News Centre, accessed 9 June 2013). Given that much of the world is in comparative poverty, there is a challenge to create enough wealth to enable everyone to achieve at least an acceptable standard of living where mortality rates are reasonable and life is better. Of course there is more than one type of solution to this challenge. All have upsides and downsides.

Doug has spent most of the past 20 years working with Professor Peter Clough to take Clough's model of mental toughness and apply it to every area where people have to be mentally active – whether it is work, play, learning, engaging with each other. Increasingly they have begun to understand how important the concept of mental toughness is and that it can contribute to the development of society as well as organizations and individuals.

Charles Elvin is the CEO of the Institute of Leadership and Management and an outspoken and public advocate of the importance of effective management and high-quality leadership for organizations and the people within them. Great managers and leaders grow business.

Charles' background has moved him through a range of industries, from banking to higher education, and countries, having lived in Japan, Malaysia, Switzerland and the United States, while always working within the education, learning and development field. Having graduated from university just before the development of the world wide web, Charles was an early adopter of and enthusiast for the opportunities online technologies present to enhance the possibilities of access to education and learning experiences.

The Mental Toughness Questionnaire (MTQ48) is a short, valid and reliable measure that assesses mental toughness in individuals and in organizations. It will be explored more fully in Chapter 3. Mental toughness is a major theme running through this book.

The Integrated Leadership Model (ILM) is a unique concept pulling together almost all thinking about leadership under one umbrella. The

ILM72 is the integrated leadership measure that measures adopted leadership style and leadership effectiveness. Developed initially with support from the Institute of Leadership and Management, it assesses the six aspects of leadership style and the three core competences for leadership effectiveness. Leadership is something that is also a recurring theme in this book.

So what are the changes in so far as they impact on a successful 21st century business? That's what we examine in the next chapter. They fall under several broad headings. These may in fact be headings that could have applied at any time in the last 500 years. The content under these headings is shifting though, as is their relative importance in the scheme of things and it is the speed at which all of this is shifting that creates challenge for the 21st century organization.

We are focusing on the following because, in our view, they are among the most important and they are interconnected.

- Leadership – understanding the new follower, trust and the need to grasp what we mean by ethics and ethical behaviour.

- Technology – understanding what kind of change is emerging, what its implications are as well as understanding how to harness what technological change can offer.

- Curiosity – 'no one is an island': The need to be inquisitive about what is happening everywhere. The West is no longer the source of most developments.

- Creativity – capturing and using our own creative power and the creative power of those around us.

References

Collins, J (2001) *Good To Great: Why some companies make the leap... and others don't*, Random House Business, London

Darwin, C (2011) *On the Origin of the Species*, Emporia Books, Kansas

Schumpeter, J A (1947) *Capitalism, Socialism and Democracy*, Allen and Unwin, London

UN News Centre [accessed 9 June 2013] *World population projected to reach 9.6 billion by 2050* [Online] http://www.un.org/apps/news/story.asp?NewsID=45165#.UvtnCPvU-us

The new factors

What are some of the challenges facing organizations in the 21st century? What do we believe might be coming over the horizon?

02

DOUG STRYCHARCZYK

This chapter examines some, and only some, of the factors that present a challenge to organizations and societies in the 21st century. We think these are the main challenges that no organization can afford to ignore.

The employee relationship

What does the employee relationship presently look like, how is it evolving and what kind of relationship might we see developing between an employer and an employee over the 21st century?

The first and, in some ways, primary development of the 21st century has been the emergence of individuals in all societies who are very different to individuals from previous generations. Observers and social scientists have noted this and it has come to be described as the 'Generation Y' and 'Generation Z' phenomena. We originally wrote that this was an obvious development, because we found so many references to it in books and articles, only to find that when speaking to business leaders, most knew the terms but didn't actually know what they meant.

At AQR, we have lost count of the number of times we have been consulted in recent years by senior executives in well-known organizations who bemoan the attitude and behaviour of 'young people'. We are often asked to help the complaining executive to change their staff and new entrants, who are variously described as demanding, unreasonably aspirational and difficult to manage, so that they can be 'more effective' employees. The answer of course is that a different kind of change is needed. It is the executive who needs to change. What the executive is really asking for is a more compliant and less demanding employee. That person is an increasingly rare beast.

The reality is that young people entering the job market these days are different to those who entered the job market 20 years ago, even, it is suggested, 10 years ago. First, they are better educated generally in the sense that many, many more go on to further and higher education than ever before. A study by the Department for Business, Innovation and Skills in the United Kingdom showed the proportion of people who entered the higher education system in the autumn of 2008 amounted to 45 per cent of all young people aged 18–19. In 1968, only 40 years earlier, that figure was around 5 per cent.

Digging more deeply into the statistics reveals that in 2008 more than half (51 per cent) of all young women were entering higher education, having overtaken males of whom comparatively fewer, 40 per cent, were entering higher education. This represents a trend within a trend.

Moreover, these overall figures mask another set of differences. Participation rates of young people entering high education also varied according to where the individual lived. In some areas participation rates reached 80 per cent! In other areas they were extremely low.

This is true internationally too. Globally the picture is similarly one of increasing participation rates and improving education standards.

So to some extent Schumpeter was right. Eventually more people have become better educated. Remember he thought that this would create problems because there would not be enough interesting work to satisfy the needs of this more able workforce.

Second, the most recent generation entering the workforce are usefully described as 'digital natives' as opposed to being 'digital visitors'. Just as a young person learns a language naturally because they are brought up in an environment where speaking that language is the norm, so they become familiar and comfortable with technology in the same way. They are completely at home with technology and technological change.

This brings two immediate and major benefits: their access to knowledge and expertise is in a totally different league to graduates of their parents' generation and also they know how to use technology to do and make things. Given that technological change is a significant factor in determining both the type and pace of change, this ability to handle technological change is important and valuable.

A digital visitor is like the person who moves to another country and must learn a new language to be able to engage in that society. That language will generally always be a second language for them, with some loss of fluency. The native speaker will always have the edge over a visitor.

Third, they are simply better informed about what is happening in the world and the quality of that information is much, much better. It is arguably harder to manipulate information now. In the 1960s, most people, if they had access to television, would watch a newsreel about world events such as the war in Vietnam. This was always several days old and it was censored and edited. It was difficult to know what was truly happening in the world. Nowadays if something happens on the other side of the globe, someone is there with a camera phone recording it and posting on the world wide web in minutes.

This can still mean that information can be manipulated but it is much more difficult to hide things now. It can also mean that we are often presented with multiple versions of the 'truth' and need to evaluate these and exercise judgement in a way that wasn't needed 50 years ago. It might be that this is a reason why trust is rising on the agenda for most organizations. In assessing information coming from different sources, the extent to which someone trusts the source of information or the messenger may influence the extent to which they will accept and adopt the source's ideas, values and visions.

This combination of factors means that young people entering employment now have a very different view of their place in the world. They can have a better understanding of what the world has to offer.

It is dangerous to generalize and it is certainly true that there are many different descriptions of the Generation Y and Generation Z cohorts. Not only do the definitions vary according to the observer but they differ according to locality. The behaviour of western Gen Ys is quite different in many ways to those in the East. But some patterns are emerging:

- They are much less likely to believe in a 'job for life'. Many don't even want this. They want to do different things at different times.
- They are less likely to be 'loyal' to a company and more likely to be loyal to a person.
- They will be more inclined to support a good boss who understands their needs.
- Most will look for a job with a purpose that provides intrinsic motivation. Arguably this is a result of exposure to global news. They seem to have a greater sense of social responsibility than previous generations – and trust politicians less.
- They are flexible in the way they work and are more adept at multitasking. Technology enables them to deal with several things at a time. They will expect flexibility in the workplace.

- They are often more questioning and less likely to accept what they are told.

- They are able to deal with large amounts of data and they work quickly. They are generally brighter than previous generations.

- They routinely use social media and expect quick responses when they do. Waiting for e-mails is not acceptable in the Gen Y/Z world.

- They learn in a different way. They are less keen on classroom-based learning. They are keener on digital technologies, especially those that use visual approaches.

- They prefer to learn by doing. They prefer interactive media rather than passive media (eg watching a TV programme or film).

- They know how to access global knowledge quickly. Finding things out is rarely a challenge.

- They are used to collaborating with others. They network freely. They don't expect to solve problems on their own.

- They have high expectations – some of which might not be realistic.

- They may be very flexible in their thinking and the way they work – and they expect employers to be flexible too.

- Importantly, they are much more likely to accept diversity wherever they find it.

- Their interests and motivations can be different. Fewer are interested in home ownership, preferring the flexibility that goes with renting (or even living with Mum and Dad for longer).

These are features that are generally positive, at least they are from the young person's perspective (although some have a downside). Many of these features are driven by developments in IT.

There are also negative features that some are beginning to identify:

- They are generally less healthy because they spend more time at a desk and on a PC, iPad, etc.

- Their involvement in gaming teaches them that when something goes wrong they can put it right by pressing a reset button. Real life doesn't have a reset button.

- Their ability to work quickly can mean they also make more mistakes.

- They will, on average, probably earn less (in real terms) than their parents did over their lifetime.

There are more features that others may bring into the picture and some may argue about the features listed above. However, the probability is that new entrants to the workforce are different in knowledge, skills and especially mindset to previous generations. The most important of these is mindset. If knowledge is easy to access and skills can be learned in many more ways than before, it is mindset that represents a challenge for everyone.

So it is not too difficult to become aware that people today are different to people in previous generations. In fact, many become aware of this subconsciously because they either like or dislike some feature of a current generation. They can't always put their finger on what that change is and they can't always define or articulate it. Identifying these features represents only one aspect of change.

What is important is that organizations and those who lead them consider:

- How fast is the situation changing? How does it link to other aspects of change (and maybe different types of change)?

- What's next? Is there anything I should be able to foresee – even if it's only in the near future?

- What does it mean for me? What is the challenge for me as an individual?

and if you are an employer:

- What does it mean for the way I will develop and run my organization?

Our experience is that few business leaders and managers take enough time to think about these questions – especially the last one. And it's not surprising. If you have learned your leadership and management skills and behaviours in previous generations and you have successfully learned, over the years, to solve yesterday's people problems then this might not be the greatest preparation for solving problems in the present situation, let alone future situations.

For the sake of adding some structure we can group the things we need to think about into three or four areas.

What is the nature of change?

In the western world, if we look at the 1960s through to the 1980s it was commonplace to talk about change and about resistance to change.

Individuals, organizations and societies found that change was something that happened to them and the primary requirement was to respond to it. Surviving change was the overriding goal and the focus was on accepting change as inevitable and sometimes painful.

Many organizations and institutions such as employers and trade unions tried to resist change, with the result being that the issue became a battle about resisting change rather than understanding change and managing it effectively. It often led to clumsy action when it became inevitably necessary to change. Redundancy would be badly handled and became something to be feared – it would often be associated with feelings of shame. Activities like this contributed to the sense that change was something to be avoided.

Gradually a continuous improvement ethos began to creep into leadership and management practice and we can see the widespread adoption of systematic approaches and total quality management (TQM) from the 1980s to the present day. Much of this was still focused on how to manage change, but at least change began to be seen as something that was recognized as a normal part of business life. From being a negative it became something that was just part of the landscape. It became neutral.

However, that's not true of all organizations and societies and doesn't fully explain the accelerating pace of change. Change is increasingly being perceived as a positive. At its least it helps to identify where organizations need to develop in order to improve what they do. At its best it creates new opportunities and creates an additional important purpose for organizations.

So perhaps the first thing for organizations to grasp is that change is constant. It is accelerating and it impacts upon and involves everyone. Everyone can, and should be, a change agent. So how does the newly emerging, highly flexible, confident employee fit in with this? What does an organization have to do to optimize this?

New generations, new attitudes

Interestingly, in early 2013, AQR recruited a 19-year-old to join the operations team. What struck us from the first was her ability to grasp quickly what we had considered moderately complicated systems. It was only a matter of days, not weeks or months, before she had mastered these systems. Most were IT based – her IT skills were by previous standards frighteningly good.

However, what came next really surprised (and pleased) us. She had been with us for about six weeks when she approached us to speak about her thoughts on our systems, particularly our customer relationship management system, and how these could be improved... entirely on her own initiative she presented us with ideas and suggestions. She was given our support to research and identify the best options, which she identified carefully and presented to her colleagues who were all considerably more experienced than she was. We empowered her to implement the selected option.

There were several things that impressed us.

First, that she had tuned into the business so quickly and that she possessed some intrinsic motivation. We have in AQR an advantage: our work is, for most people, extremely interesting. But our world is also complex: we deal with virtually every type of client imaginable across a wide range of applications. It has not always proved easy to bring people on board who can see the whole picture.

She now has an iPad and although her contract is like most traditional contracts she is accessible pretty much all of the time and she is regarded as an equal member of the whole team.

Second, that she had the confidence to come forward in this way.

And finally, that she already had a sense of continuous improvement and a sense of bringing about change.

Equally interesting was our reaction. It was initially challenging to accept that someone so 'raw' and so inexperienced could improve what we had taken years to build. But that was a temporary state. It quickly passed through intrigue (how can she do this and be so certain?) to a genuine feeling of liberation (that is one less thing I have to be personally involved with – there is someone I can trust with this aspect of the business and who seems as interested in it as we are).

Of course scale might be important here. This was one person. We are a comparatively small organization recruiting four or five people each year. How would we deal with a group of challenging people? What would have happened if we had said no? Hopefully we are ready for the next person and we are positive about encouraging them to change us too.

Employability – what this means

Another aspect is that organizations can initiate change. We tend to talk about change as if it is externally imposed upon individuals and organizations and that is indeed often the case. However, the future may belong to those who shape it.

Jim Collins describes in *Good to Great* (2001) how the 3M Company started as a mining company making sandpaper. They evolved into an adhesive and Sellotape business and are now world famous both for Post-it notes and for their ability to constantly innovate. Similarly, Kimberly Clark realized that they were good at developing products, marketing and sales but they were less good at manufacture. Yet that's what everyone believed they were good at. They no longer manufacture everything and focus on what they do best... and innovate all the time.

Change still carries challenges. Often change has a negative implication for some people. They can lose their jobs and their status. As change becomes more widely understood and more widely accepted as a normal part of the process, attention should be given to how organizations are seen as good and honest 'managers' of change.

What we see is that young people entering the market simply don't believe that most employers can give them a job for life and an increasing proportion may not even want a job for life. They accept that they will have several careers and may even have several careers at the same time (the so-called portfolio career). Yet they can be very motivated by work even when they know it might not last.

Their position to a prospective employer might be: 'I know you can't promise me a job for life. I am happy to join your organization knowing that you might turn around in three or four years' time and say "sorry but the world has changed and I might not need you any longer". I like the role you are offering and I will give it my best shot. But what I need from you, as my employer, is the opportunity to do a good and worthwhile job, reasonable terms and conditions and the opportunity to develop and grow. When the day comes that I have to leave I want to be confident that you have helped to position me so that I am not on the scrapheap and you are satisfied that I have helped you to build your business'. That's the bargain. That's the new 'psychological contract'.

The question is: are organizations aware of this and what are they doing about it? Our experience is that many are still fixated on labour turnover (low is good) while still expecting to be able to shed people when the going gets tough. Many still see the employment contract as a one-sided affair with the employer somehow in a position of strength. Employers still believe that the employee needs them more than they need the employee.

What about organizations? Are their expectations of employees changing? And how is this aligning with what employees are prepared to offer?

In 2013, AQR together with UK organization reachfor undertook a survey with employers across the United Kingdom. Around 350 organizations were asked to identify the characteristics that they had learned were associated with the most successful employees. reachfor is a federation of seven major career services that operate across most of England. The purpose of the exercise was to identify exactly what employability means to an employer. In turn we would develop a 'psychometric' instrument which would help employers identify these qualities in individuals and help individuals become aware of the extent to which they possess these apparently valuable qualities themselves.

Although skills and abilities were important in the survey – especially abilities – they did not emerge as significant as a number of personal attributes. The general feeling was that skills and knowledge can be made available to employees fairly readily. It is what training is well suited to doing. What was much more difficult to engender was what many called 'the right attitude'. Table 2.1 shows what qualities were identified (see page 24).

There were two surprises. First, most employers weren't necessarily interested in what is traditionally assessed in such measures – the so-called 'Big Five' personality model. They were very interested in specific behaviours. Second, we had carried out a similar exercise almost 20 years earlier where one factor had emerged as fairly important. That was 'obedience' or to be prepared to follow instruction (translated to 'to do as they are told'). This time it didn't appear anywhere in the survey.

What didn't surprise us was that few employers sought to assess these qualities either on recruitment or in employment, even though they knew that was what they were looking for.

The mindset items were also interesting. They equated almost exactly to our understanding of the mental toughness model, to which we will shortly come.

Interestingly, many of these qualities align with many of the emerging traits of the new Gen Y/Z employee.

Despite the fact that there is widespread recognition of what makes a good employee, few organizations appear to do anything positive to identify and capture that.

This takes us to three interrelated areas: *leadership and management*, *communications* and *organizational development*. The 21st century organization will deal with all three in new ways. In no particular order:

Leadership and management

In 2008, AQR together with support from the Institute of Leadership and Management carried out some research on leadership. The goal was to make sense of the 50 or so most popular leadership models in common

TABLE 2.1 Employability factors

Skills in dealing with people

1 Team working/Self-sufficiency: The extent to which you need or want to work with others or prefer to work on your own.

2 Altruism: The extent to which you wish to act in the best interests of others even when there may be a personal disadvantage.

3 Emotional intelligence: The extent to which you are aware of your emotions and the emotions of others and understand how to respond to these.

4 Assertiveness/Submissiveness: The extent to which you are determined to influence others, including getting your own way.

Skills in dealing with problems and issues

5 Problem solving: The extent to which you will actively identify, confront, analyse and solve problems.

6 Creativity: The extent to which you seek to add new ideas and innovation to your work.

7 The extent to which structure and order is important to the individual. This can reflect the need to be planful and preferring to working in a controlled or controllable environment.

Motivation and drivers

8 Conscientiousness: The extent to which the individual is guided by rules, standards and values.

9 Concern for standards: The extent to which you desire to identify with and work to high standards.

10 Ambition: This can be reflected in a desire for attainment or simply being the best that you can be.

11 Continuous improvement: The extent to which you will seek to reflect on what you and others are doing and seek to improve on this.

12 Professional orientation: The extent to which you accept accountability for your own learning and development to ensure that you are equipped to meet work and life challenges.

Mindset*

13 'Can do' approach

14 Goal orientation (commitment)

15 Challenge – prepared to accommodate change

16 Confidence

*These factors are described in detail in a later chapter as components of mental toughness use around the world. The research was carried out by Nollaig Heffernan under the supervision of Professor Peter Clough, then Head of Psychology at Hull University. Nollaig earned her PhD for an important aspect of this work (Browne, 2007).

She looked at adopted leadership behaviour in around 1,500 people in leadership roles in around 50 organizations, split equally between the public and private sectors. The research found that all major leadership models were rooted in one or more of six basic scales. These six scales also define leadership style. There did not appear to be a unique leadership style profile that was universally effective and it appears that leaders don't necessarily adopt their preferred leadership style. It appears that they tend to adopt a style which is consistent with the prevailing culture of the organization however it is set. Leadership style is situational. As such, perhaps leadership style and culture in organizations should be evolving to reflect new priorities.

The outcome was the creation of the Integrated Leadership Model (so called because it integrates well with all leadership models). This is not a new model in that it discovers anything new. It simply tidies up the thinking that emerged over the 20th century. The six scales are described in Table 2.2 overleaf.

Leadership is essentially about achieving performance – through motivating followers to give their discretionary effort. The suggestion is that the motivation and drivers for new and future generations are likely to be different than for those who went before. This provokes a number of thoughts and considerations.

If we accept the general description of the new Gen Y/Z employee then that will have implications for leadership style. Leadership will likely need to be less authoritarian than in the past. And there does seem to be some awareness of that as evidenced by the fact that 'obedience' is no longer seen as a primary employee virtue, although that might be a passive response because command and control tactics no longer work as well as they did in the past. The challenge will be to approach this actively.

Some of the components of style will be significant. Authority is still important in leadership but it will need to be derived from a different base than previously was the case. Positional power will no longer be sufficient – if indeed it ever was. We see this in global politics, where bad leadership is increasingly susceptible to being toppled by the masses who are better educated and less timorous.

TABLE 2.2 The Integrated Leadership Model – leadership style

The scales describe the main components of style	What the extremes represent
1 **Drivers:** The extent to which the leader believes in success or attending to the needs of individuals is a driver.	Focus on the task v focus on the person
2 **Delegation:** The extent to which the leader involves others in analysis and decision making.	Flexible v dogmatic
3 **Control:** The extent to which the leader feels they need control or they will empower others.	Centralized v de-centralized
4 **Intrinsic Motivation:** The extent to which the leader believes that people are intrinsically motivated by work.	Reward v punishment
5 **Goal Orientation:** How important hitting goals and targets are – and what they are prepared to do to deliver.	Focus on the means v focus on the end
6 **Structure:** The extent to which structure is important or there is a reliance on presence, intuition and instinct.	Structured v organic

Our research shows that the essence of what leadership is has remained unchanged since the earliest work in this area. Leadership is all about performance through engaging with followers in such a way that they are supported or motivated to give the extra effort that all of us can give if we are motivated to do so. Bennis (1961), Fiedler (1967), Adair (1969) and House (1996) all show this in their work. It is probable that this will remain unchanged. It is how leaders achieve this that will change – if the follower's characteristics change then the leader has to change too in three respects:

1 How they approach followers to engage with them

This is about leadership style and we have already discussed this.

2 How they behave in leadership roles

This is about core competence. The work carried out to develop the Integrated Leadership Model (ILM) enabled Professor Peter Clough to carry out further data analysis. What emerged was three scales that, when the contributing items were analysed, were found to be describing three competencies which are directly related to leadership effectiveness, as shown in Table 2.3.

In one sense this was not presenting anything new. If we look at most reputable models of leadership from Fiedler and House through to Adair and Covey, you will be able to see the same three themes underpinning all of these models. This is why the Integrated Leadership Model became known as such.

The analysis showed that there was a correlation between the perception of followers and the extent to which leaders demonstrated competence in the three areas. A good deal more work needs to be carried out to develop this fully, but what has emerged also tallies closely with conventional wisdom. As any good research will do, it has thrown up more questions.

One interesting thing is that these competencies are independent of each other. Another is that there may be evidence showing that there is a difference between the way males and females behave in order to provide leadership.

TABLE 2.3 The Integrated Leadership Model – leadership effectiveness

Competencies	Description
1 Determination to Deliver	Having purpose, determination and setting priorities
2 Engagement with Individuals	Equipping and supporting followers with what they need
3 Engagement with Teams	Understanding team working – especially cross-functionally

The first competency, Determination to Deliver, seemed to be universally regarded as the most important. People will follow someone who knows where they are going, looks like they are going in the right direction and stays focused. We can guess that in tomorrow's world this will remain important, especially if those who make up future generations are more purposeful in their own right.

The indication is that, hitherto, the other two qualities may have been of significance but of lesser significance than Determination to Deliver.

Engagement with Individuals means that the leader attends to the development needs of the follower, in particular to enable the follower to get up to speed as quickly as possible. This is likely to be especially appealing to Gen Y/Z .

Engagement with Teams is possibly the most underdeveloped aspect. It is not about the obvious team that sits together in an office. It is much more about the 'hidden' teams that work across functions inside and outside organizations. Business process specialists will attest to the fact that this is where most inefficiency and waste exists. Most employees are acutely aware of this and will often be frustrated if their leaders and managers do nothing about it.

The reality is that many managers simply don't see it. Many large organizations have been described as having a 'silo mentality', where managers deliberately distance themselves from their internal customers and suppliers. If Gen Y/Z is more naturally collaborative, is better at networking and is more inclined to problem-solve in groups then this area of competence is likely to be much more important than ever before.

There is another change emerging in this area. At one time the term 'leadership' applied only to a very few at the top of an organization. Everyone is part of the society we know as the organization. Everyone has a role, often several roles and everyone has a contribution to make. If not, what is their purpose? Everyone can be a leader. Leadership is relevant at every level. All employees have a role to play in encouraging the best performance from themselves and from others. Leadership development is for everyone.

3 What else they need to take into account to be effective in a leadership role

We can immediately identify three themes and there will certainly be more.

We have identified trust as a growing issue which has achieved some significance. As employees become better educated and better informed and organizations become increasingly transparent then trust in an organization and its leadership will be a fundamental requirement, if only to make future employment relationships work.

The Institute of Leadership and Management has anticipated this and carried out important research into the nature and value of trust – in top leadership and in immediate line management – as a factor in organizational and individual performance. In particular it has identified what the core elements of trust are for most people. Charles Elvin, CEO for the Institute of Leadership and Management explores this more fully in Chapter 4.

Communication

Another area where there is change in style and in substance is communication. Anyone who helps organizations run employee surveys will tell you that communication is the 'Aunt Sally' of any survey. No matter how well communication works in an organization, the people in the organization will always feel they should know more. The paradox of good communication is that people will recognize that they are well informed but that will raise their expectations and they will look for more and better communication. Where communication is poor this is always associated with poor performance.

Most organizations see communication as an exercise in dissemination of information. Most know that it is also about listening to others – staff, clients and suppliers. Very few practise this to a significant extent. However, we now have and will have people entering the workforce and people within the workforce who are well educated and who have ideas. They want and need to be heard. A big part of their motivation is to be engaged in work which is satisfying. The successful organization in the 21st century has little option but to attend to this.

Look at our example of the new recruit to AQR who came forward with improvement ideas. What would have been the consequences of paying little or no attention to her? We wouldn't have had an improvement to the business and we would have signalled to that employee that whatever else she contributed we weren't interested in her thoughts and ideas. We wouldn't have kept her for long and while we had her the contribution might have been minimal.

Dissemination of information is important. People need to trust the organization and this is a result of openness and consistency. They also need to have available to them the information they need to be able to do their jobs efficiently. If one of the factors that the employer is looking for in a model employee is the acceptance of responsibility and accountability, you only do that in a culture of first-class communication. Again, grasping the opportunities provided by technology is going to be an increasingly important challenge for all organizations in the 21st century.

Curiously there may also be a challenge in information overload. As more information becomes available and communication processes and technologies develop then it is possible to create so much information that it drowns the recipients and clogs up the organizational systems. It just becomes noise.

What organizations do about managing communication better is not immediately clear.

Organizational development

The third area is organizational development. Conventional wisdom has said that organizational structures need to be clear and... structured. The future is increasingly dynamic – new organizations emerge, new sectors develop and existing organizations are forced to change with astonishing rapidity.

New ways of doing business will create their own pressures. Retail provides a very good example. Online retail is taking over from high street retail. Or is it? What is now emerging is that a successful retailer might, in some sectors, need to offer both. However, Amazon doesn't have a high street presence – and works very well. Retailing provides an interesting insight into change and the nature of change in the 21st century. Both the question and the answer are constantly evolving.

It's self-evident that for an organization to survive and to thrive it will have to continuously adapt. For many employed in organizations and for those connected with organizations as suppliers and customers this will prove challenging. Organizations will need to be more fluid and adaptable. Employees may well find that they are increasingly members of more than one team and they might have more than one reporting line. Managers and leaders will need to be more adept at prioritizing and coordinating work – and the challenge for leaders will be to explain all this to stakeholders and to take those stakeholders – clients, staff, suppliers, citizens, etc – with them as they create modern, agile organizations. There will be an increased requirement for leadership and for engagement with staff.

It is likely that the best organizations will be those who delegate responsibility and accountability for elements of business performance to all levels of the organization and create a more interactive organization. As organization structures flatten, the communication lines from strategy maker to the deliverers of that strategy become shorter.

Leaders at all levels will not only be required to be skilled in the mechanics and principles of running an organization but they will also have to be able to pay attention to how that works, especially when engaging with the people who will deliver on their behalf.

Organizations will also need to develop new management practices and learn how to better handle existing management practices. New technology will play a part in both areas. Management processes can be increasingly systematized through the application of IT. This has the benefit of dealing with many of the more routine elements of the managerial role, freeing the manager/leader to concentrate on what is important.

Managing a better educated workforce that wants more responsibility and accountability and the freedom to grow and develop – and sees continuous professional development as an essential everyday activity – will be a very different management discipline to that espoused in the 20th century. Everyone will need to develop new skills and knowledge continuously. In many areas knowledge already has a half-life measured in months not years. As we will see, neuroscience is changing our knowledge and understanding of psychology. Undergraduates completing a 3-year degree in IT can often forget much of what they have learned in year one – it's already out of date.

An interesting development that is gathering momentum is a change in attitudes towards diversity. Throughout history we have seen groups in society discriminating against other groups, often blocking access to education and opportunity. The net effect is to prevent those who can be socially and economically active from participating fully in the social and economic development of society (and sometimes not at all). Simply from a pure economist's point of view this is wasteful and it is nonsensical as well as being distasteful.

Gender discrimination is arguably the area where most progress has been made in recent times, although as we will see, much remains to be done. Racial and ethnic discrimination remains an issue but the evidence is that Gen Y/Z is much more accepting of diversity than past generations have been. Celebrating diversity and adopting a purposeful approach towards appreciating what it can bring is likely to be a significant factor in the development of most organizations. It will also provide a challenge for many leaders and managers.

Another major area of change in the United Kingdom and elsewhere is the transformation of the role of the public sector. Often this means a transition into what are recognizably private sector organizations. Sometimes this is done in the name of efficiency and effectiveness – believing that private sector practices with their competitive ethos will provide equivalent or even better services at a lower cost to the public purse. Sometimes it is done for political and philosophical reasons. It is no longer thought appropriate that some services currently being provided by the state should be provided by the state. The state may at times be restricted to policy and strategy. Application of policy could in most cases be a normal commercial activity – it should be carried out by those who offer to do it efficiently and who survive in that role by demonstrating that they deliver effectively.

Sometimes it is done for no other reason than that the moment is right for a new approach. A good example of this is the National Health Service (NHS) in the United Kingdom. Famed the world over, no one doubts its purpose, its value and the ethos which has created a health service which is often envied. However, there are many who feel it is flawed in many regards and that number of critics is growing. The NHS puts patients on a pedestal. Treatment is free at the point of delivery. Demand for service is growing faster than it can be supplied.

There are many reasons for this. Sometimes it is simply because there is a health or medical factor that creates demand – such as the consequences of an ageing population. Sometimes the reason appears less justifiable – it is argued that more and more people are using NHS services to attend to needs which are not a good use of resources, eg attending hospitals for minor complaints which can be easily treated at home, seeking cosmetic treatments, the elderly feigning illness simply to get companionship, etc.

The NHS has a limited budget. It doesn't yet operate in a market economy responding with its services to the area of greatest or most productive need. There is a parallel market where private medicine can be bought to attend to patient needs, but most people rely on the NHS.

So this public sector organization must begin to make economic decisions. Their resources are limited so they must do all they can to operate more efficiently and more effectively to improve the supply of service. How do they accomplish this?

Another question might be: how do I allocate my scarce resources to so many competing ends? On any given day a health service will deal with a huge range of demands – from the terminally ill through to the pregnant mother through to the young person receiving their vaccinations. Where are the best places to use the scarce funds available if you don't have the funds to attend to all needs?

Attention is now beginning to turn to the role of the patient. Can the patient do more to improve the efficacy of their treatments? Can they be more self-reliant? We already see obese patients being told they are at the back of the queue for certain treatments until they have lost weight because their obesity reduces the effectiveness of treatment. The situation is similar with smokers.

There is a growing understanding that the success of many medical interventions relies as much on the cooperation of the patient as it does on the skills of medical staff. This applies both to efficiency and effectiveness. For instance, not all knee and hip joint replacement surgery is as successful as it might be. One factor is that the physiotherapy required to ensure that a new joint becomes fully effective can be awkward, uncomfortable and sometimes painful. So people give up or don't complete the rehabilitation programme. The question we are being asked is: can we identify those who might be prone to giving up easily and can we develop programmes that minimize the risk of people wasting resources? The bigger question is – can people in society play a bigger part in using the resources available to them more effectively? If so, how can this be achieved?

Increasingly these and other factors are considerations in almost every area of public services. It means that in much of the public sector around the world there is another layer of challenge emerging to that which applies to society in general.

If adopting private sector practices is a way forward for some, how do organizations that have little experience of private sector behaviour develop this? And are private sector practices and behaviours always the most appropriate? What does that part of the public sector which isn't immediately being privatized do? To what extent does it need to develop new behaviours, what are they and how do they develop them?

In Chapter 7, the directors of Academi Wales describe how the Welsh Assembly Government has approached these questions on its own behalf and on behalf of all major public sector bodies in Wales, and what is being examined for the future.

One factor that has been repeatedly mentioned throughout this chapter is technology. We are in an era of technology developing at breathtaking speed – especially in IT. This is creating consequences that will also impact on every aspect of our lives and the way organizations develop. Some of these are obvious: IT has transformed global communications, access to knowledge, sharing of information, access to markets, etc. Other forms of technology mean that we can all own cars with features that 10 years ago were only available to the wealthy.

Some are more subtle and yet just as impactful. Technology is a great leveller. Where once the Westerner had an advantage over the African or the Indian because of a superior access to knowledge (the West had libraries and books, African countries and India frequently didn't), that advantage has since disappeared. Almost all information is available to everyone wherever they are – and increasingly so.

Andrew Cuthbert will explore this in Chapter 10. But even this insightful piece only attends to one (important) aspect of the impact of development in IT. It illustrates nicely the type of change that is occurring here but readers in five years' time will look at this and regard much of it as history. There is also a danger that we look at IT as the main or dominant area of technological development.

It may not be.

If understanding people is the key to harnessing potential then we are beginning to understand how and why people think, feel and behave better and better and at an accelerating rate. That opportunity is coming about through the development of neuroscience where new technologies (admittedly yet more IT) such as functional magnetic resonance imaging – more commonly known as brain scanning – are enabling researchers to look at the brain to see how it actually works.

In the past, researchers have used techniques such as statistical methods and correlation studies to hypothesize about how the brain works. Or they have worked with people who have suffered some kind of damage to part of the brain and tried to work out what functions have ceased as a consequence. In the absence of actually being able to look inside the brain and see what is going on these are reasonable approaches. They are comparatively crude approaches which sometimes produce a good explanation, but often they don't.

Neuroscience is already answering some important questions for us and it is also generating many more questions. It is challenging what we thought we knew with some certainty. Some past certainties have gone. For instance, it used to be the case that although our personalities are formed partly through experience, it was widely believed that once we reached our mid-twenties our personalities in some way were fairly fully formed. We would change little if at all beyond that point. We now know that our brains are much more plastic than this. The brain is capable of developing new neural pathways (new ways of thinking) well into old age. It might do it more slowly than when we were young but we are very much more adaptable than we once imagined.

Moreover, we also now know that the brain doesn't always distinguish between thinking and doing in many cases. If we visualize an experience the brain will accept it as a real experience. This means that we can develop through brain training. This applies even to physical activity. One study showed that people who thought about weight-training exercise actually added muscle mass.

This alone has profound implications for understanding people's responses to change and how we might smooth the path for those who find change threatening. It also suggests that we might have the opportunity for new ways to develop people.

Neuroscience can also help to explain why we can learn things on a training programme and then forget all about them when we are back in the workplace. Studies at the University of Parma have shown that when we watch someone doing something the part of the brain that is responsible for that function becomes activated inside our brain. So perhaps role modelling does work, but... only if you then do what it is that you have seen being done. In sport this seems to have been understood for some time. Sports coaches talk about purposeful practice to embed new behaviours until they become a habit or trait. It seems the brain is good at learning in one setting but struggles to apply this learning in a new or different setting.

This has profound implications for the way we develop people and perhaps for the way we do it.

Yet another emerging area to which neuroscience is making a big contribution is our understanding of how creativity works. It seems that we are most creative when we aren't thinking about being creative! Eugene Sadler-Smith, Professor of Organisational Behaviour at the University of Surrey, suggests that the intuitive mind (which works in the background in the brain) is constantly processing data even when we don't ask it to do so. From time to time out pops an idea, which is where the 'eureka' moment comes from.

Sadler-Smith (2013) does confirm that there are conditions that help that process along. Doing something mentally stimulating is helpful as is being in a positive mood. Sleep helps too (the brain processes data even when asleep) as, apparently, do some foods. Chocolate thankfully is one of those. But the most important factor is to know your subject matter. Knowledge is important. As Sadler-Smith has noted, creativity may be about joining the dots, but you have to recognize the dots in the first place.

The point here though is that there are many technologies which are developing and emerging all at the same time, not just in IT. We will understand and apply psychology very differently in the late 21st century than we do now. This may give us much more power to shape and develop people.

Similarly, our understanding of genetics made a great leap forward in the mid-20th century with the 'discovery' of DNA and its related compounds. In the last few years we have learned that even DNA is not fixed. We can in certain conditions switch off and switch on parts of our DNA through interventions that appear to include what we eat. Some worry that this takes us into epigenetics. The point here is the same as that made earlier. We have yet another set of technologies emerging that, in the not-too-distant future, will impact on how organizations change and develop – as long as they are made up of people.

Finally, we look at what people and organizations need to develop in order to deal with the challenges of the 21st century. The reality is that there is a whirlwind of change underway. As we begin to become more relaxed about the global financial crisis we will find organizations and individuals will focus on and seize opportunities to grow, develop and prosper.

This brings us to the central theme in this book. The book is called *Developing Resilient Organizations*. But in truth resilience isn't enough. Resilience is largely a passive quality. It describes the ability to cope with adversity. When an adverse situation arises, an organization that perseveres and copes with the adversity will be described as resilient. Collins (2001) writes about that in *Good to Great* describing this quality as hardiness.

Mental toughness is a quality that describes a more proactive approach to resilience. It is a personality trait that is more commonly applied to individuals. The mentally tough are those who not only deal more effectively with adversity but also embrace challenge and change. They know that they can pick themselves up after a setback or major change, dust themselves off and carry on towards their goals. A setback or change doesn't derail them. More importantly they see change and challenge as an opportunity and not a threat. They know that some always survive change and some go under. They have the self-confidence in their abilities and in particular their ability to relate to the world around them to approach setbacks with that sense of self belief.

Given that organizations are communities of individuals, the personality of an organization, normally described as an aspect of its culture, is a function of the collective personality of its people. In that sense organizations can be mentally tough or mentally sensitive.

Mental toughness describes a mindset. The term 'tough' can sometimes mislead. Mental toughness is not about a 'macho' type of toughness. It isn't necessarily about insensitivity although we know that mentally tough individuals can let adversity 'bounce' off them as if they were insensitive. Mental toughness is much more accurately described as a state of mind where the individual (or organization) is 'comfortable within their own skin'. This comes from a sense of:

- feeling that they can rise to the occasion and 'can do' when needed;
- believing they can control the feelings and emotions of others;
- set challenging goals when others may not do so and really go for them;
- see what is happening as a challenge... not just a threat;
- have the inner belief that they have the abilities and the wherewithal to succeed.

Those that demonstrate these behaviours and beliefs will manage change, challenge and setback better than those whose response is dominated by fear, uncertainty, anger and frustration. These sap an individual's and organization's energies.

The concept of mental toughness has some of its origins in the world of sport where coaches and managers have long understood that the most able don't always win. Less able teams can beat more able teams: less able athletes can outperform more skilled athletes simply because they possess this quality.

The 21st-century organization will, as we have seen, see challenge and change as never before and will see that evolve at a pace that is faster than ever before and at a pace which is accelerating. One challenge will be to spot those changes, to anticipate their impact and where competitive advantage arises to grasp the moment and initiate change. Some opportunities will be foreseen. As we saw in 2008, some we should have foreseen and some we didn't. We can't foresee everything but we can prepare for it and be ready to deal with whatever arises.

The greatest challenge for organizations and leaders in the 21st century is to create workforces and organizational cultures that see change and adversity as ordinary, normal events and perceive them as positive situations laden with opportunities which the organization is well positioned to exploit.

That is what a resilient organization in the 21st century will do.

In the next chapter we will explore what mental toughness is, why it is so valuable and how it can be assessed and developed.

References

Adair, J (1969) *Action Centred Leadership*, Gower Publishing Ltd, Aldershot
Bennis, W (1961) Revisionist theory of leadership, *Harvard Business Review* 39(1), pp 26–36

Browne, M N M (2007) *An integrated model of leadership,* Unpublished PhD thesis

Collins, J (2001) *Good To Great: Why some companies make the leap... and others don't,* Random House Business, London

Fiedler, F E (1967) *A Theory of Leadership Effectiveness,* McGraw-Hill, New York

House, R J (1996) Path-goal theory of leadership: lessons, legacy, and a reformulated theory, *Leadership Quarterly,* 7(3), pp 323–352

Keysers, C (2011) *The Empathic Brain,* Kindle Edition

Sadler-Smith, E (2013) Toward organizational environmental virtuousness, *Journal of Applied Behavioral Science,* **49**(1), pp 123–148

Mental toughness
What is it and why is it so important?

03

PROFESSOR PETER CLOUGH, DR FIONA EARLE, DR KEITH EARLE, DR JOHN PERRY AND DOUG STRYCHARCZYK

The purpose of this chapter is to explore the concept of a mentally tough organization. It is necessarily speculative and its intention is to start a discussion rather than end a debate. In order to do this we will ask and hopefully answer some basic questions. These are:

- What is mental toughness?
- What is the '4 Cs' model of mental toughness?
- Can mental toughness be integrated with the core models prevalent in occupational and in sport psychology?
- Can we develop a mentally tough organization?

What is mental toughness?

Mental toughness is often used to describe that personality characteristic that enables people to succeed, even in times of adversity. We define mental toughness as:

> The quality which determines in large part how people deal effectively with challenge, stressors and pressure... irrespective of prevailing circumstances.
>
> (Clough and Strycharczyk, 2012, p 1)

When considering what mental toughness is, we often think of examples. These include examples of sports stars who have succeeded under great pressure (Mohammed Ali) or physically demanding environments; examples of entrepreneurs who have fought individually to make it to the top (Richard Branson); and examples of great leaders who have guided groups and whole nations to success (Nelson Mandela).

Edison and Einstein (in science and academia) and Oprah Winfrey (in entertainment) provide other notable examples.

Each has experienced setbacks and adversity – sometimes in extreme forms. Despite this they re-group, learn from their tribulations and emerge stronger, better and more effective than before. Mostly what is significant is the determination and positive mindset adopted to deal with their situation. They want to and like dealing with the situation to hand.

Two things are now clear to us: mental toughness is beneficial for performance, and it can be developed. Case studies have previously demonstrated that mental toughness development has improved performance in the workplace, education, health and sport. Improvements have included greater productivity, increased well-being, better attendance, enhanced engagement and academic performance.

Mental toughness is a concept which contributes significantly to three interrelated issues which are emerging as critically important as time goes by: performance (or attainment), well-being and positive behaviour(s). There is every indication that these are increasingly valuable and important as time goes by.

As Doug and his colleagues at AQR are finding, these seem to be emerging as the three big factors that are of interest in just about every walk of life – work, home, family, socializing, sports.

The relationship between mental toughness and performance has also been demonstrated in a number of academic studies. One clear demonstration of the effectiveness of mental toughness came from Marchant et al (2009), who examined the mental toughness of 552 workers in positions of senior management, middle management, junior management and clerical roles. The authors found that mental toughness was significantly greater in higher managerial positions and that it appeared to increase with age. Those in middle and junior management posts also showed above-average mental toughness levels but at slightly lower levels than at the senior management positions.

During the initial development of the concept, Clough, Earle, and Sewell (2002) tested the performance of participants with differing levels of mental toughness on a cognitive planning task. They manipulated the feedback to be positive or negative. Interestingly, they found that mentally tough individuals performed consistently well regardless of the feedback they received.

This suggests that mentally tough people need less affirmation to perform. In general, they are more optimistic.

Indeed, Nicholls *et al* (2008) found this when they assessed the mental toughness and life orientation of 677 sports performers. They found that all aspects of mental toughness were positively related to optimism and negatively related to pessimism. Clearly being and remaining optimistic regardless of feedback are important contributors to sustained high levels of performance.

Mental toughness is not simply a sole determinant of objective success however. As pointed out by Crust (2008), it is about making the most of one's abilities. We shouldn't consider mental toughness purely in absolute terms. That an individual is in middle management rather than senior management is not a reflection on their mental toughness. Rather, if they are mentally tough, they are more likely to reach their potential, whatever level that may be.

It is important to understand this. We can't all win an Olympic gold medal for being the best in the world at something. Only one person or team can do that.

But we can all be the best that we can be. We can be good at what we do – and with a little bit of focus and effort we can, in the words of Jim Collins, be great.

In business or in organizational development, this is the 'holy grail' of organization performance and well-being. With the best people you can build the best organizations. Developing mental toughness can provide this potential. It is a concept with the power to transform everything in society.

The world we inhabit is full of opportunity. Not everyone sees that opportunity. This is what contributes to inequality and underperformance. It appears that mental toughness is a quality that enables people to be more likely to identify and appreciate the opportunity in front of them and to grasp it firmly in both hands when it arises.

So what is the nature of this quality?

Psychologists often classify concepts as states or traits. A state is a transient experience that lasts only for a period of time and is often specific to the environment. For example, an emotion can last a matter of seconds or much longer. A trait, however, is a stable and enduring characteristic, such as being extraverted. As demonstrated best by Horsburgh *et al* (2009) at the University of Western Ontario, Canada, mental toughness lies somewhere in between.

These authors conducted a study on 219 pairs of adult twins to examine whether mental toughness is determined by genetic or environmental factors. The authors found that both genetic and environmental factors significantly related to all aspects of mental toughness. This study provides an important point in our understanding of mental toughness. In part, it is genetic, but a significant proportion of it is determined by the environment. Now, we cannot ethically change an employee's genetic makeup, but we can definitely change their environment and therefore through that develop their mental toughness.

Mental toughness: From the reactive to the proactive

Like all psychological theory, mental toughness is the result of an evolving network of research that continues to enhance our understanding of the concept. Here we discuss the evolution from constructs of resilience, hardiness, and physiological toughness that inform our understanding of mental toughness today.

Physiological toughness

Toughness generally refers to withstanding some form of strain. This is often characterized physically, be it in the form of an individual or an object. The extent to which it can withstand strain without breaking is effectively how tough it is.

The Canadian psychologist Dienstbier (1989) examined the relationship between physical toughness and mental toughness. Specifically, he examined the physiological arousal when confronted with stress, and how within-person changes could be observed over time when repeatedly exposed to physical stressors. Like many stress theorists, Dienstbier considered the interaction between the person and the environment to generate a perceived outcome, which could be positive (a challenge or opportunity) or negative (a threat or stress). Based on his observations, Dienstbier proposed that there are four physiological toughening manipulations that in turn cause psychological changes: early experience, passive toughening, active toughening and ageing.

In essence, the premise is that exposure to challenges/stressors results in a change in character. He further postulated that exposure to mental challenges/stressors would cause mental toughening. The link between mental toughness and physiological toughness has also been examined by Crust and Clough (2005), who found a positive relationship between mental toughness and pain tolerance in an isometric weight-holding task. Similarly, Levy et al (2006) noted a relationship between mental toughness and pain tolerance during rehabilitation from injury.

This brings us to an important caveat. The use of the word *tough*, and the relationship with physiological toughness, can potentially lead to a misinterpretation when discussing mental toughness. Specifically, the misinterpretation is that mental toughness is a somewhat macho concept. As pointed out by Clough and Strycharczyk (2012), this is a fallacy.

There is clear evidence from a wealth of studies that men and women are equally tough. They may employ different coping strategies, but the underlying core mental toughness remains identical across a very broad range of studies.

The meaning of the word 'toughness' in the term mental toughness is much more in tune with the notion of 'being comfortable in your own skin'. This is a quality that can give an inner strength to individuals, groups and organizations which enables them to deal with all the things that life will throw at them, including setbacks, challenges, problems and change.

But that response can happen in two ways. It can be passive: a gritted determination perhaps to overcome a setback but without having any positive feelings about it. Or it can be active or positive: an individual or organization will understand and accept that setbacks will occur and life can be challenging. Importantly they will see that as an opportunity – a challenge to be relished.

Understanding this helps to explain why there is an important difference between resilience and mental toughness – and what that difference amounts to. Moreover, it helps to explain why two individuals in an organization with similar abilities and education might approach and respond to setbacks and challenges differently.

Resilience

Resilience is a passive, reactive term used to describe someone's ability to bounce back from adversity. It is greatly important of course, as nobody has a life without adversity. There is adversity in work, in relationships, in sport, in health, in all aspects of our lives. Unfortunately, adversity often does not give warning. Resilience is the extent to which we are able to cope with and bounce back from such adversity. Connor and Davidson (2003, p.76) define resilience as 'the personal qualities that enable one to thrive in the face of adversity'.

Resilience is something that is often described as coming after adversity and before positive adaptation (Fletcher and Sarkar, 2013). This is evident from a range of resilience-based theories developed over the past two decades. One thing that most modern theories of resilience have in common is the idea that it is a dynamic process that changes over time. That is, we become more or less resilient with experience of adversity or traumatic events.

We opened this section by describing resilience as passive and reactive. Having highlighted the nature of resilience and defined it as one's ability to bounce back from adversity, it is therefore necessary to experience adversity in order to demonstrate resilience. However, mentally tough people are not simply those who respond to adversity the best. What if no problems arose? The next concept we will discuss includes a more proactive element: challenge.

Hardiness

Some people deal with stress better than others. Suzanne Kobasa (1979) recognized this when examining the stress–illness relationship in health psychology. Kobasa noticed a buffering effect between stressful life events and illness, which she termed as hardiness.

This was an enduring personality construct, which Funk (1992) calls a 'hardy personality' that consists of three interrelated concepts: commitment, control, and challenge. Hardiness theory recognizes that how we respond to stress is reliant upon a general quality that emerges through varied and rewarding experiences, often during childhood (Maddi and Kobasa, 1984). That researchers acknowledged the personality associations and generalization of these attributes was key in better understanding people's stress responses. Considering an organizational context, one of the most common stressors in organizations and in people is a result of managing change.

Change is normal. Change happens consistently from birth to death. Moreover, many work in a structure that regularly requires change to meet new demands. Hardy individuals are better at managing and coping with such change. The key to this is that they see change as normal and therefore relish it. They consider change to be an opportunity to grow: it is a challenge. Kobasa *et al* (1982) identified challenge as one-third of hardiness. Specifically, this requires interpreting potentially stressful occurrences as challenges rather than threats to security.

Committed people view potentially stressful situations as meaningful and interesting. Consequently they tend to involve themselves in what they are doing rather than become alienated from it. Cognitively the committed worker when placed in a new and/or potentially stressful situation is able to give meaning to it. At a behavioural level, because they feel they understand the situation and they are involved, they are more likely to take the initiative.

This has several implications for the way organizations should organize and behave to manage change effectively.

Through ongoing change or experiencing potentially stressful situations, hardy individuals adapt better and prosper more. This is, in part, because they are able to exert some form of control. They view stressors as changeable and will change them as they see fit. By doing so, one is able to displace the stressor outside of their responsibility, develop a plan to overcome the stressor, or eliminate it altogether. A feeling of control enables one to feel influential in subsequent proceedings, therefore encouraging them to incorporate new information (positively phrased rather than stressors) into an ongoing plan and choose a fruitful course of action.

A conceptual understanding of mental toughness

Hardiness theory presents three components: challenge, commitment and control. However, central to these components becoming effective in practice is confidence. This presents us with the '4 Cs' model proposed by Clough, Earle and Sewell (2002).

Confidence is a vital ingredient for enabling demonstration of the other components. Consider challenge, for example: the extent to which one perceives an opportunity rather than a threat. While this goes some way towards explaining mental toughness, the role of confidence is pivotal.

Imagine that there is yet another large restructure at your organization. While you may be predisposed to viewing this as an opportunity, much will depend on your own perceived ability and your confidence that you can convince others of that ability. Regardless of how much you want to view this as an opportunity, if you do not have the confidence it will inevitably pose a threat and will likely lead to avoidance behaviour.

Our conceptual understanding of mental toughness then is that it is a narrow personality trait, which can be developed. It has four components: challenge, commitment, control, and confidence. These are described below as the 4 Cs model.

What is the 4 Cs model of mental toughness?

The conceptualization by Clough, Earle and Sewell (2002) presents mental toughness as a narrow personality trait, with an infrastructure of challenge, commitment, control, and confidence. Perhaps most importantly, this model bridges an important gap between theory and practice, as the components combined enable the growth of applied research. Here we explain each of the components of mental toughness in turn.

Control

The extent to which we maintain control is key for being resilient. This component of mental toughness is divided into two sub-components: the first is life control, which indicates the extent to which we believe that we shape what happens to us, the other is emotional control, which is concerned with how we control our anxieties, frustrations, anger and other emotions.

Life control

There is a common phrase used by many that screams of a lack of life control: 'knowing my luck...'. The person beginning a statement with this phrase is typically implying that due to uncontrolled external forces, they will be unable to achieve their goal. Of course, it is frequently used without much consideration but it resonates with some of us every time we hear it because it is such a clear example of someone demonstrating a lack of perceived control over what happens to them in their life. This represents life control.

The control dimension of mental toughness is closely related to the concept of learned helplessness. Proposed by Seligman (1975), learned helplessness is a state whereby individuals perceive things that should be within their control as outside of their control.

To demonstrate the concept, Seligman tested responses from dogs. He grouped dogs and subjected them to a mild electric shock. One group of

FIGURE 3.1 Sample descriptions of high and low scores in life control

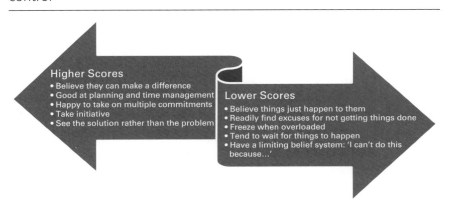

dogs was able to press on a lever to prevent the pain. However, for another group, the lever did not stop the shocks. This group learned that trying to stop the unpleasant experience was futile.

In the second part of the experiment the dogs were placed in a box that was separated into two halves by a small partition. The floor on the side the dogs were on administered the mild shocks again, while the floor on the opposing side of the partition was normal. The dogs that had previously been able to stop the shocks by pressing the lever jumped the partition. However, the dogs that were previously unable to stop the shocks simply accepted the new shocks without attempting to jump free. This group had learned (falsely) that they were unable to avoid pain and so accepted it.

Control also has links with the often-cited 'self-fulfilling prophecy'. Used by a host of philosophers, sociologists and psychologists, self-fulfilling prophecy is a prediction that directly or indirectly causes itself to become true. For example, if we believe that we are going to succeed at something, perhaps because it is under our control, we go to greater lengths to prove ourselves right.

> We are creators of our fortune, not simply foretellers.

The idea of control is also prominent in attribution theory. This was originally proposed by Heider (1944) to make sense of how we determine the cause of a personal outcome. Weiner (1972) eventually produced a common 2×2 model of attributions that distinguished between the loci of causality and stability.

The locus of causality refers to whether the outcome was caused by internal or external factors. In other words, was I the reason for this success or failure, or was it because of someone else? The locus of stability refers to how likely the cause is to remain in the future. Was this cause something consistent, like my own ability, or was it down to luck, or perhaps effort? Weiner went on to add controllability to his model.

We can see therefore that attributing something positive to internal, stable, and controllable factors means that we believe we can replicate this in the future. Our sense of being able to achieve something in the workplace is improved if we demonstrate these three attributions.

Emotional control

A great strength that we have in organizations is people. However, people are human and as such are complex, emotional entities. We experience a host of emotions regularly: happiness, sadness, anger, delight, frustration, pride, shame, joy...

We all have the ability to think logically, it is a great aspect of the human brain. At times though, positive or negative emotions can interrupt this mechanism. There may be some people who are simply predisposed to experiencing less intense emotions than others from a biological point of view. Therefore, controlling such emotions is relatively easy. However, emotions affect all of us to a greater or lesser extent. The key to maintaining high performance levels is to stay in control of which emotions to let in and which ones to keep out.

Working in any organization creates a raft of emotions for its employees. There are unpleasant emotions, such as fear, anger, frustration, aggression and annoyance. Clearly, allowing these emotions to show can be detrimental. It can be detrimental in a team environment, it can cause friction between individuals, and it also uses a lot of attentional resource. Someone internally stewing on how annoyed they are has little remaining resource to attend to more productive activities.

Alternatively, we experience pleasant emotions at work, such as pride, excitement, satisfaction, accomplishment and perhaps delight. A mentally-tough individual is also able to control these. Control does not necessarily need to be about hiding emotion, but the ability to use it effectively for performance. For example, presenting pride at a successful outcome may help to create a positive work environment, but perhaps not if the success is at the expense of an observing colleague.

In summary, experiencing emotion is not necessarily positive or negative, nor is showing emotion. The key is that the individual should be deciding which emotions should be contained and which should not. Therefore, they can be considered to be in control.

Interestingly, there may be some evidence emerging that there is a curious and potentially important organizational implication for an individual's emotional control: it is suggested that managing your emotions can also impact on the emotions of others. For instance, a manager or teacher who is feeling off might be able to mask this and appear 'buzzy' or even excited when their inner thoughts are anything but. Others with whom they are working may also feel less than positive but they can nevertheless be influenced by the emotions that the manager or teacher is presenting. Many will respond by feeling happier which lifts the mood in a group or a room and this in turn feeds back to the manager. A virtuous spiral can be established. This is a confirmation of the adage 'smile and the world smiles with you'.

Of course the opposite can occur. A moody manager or teacher can quickly diminish the mood of the group if they show those emotions.

FIGURE 3.2 Sample descriptions of high and low scores in emotional control

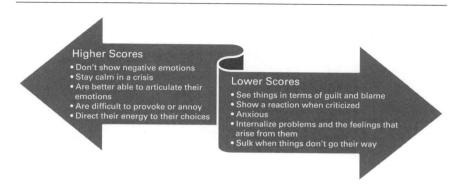

Higher Scores
- Don't show negative emotions
- Stay calm in a crisis
- Are better able to articulate their emotions
- Are difficult to provoke or annoy
- Direct their energy to their choices

Lower Scores
- See things in terms of guilt and blame
- Show a reaction when criticized
- Anxious
- Internalize problems and the feelings that arise from them
- Sulk when things don't go their way

It is interesting too to consider things like luck and superstition. When we think about life control, it seems maladaptive to adhere to superstitious behaviour. However, such behaviour could potentially be effective as an emotion-focused coping strategy that enables us to maintain emotional control.

Commitment

Commitment is about delivering. A committed person will always strive to deliver on their promises, to themselves or others. Mentally-tough individuals are prepared to make commitments and stick to them. Many occupations require individuals to work to targets. The extent to which one works hard to ensure that those targets are met is a measure of one's commitment.

We have probably all worked with individuals who we can note for their commitment (and those we can note for their lack of commitment). Committed individuals are the people prepared to take on tasks even though they may be assessed on them. Committed individuals are prepared to do what it takes to keep those promises. Sometimes a task takes longer than first expected. Sometimes it becomes a bigger task while it is being undertaken. Our committed colleague is ok with this: they might even enjoy it because the success at the end will be greater. This is not simply a decision though. It requires great mental skill to maintain motivation and focus.

Our less committed colleague might find working to targets daunting and so avoids them. When the going gets tough, this colleague is prepared to give in, citing either internal or external reasons. Boredom can sometimes be an issue, as can motivation and focus. The less committed often allow

FIGURE 3.3 Sample descriptions of high and low scores in commitment

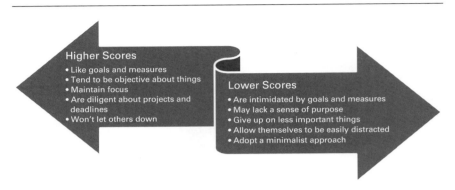

Higher Scores
- Like goals and measures
- Tend to be objective about things
- Maintain focus
- Are diligent about projects and deadlines
- Won't let others down

Lower Scores
- Are intimidated by goals and measures
- May lack a sense of purpose
- Give up on less important things
- Allow themselves to be easily distracted
- Adopt a minimalist approach

themselves to become easily distracted from the goal. We look at this more closely later in the chapter.

We often make promises to ourselves. Every New Year, millions of people resolve to better themselves by losing weight, improving their health or in other aspects of their lives. The difference between the few that achieve such resolutions and the many that do not lies in how committed they were to keeping that promise when it was made.

Commitment has been demonstrated to have the most significant relationship to the cognitive base of mental toughness. In a study by Dewhurst *et al* (2012) 60 participants were read two lists of words that they then had to recall. After the first list was read, participants were told that this was just for practice and they were not required to remember it. However, after the second list of words had been read, participants were told to recall words from both lists.

When recalling words from the first list, which they had been told to forget, mental toughness (as assessed by the MTQ48 measure) accounted for less than 1 per cent of variance. In effect, people who were mentally tough were no better than those who were not. However, when recalling words from the second list, mental toughness accounted for more than 20 per cent of the variance. This was largely explained by the commitment component.

Recent research has also found commitment to be an important determinant of cognitive inhibition and mind wandering. This means that those with high levels of commitment are better able to block out distractions and stay focused compared to those with lower levels of commitment. Clearly this is important when undertaking lengthy and/or complex tasks. This is particularly important when examining the productivity of a workforce.

Work by Clough *et al* shows that scores on the commitment subscale are positively correlated with key elements of brain structure. A cluster of significant positive correlation is also present in the brain area called the anterior cingulate gyrus (the area associated with control over anxiety), most likely reflecting a higher level of control over anxiety, a factor that plays an important role in commitment. High control over anxiety facilitates individuals' performance and commitment to a given activity due to an ability to control the potential anxiety associated with it.

Commitment is therefore the element that enables individuals and organizations to be mindful to set goals and targets for many of the things they need to do. In a world where measurement and key performance indicators (KPIs) are becoming *de rigueur* this is more than a useful response – it is essential.

But that is only half of the equation. Many who set goals and targets don't keep those promises. A truly committed person does. Arguably as the world spins faster and we get judged by our reliability in dealing with others, this becomes a more important quality.

Resilience

We have described resilience as a passive but important quality. It provides some capability to cope with setbacks. Resilience is often defined in terms of these two factors – control and commitment. Neither conveys necessarily the sense that the individual sees these as positive factors. It is simply a matter of 'gritting your teeth' and getting on with it until the situation is brought back under control and some semblance of normality is restored.

However, it is possible to approach the same situation more positively and have the confidence to see the situation not as a problem that needs to be sorted but also as an opportunity where the outcome can be beneficial for all. This is where the remaining two factors come to the fore and transform resilience into a more powerful concept – mental toughness. These are now described below.

Challenge

This component of mental toughness represents how individuals respond to challenge. This is commonly brought about by change. It is the beginning of a very divergent path. The perception of a change as challenge is the interpretation of it as an opportunity to learn, grow and thrive and meets it with a host of positive emotions. These include positive physiological response,

FIGURE 3.4 Sample descriptions of high and low scores in challenge

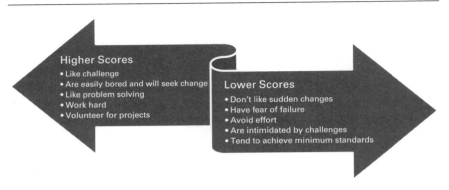

optimism and behaviour. Conversely, the interpretation of this change as a threat yields negative emotions, reduced positive physiological activity, pessimism and avoidance-type behaviours.

This component is also about seeking challenge. It is proactive, more so than described in theories of psychological resilience. Those with high scores in challenge will seek out achievement situations where there is the potential to accomplish more.

Individuals who actively approach challenge provide themselves with the opportunity for greater rewards. This concept dates back to McClelland's learned needs theory (1962) which identified three primary needs: affiliation (desire to establish social relationships), power (desire to control environment) and achievement (desire to take responsibility). It was from this theory that researchers observed how some individuals strive to approach achievement situations while others shy away. Clearly, for one to reach their potential, they must approach challenges that carry both risk and reward.

There is evidence to suggest that mental toughness is associated with risk taking, which is discussed later in this chapter. Logically, it is the challenge component that motivates us to take risks. Moreover, it is taking such risks that brings the greatest rewards. To progress, it is necessary to sometimes move out of your comfort zone.

If you do what you've always done, you'll get what you've always got.

So challenge is the element that enables us, whether as individuals or organizations, to desire to push out of a comfort zone and stretch oneself, even though this carries risk. Importantly, those who approach challenge in this way are also those who will accept that all outcomes, including failure and setbacks, have a positive element. Even a failure becomes a learning experience and potentially enables us to be more successful the next time we push back the boundaries and step into the relative unknown.

Confidence

Of all psychological concepts, confidence is one of the most commonly referred to. In essence, it is the extent to which we believe in ourselves to reach an identified target. This is clearly vital to performance, but perhaps even more so when setbacks occur. In the 4 Cs model, we distinguish between two types of confidence: confidence in abilities, which is the extent to which we believe that we have the capacity for success, and interpersonal confidence, which defines how comfortable we are at interacting with others.

Confidence in abilities

Few things are more powerful in the human psyche than belief in one's own abilities. When we believe that we have the ability to succeed, success is then only dependent on opportunity. When an opportunity arises, a confident person knows that this is a chance to shine and will exert effort in a bid to demonstrate competence.

When setbacks inevitably occur, because few things in life resemble a completely smooth journey, those confident in their abilities believe that persistence will ultimately be rewarding. Such effort and persistence consequently lead to very different outcomes to those who have less confidence in their abilities and therefore exert less effort and persistence.

FIGURE 3.5 Sample descriptions of high and low scores in confidence in abilities

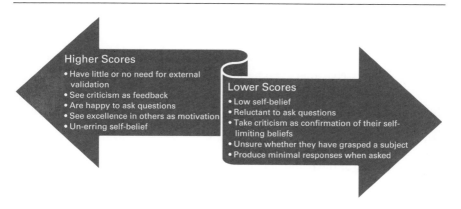

Higher Scores
- Have little or no need for external validation
- See criticism as feedback
- Are happy to ask questions
- See excellence in others as motivation
- Un-erring self-belief

Lower Scores
- Low self-belief
- Reluctant to ask questions
- Take criticism as confirmation of their self-limiting beliefs
- Unsure whether they have grasped a subject
- Produce minimal responses when asked

One of the prominent theories in the domain of confidence is self-efficacy theory. Developed by Albert Bandura (1977), self-efficacy is 'the belief in one's capabilities to organize and execute the courses of action required to manage prospective situations'. In other words, it is a person's belief in their ability to succeed in a particular situation. It is important to note that self-efficacy is specific to a situation, rather than a more general confidence. The most cited aspect of Bandura's theory is what he refers to as the four key determinants:

- performance accomplishments – we gain self-efficacy from having previously been successful at the task;
- vicarious experiences – we gain self-efficacy having seen other people of perceived similar ability being successful at the task;
- verbal persuasion – we gain self-efficacy by being convinced of our ability to be successful at the task;
- emotional arousal – we gain self-efficacy by being emotionally ready to take on the task.

Finally, it is important to note that not all who have confidence in their abilities are actually able. We have all met the overconfident 'know-it-all'. Conversely, there are those who are able and unfortunately do not believe in themselves, which obviously impacts on their attainment and well-being.

Interpersonal confidence

Being confident in your abilities is a great asset. However, its impact is much lessened if the individual does not have the confidence to express their views to others.

Confidence in interpersonal interactions is required to assert oneself and present work. A clear demonstration of interpersonal confidence can be observed at most meetings. Some will take a back seat, unsure whether their opinion is correct (confidence in abilities), or unwilling to express this view to others, as they feel unable to assert themselves orally (interpersonal confidence). Conversely, others will happily assert their views, confident in both the validity of their statements and in presenting them. In some instances they will control those meetings by dint of their confidence to be able to influence others.

It is worthwhile noting of course that confidence can be misplaced. One need only think of the deluded contestants on many 'talent' shows regularly shown on television for examples.

FIGURE 3.6 Sample descriptions of high and low scores in interpersonal confidence

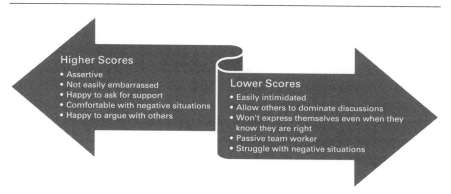

Higher Scores
- Assertive
- Not easily embarrassed
- Happy to ask for support
- Comfortable with negative situations
- Happy to argue with others

Lower Scores
- Easily intimidated
- Allow others to dominate discussions
- Won't express themselves even when they know they are right
- Passive team worker
- Struggle with negative situations

While believing that one has great ability does not make it objectively true, it is necessary for the individual to present the other components of mental toughness. With this confidence, they will seek challenge, commit themselves to the task and believe that they are in control.

Extraversion is a personality trait often associated with leaders. Unsurprisingly, mental toughness is related to extraversion. In particular, Clough, Earle and Sewell (2002) found that interpersonal confidence is positively associated with extraversion as well as assertiveness and independence. If an individual has ambitions to move into leadership, these are clearly useful characteristics.

The 4 Cs summary

While discussed separately above for ease of understanding, it is important to recognize that each component is not entirely independent of the others. There are clear structural crossovers in the model, which is why it is possible to consider overall mental toughness by aggregating each component. In effect, each component adds to overall mental toughness but also influences the other components. For example, by raising our confidence we are more likely to believe we have control and therefore be more likely to take on challenges and be committed to achieving our goals.

Consequently, interventions to build mental toughness may be geared more towards one aspect but developing one component is often likely to have a positive knock-on effect on the rest of those needed for mental toughness. Hence developing mental toughness using the 4 Cs model can be a powerful tool.

Measuring mental toughness

It is worth noting that most of the research cited in this chapter and elsewhere in this book has examined mental toughness by using MTQ48. This is a 48-item questionnaire that requires the respondent to identify the extent to which they agree or disagree with each statement. Originally developed by Clough, Earle and Sewell (2002), what is now known as the MTQ48 is a popular research tool.

Taken up by AQR, the MTQ48 has been developed into a commercially available measure with minor modifications in some instances to ensure its easy application in specific markets. It is well suited to being used by almost any potential users in almost every sphere of activity you can imagine. It is an excellent example of how modern psychometrics is evolving to meet the needs of users. It is now used in more than 40 countries and translated into 15 languages. Its commercial use for business and management organizations is vast. By the end of 2014 it is expected to be used by more than 3,000 significant organizations in over 80 countries.

Moreover, it can be applied wherever people have to do something and is therefore significant in almost everything an individual does. It is used in sport, health, education and social work. Of late there has been a large uptake in its use for employability and social mobility.

The MTQ48 expert report system provides detailed reports on overall mental toughness as well as each component of the 4 Cs model. It has been shown to be valid and reliable in a host of studies. For example, the predictive validity of the MTQ48 has been demonstrated in pain tolerance tests (eg Crust and Clough, 2005). Robust support for the validity of the measure came from Perry *et al* (2013) who examined the factorial validity and scale reliability on a sample of 8,207. This sample included senior managers, middle managers, clerical staff, sportspeople and students. In all groups there was support for the validity and reliability of the MTQ48.

Can mental toughness be integrated with the core models prevalent in occupational and in sport psychology?

Publishable research from sport and health domains

Much of our conceptual understanding of mental toughness has derived from studies in sport and health settings. These have been excellent vehicles for establishing the applications in organizations for developing mental toughness for performance and well-being. As discussed earlier, much of the early hardiness research focused on health. In sport, mental toughness is used regularly to explain peak performance. As sport involves frequently-changing circumstances and stressful situations it is an effective ground for testing theory. This has led to several studies examining coping.

Nicholls, Polman, Levy and Backhouse (2008) examined coping strategies used by athletes. They found that mentally-tough performers used more task-focused coping strategies, while those with lower levels of mental toughness adopted more distraction- or disengagement-focused strategies. In other words, mentally-tough performers took on problems while more mentally-sensitive individuals shied away from them.

In a follow-up study, Kaiseler, Polman and Nicholls (2009) also found that mentally-tough performers were more likely to tackle a problem rather than use emotion-focused methods or avoidance techniques. This again supports the notion that mentally-tough performers cope better with stressful situations.

It has long been understood how important well-being is in the workplace. Of late, there has been a host of studies examining the effects of mental toughness on health. Specifically, researchers at the University of Basle have been exploring the role of mental toughness in adolescent health. They have found that adolescent exercise and physical activity are associated with mental toughness (Gerber *et al*, 2012), that mentally-tough adolescents are more resilient against stress and that they adapt better to stress over time (Gerber *et al*, 2013).

Integrating mental toughness with some of the key models in applied psychology

There are a number of proven advantages of being mentally tough for individuals. They are clearly more able to function effectively in high-pressure situations. We believe that the same is true of organizations as a whole, as they are clearly the sum of the skills and talents of the people who work within them.

One way of exploring the advantages of mental toughness in the workplace is to link this concept to some of the key concepts in applied occupational and sports psychology. Here we examine five main concepts:

- motivation;
- team working;
- stress;

- leadership;
- emotional intelligence.

Motivation

The core concept in performance psychology is motivation. Occupational psychology has a clear track record in this area. A number of key motivational theories have been developed that have been used widely to get a better understanding of workplace performance. The motivational theories can be subdivided into two main categories: need theories and process theories.

Arguably the most well-known need theory can be seen in the work of Abraham Maslow (1943). He speculated that individuals have a set of needs that need to be satisfied in order for them to fully function. These needs are: physiological, safety, social, esteem and self-actualization (living up to one's full potential).

Although the model has little empirical support it does cast a huge shadow over, or better still illuminates, the world of business. It seems very reasonable to suggest that mentally-tough individuals should be self-actualizing. They have a natural tendency to achieve and strive. If the self-actualized person is the core of organizational success, then so perhaps is the mentally-tough employee.

Another influential need theory is McClelland's learned needs theory. He argued that an individual's need to develop is a result of their early environment and it is this need that then drives behaviour. The most widely-researched needs are achievement, affiliation and power. Again there is a close tie-in between these and mental toughness. It is clear that mentally-tough individuals are often comfortable being in management and/or leadership roles and they are driven by a need to achieve and succeed. There are also close links with affiliation. These links will be discussed later in this chapter.

McClelland developed a model that provides organizations with an effective way of helping their employees meet their needs. Many of these are widely used and they clearly could be used in developing a mentally-tough organization.

McClelland championed:

- allowing feedback;
- using achievement heroes;
- the importance of improving the self-image of employees; and
- the importance of introducing realism into the workplace.

He was clear that employees should both think in realistic terms and think positively. The latter of these 'prescriptions' especially is at the core of many interventions designed to enhance mental toughness.

The other broad area of motivational theories encompasses process. It tends to assume that individuals make rational decisions about how much effort they put into their activities. Vroom's expectancy model is perhaps the seminal piece of work in this area (Vroom, 1964). He argues there are three main aspects that need to be considered. The first is expectancy. Expectancy relates to the judgement of an individual's chances of reaching their performance goals. The second is instrumentality. What are the chances of getting various outcomes if a performance goal is achieved? Finally there is valence. What value does the outcome hold for the individual?

The research evidence to date shows that mentally-tough individuals are more logical and analytic. They tend to take a more balanced view of the workplace and are less influenced by emotional variations. Clearly many, probably most, organizations adopt this rational approach to motivation. The mentally-tough individual will thrive in this type of environment.

A final process theory we will examine is that of equity theory. Again, at the heart of equity theory is the idea of the rationality of the workforce. This theory argues that employees compare their efforts and rewards with those in similar situations. Equity exists when employees perceive that the ratio of their inputs (ie effort) to their rewards is equivalent to the ratios of other employees. Inputs include many things, for example education, skills, age, seniority and creativity. Outcomes encompass such things as pay, job security, promotions and recognition.

Putting the two areas of need and process together provides a template for maximizing motivation. It is the leader's job to identify what a person desires and then clearly identify how to achieve these outcomes while helping the individual to have a sound and realistic understanding of the ratio of inputs to outputs.

It is perhaps time to move on to mental toughness and working with others. How might a mentally-tough workforce operate in respect to these softer, but vital, aspects of the workplace?

Team working

The importance of working effectively with others is clear. However, the duality of the concept of team working is shown in the well-used adage:

There is no I in team – but, if you look carefully, you will find m-e.

Mentally-tough individuals are often driven by the need to achieve and are, by definition, rather competitive. Does this mean that they are not team workers? We don't think so and will explore some of the issues in the following section.

In an organization, teams carry out a number of functions. For example, they allow it to accomplish complex tasks, they generate creative solutions, they implement complex decisions and socialize with and train newcomers.

Interestingly, it has been argued by Tuckman (1965) for a group to work effectively it has to have a storming stage. In this stage of group activity conflicts emerge, there is clear disagreement and some members may withdraw. It is suggested that mentally-tough individuals will be more likely to prosper in a storming group and will probably be the instigators. A team lacking toughness may never get past its storming stage and therefore never really perform.

When most people talk about team working they tend to relate this to cohesiveness. In reality teams can be socially cohesive, task cohesive, both or neither. Most people appear to concentrate on social cohesion, although interestingly there is little evidence that this impacts on performance. Basically, social cohesion revolves around friendliness and being liked. Task cohesion is about working effectively together and does not necessarily rely on social cohesiveness.

Ideally, organizations would have both, but we would argue the ability to work with people who you do not necessarily like is the true core of successful team working. Mentally-tough individuals have a strong self-concept and are internally validated. This allows them to make less popular decisions, which may be needed. It is not that mentally-tough individuals are unpopular. They are usually not as there is an inherent attractiveness in confident people. However, they are not driven by the desire to fit in.

We will briefly discuss a few 'classic' aspects of organizational psychology to illustrate the point. The first is social control. The work of Asch (1956) and Milgram (1963) has clearly shown that many people can be pressurized into doing things that are clearly wrong, and in the case of Milgram's research, abhorrent.

Both these classic studies reveal that humans are very easily led. More positively, they also show that if only one individual stands up to social control the majority of others will do so as well. Basically, mentally-tough individuals are less susceptible to social pressure and should therefore be more objective and reliable problem solvers.

In any team one problem that exists is social loafing. It is easy to hide in a crowd and this underperformance by individuals, even in a high-performing team, can be costly. The commitment element of the 4 Cs model protects against this tendency. Committed individuals will normally give their work 100 per cent effort, even though they cannot be seen doing it.

Finally we will briefly discuss groupthink. This is the pressure that highly-cohesive groups exert on their members, resulting in uniform and actable choices that actually reduce their capacity to make effective decisions. Two of the key antecedents to groupthink are classically at the centre of old-fashioned teamwork thinking: high cohesion and insulation from other teams and groups. Groupthink produces a number of worrying symptoms. These include illusions of invulnerability, belief in inherent morality, self-censorship and illusions of unanimity.

Organizations often create problems when chasing classic social cohesive team working. They open themselves up to high levels of social control and incomplete problem solving.

There are a number of ways to try to reduce problems like groupthink. Mentally-tough individuals will often be needed to put these in place. For example, members of a team should be encouraged to evaluate ideas openly and critically. This takes social confidence, tenacity and an enjoyment of challenge. Similarly, someone will often have to take a devil's advocate role. In reality this is quite similar to the monitor–evaluator role in Belbin's categorization of team roles (Belbin, 1981). The person playing this role will rarely win a popularity contest and it is hard to see a sensitive person thriving in it.

Related to many of these issues is risk taking. An effective organization is neither risk averse nor is it 'gung ho'. It achieves a balance of risk taking that is appropriate for the sector. There is some evidence that mental toughness has an impact on risk-taking behaviour. Crust and Keegan (2010) speculate that tough individuals appear to be future-orientated decision makers who seek out challenges and approach, rather than avoid, potential anxiety-producing situations. In other words, they tend to take controlled risky decisions – with the emphasis on control.

An area that ties in with risk taking is fatigue. When people are tired they tend to make riskier decisions (Hockey *et al*, 2000). It appears that mentally-tough individuals are less prone to fatigue and hence they should remain more consistent in their risk taking.

Stress

Stress at work is consistently identified as a major problem impacting on the effectiveness and efficiency of individuals and organizations. Or should we say, inappropriate levels of stress are. It is the employers' responsibility to ensure that unnecessary stressors are removed from the workplace or minimized if they cannot be removed. Unfortunately, many roles have an element of stress attached to them.

Stress can be seen as:

> ... an adaptive response, mediated by individual characteristics and/or psychological process, that is a consequence of any external action, situation, or event that places special physical and/or psychological demands on a person...
>
> (Ivancevich and Matteson, 1980)

There is a vast array of stressors. At the individual level these include job demands, role conflict, role ambiguity and workload. At the group level there are such things as leader behaviour, lack of cohesiveness and intra-group conflict. The organization itself produces many stressors emanating from its culture, its structure, technology and change. Finally, and often overlooked, are extra-organizational stressors. These include family issues, the economy and commuting.

Inappropriately high levels of stress can have very many detrimental effects on an organization. It can lead to psychological problems such as low job satisfaction, depression and even burnout. These are obviously closely related to behaviour issues, which include absenteeism, turnover, poor performance, accidents and substance abuse. There are clear links with physical illness.

Arguably the most insidious problems associated with stress are those related to cognitive function. Stress levels that are beyond what a person can deal with can severely impact on cognitive processing, leading to poor decisions, poor concentration and forgetfulness. Unlike objective data such as turnover the real costs and damage of these cognitive deficits are difficult to quantify. A poor decision by a senior executive can bring an organization to its knees.

Work-related stress is not simply a reflection of workload. The key is controllability. High demands and high control can produce an environment best described as 'arousing'. To the mentally-tough individual this type of culture may be seen as some form of Nirvana. They fear 'brownout' – rusting away – much more than burnout.

There is no such thing as a definitive stressor. What stresses out one person enables someone else. Some people are simply better suited to highly stressful environments. Normally this means that individuals best suited to the demand context simply keep going. The less suited are driven from that workplace. It is clear we can do much better than this. This will be discussed later in the chapter.

Sensitive individuals cope in a fundamentally different way than their mentally-tough counterparts. They rely more on emotional coping, seeking out social support. Tougher individuals will adopt a more active coping perspective, striving to change things. Both approaches work for different individuals. Too often however organizations take a 'one size fits all' approach.

Leadership

Leadership is a stressful activity. In order to lead successfully we can comfortably argue that an individual has to have high levels of mental toughness. This is supported by the work of Marchant *et al* (2009) who showed a clear relationship between level of seniority in an organization and mental toughness level. The higher the grade, the higher the mental toughness. This does not show that mental toughness is related to great leadership but it does suggest that a degree of mental toughness is necessary for being put in a position where you can be a highly effective leader.

Leadership has been described in many ways. One of our favourite definitions was developed by Bass (1990) who states:

> Leadership is an interaction between members of a group. Leaders are agents
> of change, persons whose acts affect other people more than other people's acts
> affect them. Leadership occurs when one group member modifies the motivation
> of others in the group.

This could almost be an alternative definition of what we think of as mental toughness. It is about influence and change.

There are very many models of leadership. Working with Doug Strycharczyk, Professor Clough has developed a model and measure (the ILM72) that seeks to bring together all the core elements of the myriad of ideas within the leadership domain. This too has been transformed by AQR into a commercial measure and is used all over the world. The model and measure has two components.

The first identifies six specific scales, which describe the key facets of leadership style. These describe how a leader behaves when going about their business. Moreover it describes adopted style, not necessarily preferred style. Our work showed that there was no such thing as a unique style which was more effective than any other description of style. Indeed, the suggestion is that leadership style is situational.

The specific scales are:

1 **Task v person:** how much the leader is oriented to meet the needs of the task or individuals. This reflects the leader's belief about an aspect

of motivation. Does success breed success (task focus) or do you work on the person?

2 Flexible v dogmatic: how much the leader involves others in analysis and decision making.

3 De-centralized v centralized: how much the leader feels central to the operation or is willing to delegate authority to others.

4 Reward v punishment: how much the leader believes people are motivated by reward or punishment.

5 The means v the end: how important hitting goals and targets are to the leader and what they are willing to sacrifice to get there.

6 Structured v organic: how much structure, planning and personal organization are important to the leader compared to relying on intuition and instinct.

The second component describes three global scales. These are three competencies which emerge as central to leadership behaviour. This time there is some suggestion that having more of these competencies does translate into better followership. In turn, this should lead to better performance as followers give up, willingly, their discretionary effort.

A Determination to deliver: measures single-minded determination to achieve.

B Engagement with individuals: how much the leader focuses on the confidence and commitment of individuals to enable them to contribute to the organization and fulfil themselves.

C Engagement with team working: how much the leader harnesses all the potential in an organization with a particular emphasis on cross-functional team working.

Those familiar with the major leadership models (Fiedler, 1967; Adair, 1984; and House, 1971) will recognize these as central concepts in all of these models.

Mental toughness both informs the leadership style used and enhances the effectiveness of the preferred approach. We are not prescriptive on which style is best. It is clearly dependent on the situation. But mental toughness can facilitate the approach used. To some extent at least, 'it's not what you do, it's the way that you do it'.

The global competencies are different. Ideally the truly effective leader would focus on all three. The central themes of these can be easily linked to the central themes of the 4 Cs model.

It is not possible in a chapter like this one to cover all aspects of leadership. As an illustration of how mental toughness and leadership can be linked we will briefly focus on transformational leadership. This model has been dominant in the last decade. There is a debate about what transformational leadership is but it can be suggested that a transformational leader:

- establishes a vision;
- stretches the minds of their teams;
- helps people overcome obstacles;
- helps people overcome failures;
- shares success.

Some will argue that this is really about emotionally intelligent active coping, that is, it relies on understanding people and helping them cope. In our terms, it is a combination of task and interpersonal confidence, coupled with challenge commitment and control.

This is consistent with a growing awareness among researchers and practitioners (such as Paul Brown) that the notion of emotional intelligence might need to be described in a fresh way and that we may be talking about intelligent emotions. It is an area that needs and deserves a good deal more exploration.

Emotional intelligence

When writing a chapter like this one it is impossible, and inadvisable, to avoid discussing what is popularly understood to be emotional intelligence and its relationship with mental toughness. Toughness can often be misrepresented as a macho and unsubtle concept. This is entirely wrong. We will try to illustrate this point by relating the 4 Cs model to the original definition of emotional intelligence (EI) produced by Goleman (1998). He identified five characteristics of EI. It should be noted that none of them relate directly to being emotional – actually they are far from this.

The first characteristic is termed *self-awareness*. This is about knowing yourself, recognizing feelings as they occur and discriminating between them. It might be expected that mentally-tough individuals are less good at this but this does not appear to be the case. For example, Crust *et al* (2009) carried out a study that suggested mentally-tough people are as emotionally literate as anyone else. They experience the same intensity of effect, but deal with it more effectively. This suggests that they may be as good, or better, at understanding themselves.

The second characteristic was identified as *mood management*. This involves the ability to deal with feelings and respond appropriately. This is clearly linked to emotional control.

Third there is *self-motivation*. This is directing yourself towards a goal despite self-doubt, disinterest and distraction. This is an excellent definition of the commitment scale.

Fourth there is *empathy*. We acknowledge that mentally-tough individuals may be less good at this. Empathy is about recognizing and responding to the feelings of others. It is probable that mentally-tough individuals would have to work at this.

Finally there is *relationship management*. This is all about a positive and mutually-beneficial set of interpersonal interactions, conflict resolutions and negotiations. The mentally tough may have an advantage here.

Mentally-tough individuals and organizations are not emotionally illiterate., rather they are simply not driven by emotion.

Can we develop a mentally-tough organization?

As outlined in the section on stress, there are four levels of potential stressor: individual level, group level, organizational level and extra-organizational level. This broad conceptualization can be useful when looking at ways of producing a truly tough organization.

Before beginning to develop organizational toughness, it is vital to carry out an organizational diagnosis. Basically, this involves three broad questions:

- What are the performance issues within the organization?
- What are the implications of these issues?
- What will be targeted to develop and/or improve?

After this stage then interventions can begin if desired. Finally, the impact of the interventions needs to be carefully evaluated and the cycle begins again.

Interventions focused on the individual level

Selection

Selecting mentally-tough individuals is a straightforward way of increasing the toughness levels of a business. It can be seen as somewhat akin to 'herd immunity'. If you have a critical mass of toughness then you reach a tipping point of this valuable skillset.

A tight definition of toughness allows the development of clear and concise competencies. These provide a vital foundation on which to build appropriate assessment exercises. The MTQ48 offers an excellent way into assessing the toughness of a candidate.

Training and development

There is some evidence that mental toughness has a genetic component. For example, Horsburgh *et al* (2009), using a sample of twins, showed that there was a clear hereditary basis. However, it is never as simple as nature versus nurture. Both have an influence. Some people are born tough, others may develop toughness. Early experiences can lead to toughening, but they can also lead to a reduction in toughness. It is not true that putting people in stressful situations will automatically toughen people.

Crust and Clough (2011) identified three factors that might enhance mental toughness:

1 providing a challenging yet supportive environment;

2 having an effective social support mechanism;

3 encouraging reflection: emphasizing the importance of experiential learning.

One question is: can formal training increase toughness? There is some evidence that mental skills training can indeed do this (eg Sheard and Golby, 2007). There are a number of mental skills that form the core of these interventions. These fall into five broad categories:

- positive thinking – affirmations, turning negatives into positives, etc;

- visualization – guided imagery, etc;

- anxiety control – relaxation techniques;

- attentional control – focus, dealing with distractions;

- goal setting – SMART.

In addition to formal training sessions, mental toughness can be developed through coaching and mentoring. At first sight this might appear to be slightly counterintuitive: using a 'soft' skills approach to develop toughness. However, it is certainly possible. There is broad agreement that it is about helping a person achieve their goals or improve their performance through structured one-to-one conversations. Developing some aspects of mental toughness is inherent in many coaching sessions.

Group level interventions

Teams

People who rise to the top of an organization are almost inevitably more mentally tough than the average person. However, being mentally tough usually implies a degree of personal achievement and a degree of mental insensitivity – a tendency to be 'thick skinned' and not be too sensitive to things that might get in the way of performance. Not the best recipe for team working!

The challenge is to maintain the mental toughness of these high performers while helping them to develop the behaviours which are consistent with effective team working.

AQR, in collaboration with Dr Clough, has researched this area for more than 20 years and have together concluded that high-performing teams appear to do the same things wherever they are. Examining the behaviour of high-performing teams – whether they are from the sports, social or the business worlds – shows that there are certain characteristics that are consistently present if that team is truly 'world class'. These characteristics fall into five broad and interrelated areas, captured in what AQR calls its 5 Circles model:

- setting and working to common goals and objectives;
- good communications – listening to each other and sharing what we know;
- continuous improvement and problem solving – facing up to setbacks and wanting to put them right;
- developing and maintaining good interpersonal relationships – irrespective of whether or not you like the others in your team;
- creating feelings of success and involvement – contributing to the positive mood of the team.

We believe it is possible to develop 'team toughness'. This revolves around action targeted at the 4 Cs.

Interventions to bolster the challenge domain include:

- Review and prioritize work together.
- Communicate with each other.
- Identify each other's strengths and weaknesses. Coach and delegate where necessary.

- View challenges and obstacles as opportunities at both a team and individual level.

- Break down assignments into smaller, manageable chunks and delegate.

- Recognize when you need to take time out and recharge as a team and as individuals.

Interventions aimed at the control domain include:

- Agree on who is doing what.

- Accept that setbacks are normal occurrences.

- Agree on a plan together and support each other in sticking to it.

- Give each other the space, time and support you each need to recover from setbacks.

- Some things will always be outside of your control – work as a team to work around that which you can't change.

Interventions aimed at the commitment domain include:

- Take time to recognize each other's contributions and give praise where due.

- Accept that some tasks can't be completed. Review resources and energy – could they be better directed?

- Identify what motivates you as a team and as individuals and incorporate this into your planning.

- Agree on your goals and deadlines. They should be specific, measurable, achievable, relevant and time bound.

- Don't be afraid to ask each other for help when you need it and encourage each other to suggest ideas.

- Have regular meetings or contact to monitor progress. Things change and so might your goals with them.

- Listen to each other and ask each other questions. Communicate.

Finally, interventions aimed at the confidence domain include:

- Recognize each other's strengths, acknowledge them and use them.

- Don't dwell on mistakes and overgeneralize them. Not everything is black and white, mistakes can be learned from.

- Be aware of over-confidence.

- If confidence is knocked, recognize the need for time off to recover. Give each other the additional support you need.
- Give constructive criticism, corrections and encouragement instead of verbally beating someone down.
- Give teammates the support they need to improve their skills and increase their confidence.
- If a teammate or colleague needs chastizing, do it in private and provide them with the opportunity to remedy their error.

All these disparate ideas and actions can be drawn into producing a 'team charter'. The purpose of this charter would be to produce a team with a range of mental toughness scores that performs in a tough way.

Leadership

Obviously leaders are individuals but they also belong to the group of management. The tone they set impacts on others and creates its own microclimates. Leaders can work to develop their own mental toughness and the mental toughness of their employees.

A key question not yet discussed in this chapter is that of the 'mental toughness balance'. Diversity is the lifeblood of any group. It is not suggested that all employees are, or should be, mentally tough but rather that the group should operate in a resiliently tough way if it is to perform in a challenging environment and do this in a way preserves the well-being of its members.

Making effective use of more sensitive individuals is, counterintuitively, an excellent way of doing this. Difference reduces conformity which in turn leads to creativity and respect. The leader's role therefore encompasses ways of dealing with mental toughness differences as well as managing the myriad of other differences that make up the workforce.

The organizational level

A key question is: do you alter the worker or the workplace? As a rule it is harder to alter the workplace, but altering the organization in certain ways may help it become a more mentally tough entity.

The classic approaches to organizational design have been job enlargement and job enrichment. Job enlargement is about increasing the number and variety of tasks a worker performs. Job enrichment involves giving the employee more autonomy. At the heart of both of these is the belief that people work better when they have a sense of achievement. Control and challenge are at the heart of this philosophy and at the heart of the 4 Cs model.

It can be speculated that providing more challenging jobs may develop the mental toughness of those doing them. Less speculation is needed when suggesting that mentally-tough individuals will find these jobs well suited to their skillsets.

Attempts to improve organizational performance by enhancing autonomy have met with mixed results. We would suggest that in order to get this approach to work effectively it is necessary to consider individual differences within the workforce. One key difference would be mental toughness.

Organizational development (OD) is about ways of increasing an organization's effectiveness. One of the key roles in any OD activity is the change agent. This individual identifies the need to change and drive it through. Without them it simply will not work. Mentally-tough individuals are ideally suited to carry out this very demanding role. In reality, they will often do it spontaneously.

We felt a brief note on job satisfaction might be helpful. Job satisfaction refers to what employees think about their jobs. In reality it reflects individual differences as much as it reflects differences between jobs. Hulin (1991) stated 'Jobs with responsibility may be dissatisfying to some because of the stress and problems that co-vary with responsibility: others may find responsibility a source of positive affect' (p 460). Low satisfaction scores may indicate an issue with work or may be a reflection of the worker themselves. When identifying problems and planning interventions this needs to be taken into account.

In summary, an organization can create the psychological space for mentally-tough working, providing an atmosphere of challenge and autonomy. This in turn will produce mentally-tough employees but some may not prosper in this demanding environment. Organization development must be predicated on individual development to be truly successful.

The extra-organizational level

This important area is usually overlooked. Issues at home transfer to the workplace and issues in the workplace transfer to the home. When building mental toughness it should be remembered that the skills learned can easily apply to non-work aspects of a person's life and, of course, skills learned at home and at play are nearly always transferable into the workplace and into education.

In the early 1990s, Doug and his colleagues at AQR worked with Champion Spark Plug on a pioneering continuous improvement programme which was built around people identifying and solving problems in small groups, something that is fairly common today. The then-CEO of Champion Spark Plug John Shapley believed strongly that the notion of team-based continuous improvement activity should be extended to *all* staff in an organization, irrespective of level. Until that point improvement teams, at least in the West, had been largely confined to management and senior staff.

Indeed, within the organization many senior managers doubted that employees at all levels could be engaged in this way. The human resources manager for the largest operation decided to carry out an interesting exercise. He arranged to interview almost 750 staff (clerical and shop-floor) about their hobbies, interests and activities outside the workplace. These were people who carried no managerial or supervisory responsibility in the organization's structure.

To everyone's surprise, he found that more than a third were involved in activities that required supervisory, managerial or organizational skills that they were never allowed to use in the workplace. They were involved in running scout troops, voluntary activities, care of the elderly, etc. Many sat on committees and governing bodies for schools and local organizations. In almost all of these roles they had responsibility for doing what they did as efficiently and as effectively as possible.

This indicated a huge reservoir of talent that wasn't being utilized.

John Sharpley's response was to put every single employee – director, manager, employee – through the same team-building programme and to challenge everyone to identify how to improve performance and eliminate irritations at their level. To support this he offered accredited supervisory skills and 'soft' skills training to *any* employee irrespective of level. The message was 'you are all important members of the organization – and in this respect you are equally important'. Hundreds took up the offer. Every single employee began to become involved in continuous improvement activity. The savings generated and waste eliminated yielded a payback measured in months not years. One idea alone (generated by a team on the shop floor) more than paid for the cost of the whole development programme.

One interesting side effect was that absenteeism dropped from around 11 per cent per annum to less than 2 per cent. Engaging employees in their work and empowering them in this way produced a remarkable transformation in attitude and behaviour. People wanted to come to work because it interested them.

Another was that many employees when working in teams would often come into work on Saturday mornings in their own time (without pay) to carry out problem-solving activity. We first learned of this because the takings in the company canteen began to increase although there was no scheduled increase in numbers in the operation.

Champion Spark Plug's groundbreaking programme was featured on BBC TV, where Professor John Adair commented that it was (at that time) 'unique' and 'highly effective'. What Sharpley and his colleagues had achieved was creating a 'can do' mindset in the workplace at all levels and the leader of the organization was taking the mentally tough and the mentally sensitive with him. There were cynics, there were the fearful and there were the outright hostile, but creating a safe and supportive environment in which change could take place did work.

There is generally a lack of research and understanding about how work and the life we lead outside of work interact.

An enlightened employer will consider this and develop ways to support the tough and the sensitive to deal with the interface. While mentally-tough individuals may want to work longer hours and avoid holidays, there should be checks put on this. Does this impact negatively on the rest of their lives?

It is not certain what role an employer should play in employees' non-working activities. It should be a question that is asked and is likely to bubble to the top of the agenda over time. We are already in a 24/7 world where all kinds of flexibility are needed for someone to perform effectively. Sometimes it is possible to organize work so that it fits well with the need of employees. Increasingly this is difficult to achieve.

In the world of business 'the customer is often king'. Some customers are understanding, many are not. They have a problem and want you to solve their problem without bringing yours to their attention.

Some final thoughts

In conclusion, we believe that the mentally-tough organization can be developed. This is not about restricting diversity but rather providing a firm foundation of realism and skills.

Peak performance is the ability to function efficiently at your best, enabling you to express your full potential. It can be argued that this is the 'flip side' of stress management. Often mental toughness is simply seen as 'surviving the bad', but we would argue it is as much about maximizing 'the good'. Optimizing performance means responding positively to challenges. It will often involve dealing with adversity and setbacks.

Similarly, there is a significant crossover between mental toughness and positive psychology. Positive psychology was created as it was believed that there was simply too much focus on the negative aspects of the human condition. While this is undoubtedly true, we believe it would be wrong to ignore the negatives – the real world has those too.

There is more focus nowadays on happiness. Who would argue with that? Well, we would. Happiness is really about subjective well-being. It is transient and perhaps it is naïve to put this as an end goal. It is sometimes termed the 'hedonist treadmill', with people running on the spot to chase something rather ephemeral. An organization chasing the happiness agenda may find this a fruitless task.

We prefer in our work to focus on contentment. This is achieved by facing challenges and accepting risk. It arguably has more depth and is more sustainable. It is tied in with the classic need theories of motivation and organizational development and provides a valid end point. It is close to the idea of self-actualization. In order to arrive there individuals have to develop and deal with problems and that brings us back to mental toughness.

An important point

Do we *need* to develop more mentally-tough organizations and more mentally-tough individuals? We think so. The direction of travel is pretty clear. There are more challenges of different kinds than ever before.

But you, the reader, can judge for yourself. We can describe a mentally-tough individual in fairly simple language. Look at Table 3.1 on page 75. Does this describe the kind of person who will prosper today and will prosper tomorrow in a world that appears to be asking people to be more individually responsible and more accountable for their own prosperity, their health and their well-being?

We've yet to meet someone who says not. QED, as they say.

So... what about the future?

If we make some simple assumptions about the future and, probably with confidence, predict that the world will become challenging in new and different ways and at a faster pace than ever before, then there is a strong

TABLE 3.1 Practical descriptions of mental toughness

Scale	What will be running through the mind of a mentally-tough individual
Control	I really believe I *can do* it. I can *keep my emotions in check* when doing it.
Commitment	I *promise* to do it – I'll set a goal. I'll *do what it takes* to deliver it (hard work).
Challenge	I will *push back* the boundaries – I will take a chance. *Setbacks make me stronger.*
Confidence	I *believe* I have the ability to do it. I can *stand my ground* if I need to.

likelihood that being able to deal with this positively will be a key requirement for individuals and organizations. To be positive about it and embrace it will be better still – it is likely to produce the best outcomes for all.

An evolution from a stoical response to change (resilience) to a more proactive and enthusiastic response (mental toughness) might be both inevitable and desirable. If we look at the description of the so-called Generation Y and Generation Z cohorts in Chapter 2 you might say that this is already underway.

The 20th century saw some interesting developments in society in many countries around the globe. In the early part of the 20th century we saw the beginnings of the state taking a role in the well-being of its citizens, which was accelerated in the post-war enthusiasm for nationalization of so-called key industries and sectors.

For a while the notion of a job for life and the state safety net held sway – certainly in the United Kingdom. However, there is now a reversal of some of that. Few expect a job for life, most expect that they will have many jobs and many forms of employment over their lifetimes and there is a growing awareness that most will need to be more self-sufficient in many ways. Even where the state does provide some support it will be less than before. Rising retirement ages and diminishing levels of pensions are good examples.

We are already seeing a growing interest in developing factors such as character, grit, mindset and resilience in improving employability and social mobility for young people – and this is pretty much universal. It is a global issue.

Organizationally we think the challenge will lie in two areas. Leadership is one. As leading an organization becomes more challenging there will be a need for tenacious leadership. Selecting, developing and motivating workforces to provide the flexibility to respond to future needs will be another.

Will the mental toughness concept shed more light on our behaviours, abilities and qualities? It is in the nature of academics not to claim something until there is reasonable evidence for its existence. However, we are already noticing some interesting by-products from current research and applications of the MTQ48 measure. These need much more investigation but even now they raise interesting and useful questions. When you are at the leading edge you often have to make an educated guess which becomes your hypothesis.

As indicated earlier, the mentally tough aren't necessarily macho and tough in that sense. Nor are they necessarily emotionally insensitive or emotionally illiterate. It appears that the mentally tough are often 'comfortable in their own skin' and do not need to deal with stressors, pressure and challenges in an aggressive manner. They appear to be able to take these in their stride and can be as emotionally aware as any other.

It is now being suggested that intelligent emotions may be a more appropriate concept than emotional intelligence: the suggestion being that it is the individual experiencing the emotions who impacts on the world around them by managing those emotions. Imagine a manager who doesn't feel happy. When he or she goes to work, the staff will soon learn that their manager is unhappy and are often likely to pick up that mood unless he or she presents a more positive set of emotions. If the manager presents a more positive set of emotions then this might impact positively on the mood of the people around them which, it is suggested, creates a virtuous spiral in lifting the mood of the manager. This corresponds well with our understanding of the emotional control subscale in our model of mental toughness.

The implication here is that mental toughness might be important for relationship building – especially in developing productive team working as opposed to the traditional notion of teams where people rub along with each other. That may be nice but is it as productive as it can be? Can mental toughness development add to performance and well-being in this area too?

In summary, mental toughness is like most personality traits: it has always been there. It has always been the quality that helps people to deal with change, challenge and setback. It is not a big stretch to suppose that it will become much more important as the 21st century rolls out and will find many more applications and connections for developing organizations.

References

Adair, J (1969) *Action Centred Leadership*, Gower Publishing Ltd, Aldershot

Adair, J E (1984) *The Skills of Leadership*, Nichols Pub Co, New York

Asch, S E (1956) Studies of independence and conformity: a minority of one against a unanimous majority, *Psychological Monographs*, 70

Bandura, A (1977) Self-efficacy: toward a unifying theory of behavioral change, *Psychological Review*, 84(2), pp 191–215, doi: 10.1037/0033-295X.84.2.191

Bass, B M (1990) *Bass and Stogdill's Handbook of Leadership: Theory, research, and managerial applications*, Free Press, New York

Belbin, R M (1981) *Management Teams: Why they succeed* or *fail*, Butterworth-Heinemann, London

Bennis, W (1961) Revisionist theory of Leadership, *Harvard Business Review*, 39(1), pp 26–36

Clough, P J, Earle, K, and Sewell, D (2002) Mental toughness: the concept and its measurement, in *Solutions in Sport Psychology*, ed I Cockerill, pp 32–43, Thomson, London

Clough, P J and Strycharczyk, D (2012) *Developing Mental Toughness: Improving performance, wellbeing and positive behaviour in others*, Kogan Page, Philidelphia

Connor, K M and Davidson, J R (2003) Development of a new resilience scale: the Connor-Davidson Resilience Scale (CD-RISC), *Depression and Anxiety*, 18, p 76

Crust, L (2008) A review and conceptual re-examination of mental toughness: implications for future researchers, *Personality and Individual Differences*, 45(7), pp 576–583

Crust, L and Clough, P J (2005) Relationship between mental toughness and physical endurance, *Perceptual and Motor Skills*, 100(1), pp 192–194

Crust, L and Clough, P J (2011) Developing mental toughness: from research to practice, *Journal of Sport Psychology in Action*, 2(1), pp 21–32

Crust, L and Keegan, R (2010) Mental toughness and attitudes to risk-taking, *Personality and Individual Differences*, 49(3), pp 164–168

Dewhurst, S A, Anderson, R J, Cotter, G, Crust, L, and Clough, P J (2012) Identifying the cognitive basis of mental toughness: evidence from the directed forgetting paradigm, *Personality and Individual Differences*, 53, pp 587–590

Dienstbier, R A (1989) Arousal and physiological toughness: implications for mental and physical health, *Psychological Review*, 96(1), pp 84–100

Fiedler, F E (1967) *A Theory of Leadership Effectiveness*, McGraw-Hill, New York

Fletcher, D, and Sarkar, M (2013) Psychological resilience: a review and critique of definitions, concepts, and theory, *European Psychologist*, 18(1), pp 12–23, doi: 10.1027/1016-9040/a000124

Funk, S C (1992) Hardiness: a review of theory and research, *Health Psychology*, 11, pp 335–345

Gerber, M, Brand, S, Feldmetha, A K, Langa, C, Elliota, C, and Holsboer-Trachsler, E, Pühse, U (2013) Adolescents with high mental toughness adapt better to perceived stress: a longitudinal study with Swiss vocational students, *Personality and Individual Differences*, **54**(7) pp 808–814

Gerber, M, Kalak, N, Lemola, S, Clough, P J, Perry, J L, Pühse, U, Elliot, C, Holsboer-Trachsler, E and Brand, S (2012) Are adolescents with high mental toughness levels more resilient against stress? *Stress and Health*, **29**, pp 164–171, doi: 10.1002/smi.2447

Goleman, D (1998) *Working with Emotional Intelligence*, Bantam, New York

Heider, F (1944) Social perception and phenomenal causality, *Psychological Review*, **51**, pp 358–374

Hockey, G R J, Maule, J, Clough, P J, and Bdzola, L (2000) Effects of negative mood states on risk in everyday decision making, *Cognition & Emotion*, **14**(6), pp 823–855

Horsburgh, V, Schermer, J, Veselka, L, and Vernon, P (2009) A behavioral genetic study of mental toughness and personality, *Personality and Individual Differences*, **46**, pp 100–105

House, R J (1971) A path–goal theory of leader effectiveness, *Administrative Science Quarterly*, **16**(3) pp 321–338

House, R J (1996) *A Theory of Leadership Effectiveness*, McGraw-Hill, New York

Hulin, C (1991) Adaptation, persistence, and commitment in organizations, in *Handbook of Industrial and Organizational Psychology Vol 2* eds D Marvin and L M Hough (2nd ed) pp 445–505, Consulting Psychologists Press, CA

Ivancevich, J M and Matteson, M T (1980) *Stress and work*, Scott, Foresman, Glenview

Kaiseler, M, Polman, R, and Nicholls, A (2009) Mental toughness, stress, stress appraisal, coping and coping effectiveness in sport, *Personality and Individual Differences*, **47**, pp 728–733

Kobasa, S C (1979) Stressful life events, personality and health: an enquiry into hardiness, *Journal of Personality and Social Psychology*, **37**, pp 1–11

Kobasa, S C, Maddi, S R , Puccetti, M C (1982) Personality and exercise as buffers in the stress–illness relationship, *Journal of Behavioral Medicine*, **4**, pp 391–404

Levy, A R, Polman, R C J, Clough, P J, Marchant, D C, and Earle, K (2006) Mental toughness as a determinant of beliefs, pain, and adherence in sport injury rehabilitation, *Journal of Sports Rehabilitation*, **15**, pp 246–254

Maddi, S R and Kobasa, S C (1984) *The Hardy Executive: Health under stress*, Dow Jones-Irwin, Homewood

Marchant, D, Polman, R, Clough, P J, Jackson, J G, Levy, A and Nicholls, A R (2009) Mental toughness: managerial and age differences, *Journal of Managerial Psychology*, **24**, pp 428–437

Maslow, A (1943) A theory of human motivation, *Psychological review*, **50**, pp 370–396

McClelland, D C (1962) Business drives and national achievement, *Harvard Business Review* (1962), pp 103–105

Milgram, S (1963) Behavioral study of obedience, *Journal of Abnormal and Social Psychology*, **67**, pp 371–378

Nicholls, A R, Polman, R C, Levy, A R and Backhouse, S H (2008) Mental toughness, optimism, and coping among athletes, *Personality and Individual Differences*, **44**, pp 1182–1192

Perry, J, Clough, P J, Crust, L, Earle, K and Nicholls, A (2013) Factorial validity of the Mental Toughness Questionnaire-48, *Personality and Individual Differences*, **54** (5), pp 587–592

Seligman, M E P (1975) *Helplessness: On depression, development, and death. A series of books in psychology*, W H Freeman/Times Books/ Henry Holt & Co, New York

Sheard, M and Golby, J (2007) Hardiness and undergraduate academic study: the moderating role of commitment, *Personality and Individual Differences*, **43**, pp 579–588

Tuckman, B W (1965) Developmental sequence in small groups, *Psychological Bulletin*, **63**(6), pp 384–399, doi: 10.1037/h0022100

Vroom, V H (1964) *Work and Motivation*, Wiley, New York

Weiner, B (1972) *Theories of Motivation: From mechanism to cognition*, Rand McNally, Chicago

Trust-based leadership and resilient organizations in the 21st century

The growing importance of trust in developing successful organizations

CHARLES ELVIN

The purpose of this chapter is to illustrate the important connection between leadership, trust and organizational resilience. It looks at a number of dimensions of trust, although not all of them and by doing so seeks to divide the complex subject of trust into some more manageable chunks. Trust is a fundamental element of leadership: for leaders to be genuinely effective, a deep awareness and understanding of trust is essential. The vital importance of trust as a topic for all organizations has never been clearer than in the complex world which is the 21st century.

Surviving the unexpected

'Events, my dear boy, events!' is how British Prime Minister Harold Macmillan is said to have responded when asked by a journalist what he feared most. Although there is some debate over whether Macmillan actually said this, the significance of unforeseen events and the ability to respond to them is as important for the survival of organizations today as it was for British politicians and their governments in the 1960s, probably more so. Although it is a cliché, it remains true: one of the things we can be certain of is that we do not know what could happen which might divert us from a well-laid plan or strategy.

Helmuth von Moltke, a 19th century Prussian Field Marshall, is recognized as one of history's greatest military strategists, whose thinking was a forerunner for the approach that evolved into what is now known as Mission Command. He observed that 'no plan survives first contact with the enemy'. This is further reflected by the observation from Dwight D. Eisenhower, the US President and Supreme Commander of Allied Forces in the Second World War when he said 'in preparing for battle, I have always found that plans are useless but planning is indispensable'.

The importance of being able to respond, adapt and react quickly and effectively to changes in circumstances extends far beyond the political or military arenas. Organizations in the public, private and third sectors are faced with ever-increasing changes and challenges that they need to respond to and that they did not expect or plan for. In these instances, plans, however carefully crafted, will not provide the solution.

It is clearly ridiculous to try to predict the unpredictable. What we can do, however, is put into place practices and behaviours that will give any organization a much greater level of ability to respond to those events. Moreover, they can do this in such a way so as either to prevent them from being catastrophic for the organization or, preferably, to enable the organization to use those events to enhance and strengthen itself in the future.

In his book *Adapt* (2011), Tim Harford illustrates (among other things) two essential points: the importance of adaptation and the essential role that leadership plays in enabling an organization to act, survive, learn, adapt, and then continue. Within the leadership function of an organization sits a vital component without which this would not be possible. If the approach to leadership does not contain a focus on this particular component, then the ability of an organization to truly adapt and respond to events and so have the resilience it needs to survive will not happen effectively. That vital component is trust.

Within the same book, Harford illustrates an inherent weakness of one particular approach to leaders and leadership in situations where unexpected events hit an organization. This is the tendency of people to look to leaders to provide a grand vision or to be gurus who will provide an infallible solution – and for the leaders to see themselves in that light and seek to provide such a plan or solution. Harford provides excellent illustrations as to why this approach is not right for a world which is now highly unpredictable, extremely complex and very fast moving.

The need now and into the future is for a much more 'bottom-up' approach with trial and error being at the heart of this and with trust being necessary to enable it. This calls for leadership and leaders that encourage this approach, that actively work to make it happen and that do not seek to provide answers to every question they are presented with. This requires leaders to both accept and believe that neither they, nor maybe anyone, are the experts when it comes to responding to new challenges or events that hit their organization. Knowing when you don't know is one of the most important leadership strengths.

This kind of trust as a necessity for great leadership is not necessarily a new concept. It resonates strongly with what Jim Collins describes in *Good to Great* (2001) and his finding that the most sustainably successful organizations possess what he calls 'Level 5 leadership'. These he describes as leaders with 1,000 helpers. These leaders, he writes, 'look out the window to attribute success to factors other than themselves'. Collins found that only a tiny proportion of the businesses he examined, even among some of the apparently successful, possessed this level of capability. He confirmed that this was essential for sustained success.

If one of the essential requirements for any modern organization is the ability to adapt, then the leadership approach needed is one which requires a deep understanding of and development of trust in all its dimensions to allow this to happen. It is not only a question of having trust, it is essential to actively understand it, openly address it and work on developing it as a core feature of leadership practice and behaviour. For leadership to be able to deliver an organization safely out of the unexpected, unknown or unpredictable events it encounters, it must be trust centred.

Technology and innovation will almost certainly continue to develop ever more quickly and thus change the world we live in and increase the complexity of problems, their speed of impact and their potential consequences. However, it is worth highlighting that not all events that organizations will need to deal with are negative. The ability to take advantage of opportunities is as much a challenge as addressing threats and trust plays a central role in these as much as it does in withstanding the threats. Furthermore, it is not always as black and white as this suggests. What one sees as a threat another sees as an opportunity. The two often go hand in hand and, again, trust is a key element in seizing the opportunity in an event rather than being paralysed by its threat.

The leadership skills for the 21st century require a proactive approach to enabling those within an organization to solve the problems of the organization as well as take advantage of the diverse opportunities that arise at the same time. The days of the leader being the source of all answers are long gone and have now firmly migrated to being the days of enticing the best out of people and teams as well as having the understanding and self-awareness to truly see situations for what they are. Central to those leadership skills is an understanding and engagement with the complex issue which is trust.

Two categories of trust relevant to organizational resilience

The link between trust in all its forms and the ability of organizations to not only survive in the modern world but thrive in it is a theme which has, rightly, gained a great deal of attention and focus in management and leadership research over the past decade. Stephen M R Covey's book *The Speed of Trust*, first published in 2006, thrust trust as a subject requiring attention in its own right very much into the mainstream by showing how it touches and affects every part of an organization. Covey also provides a journey through the behaviours that both build and damage trust as well as a reassuring chapter on re-building it once it is damaged.

Beyond a focus on trust alone, almost every book on leadership that examines the skills, actions, attributes and behaviours needed to have people willingly follow you refers to trust in its many forms. Consistently, they draw the huge difference between being in command (which many who call themselves leaders actually are) and truly leading (which is being willingly followed, in particular into the unknown and unknowable). One of the defining differences between these two very different states of 'leadership' is the level of trust in the leader and trust in their personal attributes as a person of genuine integrity and good intent. Although this trust is often in a leader's capabilities, it is trust in the leader's intent that is the defining difference. This has to be combined with a very high level of trust that the leader has in those that follow him or her, and the levels of trust that exist between members of the same team.

Although trust has taken its place in business and management literature and research as a serious topic in its own right, it is neither a single thing nor a simple thing and this can make it seem elusive or vague. It can be also overwhelming as a subject area. Moreover, everyone has an opinion on the subject, which can make objective analysis and discussion a major challenge.

Manifestations of different types of trust are seen on a daily and personal basis. We trust not just on a daily basis but every second of every day in some form. We trust drivers to keep to the rules of the road, water companies to ensure our water is clean and arrives to our houses and mail services to deliver what we post.

Trust has become a central theme in the complex and expanding world that is the internet. We have 'trusted' sites and 'trusted' relationships between computers and websites. We trust our supply chains and trust the government monitoring of food manufacturing. We trust the expertise of engineers and physicists in the design of aeroplanes and skyscrapers. We trust our communities and our families.

We place immense trust in our schools to teach our children but also in babysitters to care for them when we go out. We trust recommendations made by others, even (as in the case of many websites that provide consumer reviews, such as TripAdvisor) if we have no real idea who the person is who is giving the recommendation. Trust is a fundamental feature of human life and society and that means it is also a fundamental feature of all organizations. In that lies its importance but also its complexity.

Although trust comes in many forms it is possible to define it in general terms. Most commonly this is done in connection with the relationship between two parties or people – who can be called the 'trustor' (the party doing the trusting) and the 'trustee' (the one who is trusted) – and the consequences or impact if that relationship does not deliver what the trustor expects. Additionally there needs to be an impact or consequence on the trustor, usually either harmful in some way or a failure to have an expected positive outcome, which would come into being if the trustee did not act in the way expected or desired by the trustor. Underlying all concepts of trust sit these three features: the party trusting, the party trusted and the risk or consequence if the trust expectation between them is not fulfilled or alternatively a benefit to one or both if expectations are fulfilled or exceeded.

There are so many different forms of trust that it is helpful to focus specifically on two categories of trust that have special relevance to the resilience of organizations. This does not in any way devalue other approaches to trust or their importance, it simply illustrates how complicated the topic is and therefore the need to approach it in a more manageable form.

The two broad categories of trust that are of the greatest significance to organizational resilience can be described most simply as 'external trust' and 'internal trust'. These are then subdivided into different forms of trust within each category. Within these terms the perspective being taken is to look at how trust enables and supports organizational resilience. These two categories of trust interrelate and should always be seen as deeply connected and co-dependent. Trust is, however, primarily about and between people and they play the central role.

External trust

External trust describes the relationships between an organization and the people within it and people and organizations outside it. Importantly, those outside it can know very much less about the organization than those within it. This can be both a good thing and it can be a bad thing. It can serve to mask true dedication and intent within a company, but also allow an organization to have better external relationships that perhaps the internal state would suggest.

On a technical level it is worth observing that organizations are able to 'trust' other organizations in a number of ways – most notably through computer systems that allow access to data, a specific activity or a financial transaction. Setting up a Direct Debit is a common form of organizational trust through systems rather than people. Extending lines of credit and payment terms are also methods of showing trust between organizations in simple, measurable ways.

To explore external trust further it is helpful to subdivide it into three areas. The three of greatest significance are:

- the trust relationship between the organization and its customers (in the broadest sense of a 'customer' being someone or something the organization supplies or serves);
- the trust between an organization and the companies that supply it with products and services;
- the nature of trust between the organization and its broader market in which it works and operates.

Customer trust, supplier trust and market trust are all worth a slightly closer look.

Customer trust

Customer trust goes beyond keeping your promises (such as either meeting a contract or simply being reliable), although consistently failing to keep them is a fairly good way of damaging trust. The area of greatest interest is the degree to which the customers trust the people in the organization.

It is, however, worth noting that organizations need to trust their customers and the online world is making this a growing area of development.

A good example of organizations trusting their customers is highlighted in online shopping from supermarkets. When something delivered turns out to be damaged, such as eggs, the supermarket trusts the customer who has commented that they are damaged and credits them the price of the eggs. They trust that what the customer is telling them is the truth. A cynic could point out that they have no choice other than to trust the customer and that it is cheaper to do so and accept a certain level of dishonest claims. However, the feeling that you are trusted when you tell the supermarket something is broken and not asked to prove it was delivered that way is valuable to the customer and often commented on by those who shop online.

An organization's customer trust is greatly influenced by how the organization approaches its customers, how it views them, treats them and thinks about them. If it 'de-personalizes' them by forcing them to communicate via technology (such as the dreaded automated telephone support system) or fails to engage with them on a human level it may have plenty of customers, but when things do not go perfectly the chances are these will not trust the organization. Not having that customer trust can have serious consequences... they leave!

Loyalty is a big issue for organizations and considerable sums are spent on it. The customer relationship and loyalty are built, in part, on a feeling of trust in the organization you are a customer of. If the organization has that trust, it may be one of the things that save it from very serious consequences.

The importance of customer trust to the resilience of an organization can be illustrated by an experience the Institute of Leadership and Management had in 2012. In May 2012, the Institute went live with a new central IT system to support its business, through which its customers needed to work on a regular basis. The Institute is an organization permitted to grant formal qualifications and those qualifications are delivered by approved organizations, which are mostly private training providers or colleges. The training providers or colleges had to register every candidate studying for an Institute of Leadership and Management qualification through this IT system, which also managed payments to the Institute for these qualifications and for issuing the all-important certificate at completion. For the training providers and the colleges this can represent a major part of their business.

The system, when implemented, did not work as planned – far from it. Problems with the system stopped the registering of students to study for the qualifications and interrupted the issuing of certificates for qualifications. It not only caused major issues for the Institute but also for its core customers, the training providers and colleges, as it impacted on their relationship with their customers and learners.

Understandably, the training providers and colleges were extremely unhappy about this and the impact it had on them and their businesses. It was far from simple: as one issue resolved, others emerged. The Institute's customer service team and the IT team worked around the clock to resolve issues, change data and find workarounds. It took months to fully resolve and work through the backlog.

However, almost all of the Institute's customers remained with them (there are alternatives in the market). They trusted not only what it was saying about the problems but also the deep dedication of the customer services team to do what they said they would do to address the issues. The Institute survived a very serious 'event' that was mostly outside its control and certainly unexpected and unplanned.

The trust the Institute's customers had in it and more significantly its staff was a key feature which supported its survival through that episode. The customers trusted the integrity and commitment of both the individuals and the organization in addressing the problems as quickly and effectively as possible. That trust was well placed as the Institute and the teams within it moved heaven and earth to solve the problems.

Supplier trust

Supplier trust refers to the relationship an organization has with other organizations it receives products and services from. This includes contracts, service agreements, payment terms and also informal arrangements and activities which emerge over time. This can be as simple as being invited to events hosted by the supplier (such as staff parties, launch events and campaign events) to providing additional services, information and support.

Why does this matter? Why should an organization care too much about the relationships it has with suppliers? If suppliers get too close it may be hard to cease using them and replace them should the need arise. This is generally true. Most of the time having good relationships with suppliers is simply a more pleasant and human way of doing business.

On occasion, however, having a deeply trusting relationship with a supplier can make the difference when you need them to go significantly beyond your agreement or provide you with something exceptional, through them understanding your business and what is important to you. This can come in many forms, such as informally extending agreement terms, agreeing to work together on something different and innovative to allow you to respond to new circumstances, providing information or knowledge beyond any agreement when the supplier learns something about your market, a competitor or a potential situation coming up. This can be a vital informal source of warning or even advantage. A truly trusted supplier provides much more than a service delivered to contractual specification. Having a deeply trusting relationship with a supplier can make the difference just when an organization needs it. Trusting your suppliers and having them trust you – beyond the scope of any formal agreement – gives any organization an additional level of resilience. It is worth developing and investing in.

The cultural influences on trust are also often nicely highlighted in the area of supplier trust and these have significant implications for how agreements are set up and managed. In the Middle East, for example, developing a relationship and building trust is just as important as the paper agreement. The psychometric assessment company AQR does not have a single formal agreement with anyone in that region but has a lot of business. It took over seven years to build the relationships. AQR get paid on time and their portfolio of work is growing.

The same is frequently said of doing business in South-east Asia and China: the trust and personal relationship is far more significant than any written agreement. In fact, there are occasions where demanding a written and signed contract can be seen as not trusting the other party and viewed as insulting. With differing levels of effectiveness in legal systems, as well as the challenges of jurisdiction and interpretation across languages, trust may well be the best route to a successful business relationship.

Market trust

The third and slightly less tangible dimension of external trust that organizations need to pay attention to is market trust. It is the extent to which those who operate in or around your market trust the persona your organization projects. This is slightly harder to measure, but has a very significant bearing on how people talk about an organization and their view of it. Inevitably it is deeply connected to an organization's brand, as this is how those in the market you operate in see you and respond to what you do and say as an organization.

This has an effect on the degree to which you are attractive to applicants for jobs, as well as the significance attributed to your organization's comments or views about the market you work in and that in turn influence the whole market and the actions of others within it. You are seen as a leading organization in your field or industry if you have a high level of trust from that market. People outside your organization will take note and act based on what you as an organization say and do or what specific individuals in your organization say and do.

How does market trust make you more resilient to unexpected events? In addition to making your organization a place people will want to work, it will also allow quicker and deeper engagement in areas of influence. You want to be the organization governments look to for advice and opinion in your market – it gives you not only early sight of developments and changes but also the chance to influence them. Staying with the governmental angle, if there is an intention to introduce regulation into a market that was previously free of it, you will not only create the opportunity to influence the nature of that regulation and how it is implemented, but also give yourself the greatest amount of time to change and adapt to it.

Within the idea of market trust I would exclude share prices and bond prices and other financial instruments, not because they are not relevant or important to an organization – they are – but because they represent a different form of trust related to investment and potential financial performance. The market for shares and financial products is often very distant from the markets organizations work within on a day-to-day basis. The speed of trading is now so fast and so automated that this market takes a very different view of an organization based often on different objectives and drivers.

External trust summary

Developing and understanding the nature of external trust in an organization plays an important role in creating the best possible environment for an organization to be able to respond, adapt and cope with unplanned events or situations. Some aspects of it, such as the trust customers have in your organization, can play a vital role. Others, such as supplier trust, may simply be tipping the scales slightly in your direction.

Those leading and managing organizations in the 21st century need to use every tool available to them to support their organizations. External trust can be understood and measured and needs to be on the agenda as an area of focus. External trust matters and organizations need to ensure that not only are they aware of it and seeking to measure and understand it, but also that they need to actively work to improve it. By doing this, they will be starting to use the understanding of trust in organizations to add resilience.

All forms of external trust are deeply linked to how an organization builds and develops internal trust. In particular, customer trust is often a reflection of internal trust and, as the Cineworld case study below (see page 95) illustrates, it is easy to see how the development of internal trust directly influences customer experience and trust.

Internal trust

Internal trust focuses on the nature and dynamics of trust that exist and the interplay within an organization, primarily between the people in it. It is a complex and constantly changing environment but there are three significant dimensions of internal trust that have a dominant role and are the focus of greater attention. These dimensions interact with each other and do not exist in isolation. For any organization, understanding the interrelationships between each of these is as important as looking at each of them individually. The three are:

- the trust in leaders by those being led;
- the trust leaders have in those they lead;
- the trust between team members in the same team or group.

Internal trust is complicated to evaluate and address but it has such a profound impact on organizations that it is essential that modern leaders actively address it and build it in theirs. It also can suffer from the paradox where finding out an organization has low internal trust can be hard because the people inside do not trust each other or their leaders sufficiently to tell them.

Trust is not binary like an on/off switch. It is better to view it as a dimmer switch for a light, with a wide range of settings from fully bright to only just on and every noticeable intensity between. Additionally, although trust is often rightly seen as a reciprocal feeling or feature of a relationship, it is not always the case that there is the same level of intensity in both directions. I might trust you a lot more than you trust me. These factors add complexity to any investigation into trust and they are mentioned here simply to illustrate that when looking at trust in an organization these considerations need to be taken into account.

Trust in leaders by those being led

This is one of the fundamental and defining differences between being a true leader and simply being in command or in authority. If a leader is not trusted then they may be obeyed but they will never get the best out of any team and will not see that team respond and rise to challenges of the unexpected. It is probably fair to say that if you are not trusted then you are not a leader.

In *The Leadership Challenge* by James Kouzes and Barry Z Posner (2012), the fourth of their five 'Practices of Exemplary Leadership' is for leaders to 'enable others to act'. To do this, leaders have to 'create a climate of trust'. This is backed up by strong evidence that high-trust organizations significantly out-perform low-trust ones. Trust in a leader goes to the heart of leadership, which is about integrity of purpose and the integrity of the leader as a person. This is the 'being' part of leadership. It is all very well to know a great deal and do the right things in terms of actions, but the spark that ignites the genuine and deep trust in leaders is the understanding that they truly believe in what they are doing and the best interests of those they lead. This builds trust and once a leader is trusted by those they lead the result is transformational.

At an event with the Institute of Leadership and Managements in 2013, Professor John Adair, one of the icons of leadership studies, illustrated this point through a story he told about being at sea in a trawler in a very severe storm. He highlighted the immediate and unwavering trust that the crew had in the judgement, experience, ability and intent of the captain to get them through the storm and back home safely. Fundamental to that was the crew's trust in his deep intent – that he, the captain, was entirely focused on the mission of getting them safely through the storm and home. It was a mission they all shared.

This meant that even orders that a crew member might not fully agree with or understand the reason for were accepted willingly and with full commitment. It was the trust not only in the captain's ability that was evident, it was the trust in his intent that gave him the unwavering, willing followers that were so important at that particular time of crisis. The captain, Adair noted, was not particularly liked by his crew and was not a friend to any of them, but he was deeply trusted and respected. This meant his crew had gladly served with him for a long time and delivered extraordinary performance for the whole boat and crew. The defining characteristic of the captain's success as a leader able to deal with the storms that hit the ship was that he was trusted and that he trusted his crew. Although not explicit in the story, it is highly likely that the crew trusted each other as well.

Being trusted as a leader enables a leader to ask those they lead to do extraordinary things, sometimes without time to explain why. Organizations can encounter the equivalent of a ship being hit by a storm. A trusted leader is believed when they say there is a storm coming or the organization are already in a storm (not everything that hits an organization is as obvious as a storm hitting a boat) and there is a need to react and respond.

This allows rapid re-focusing on the new problem. It may be cancelling a loved project, diverting resources, changing terms and conditions or any number of actions. If the leader is trusted and the integrity of their purpose and of them as a person is trusted, they will be able to do this quickly, effectively and with the support of those they lead. That speed, that ability to re-direct resources and people and have them willingly do so is a vital tool for any leader of any organization.

If the leader is not able to respond in that way the consequences could be damaging or possibly catastrophic. Being trusted as a leader is essential if you are to get the response you need. If you are not trusted then you are not a leader, you are simply in authority – and a crisis is not a good time to find that out. You may get people to switch quickly to new circumstances, but if you don't have their willing buy-in the response will be lacklustre and may not give the organization what it needs to survive. It is highly unlikely that a leader will be trusted if they do not trust those they lead. Leaders go first – they model the way – so to be trusted and gain the huge value that comes with that, leaders have to trust.

The trust leaders have in those they lead

This is the other side of the equation between those leading and those being led and is equally as important. Leaders need to trust those they lead, not simply to follow a command but to do what is best for the mission and the direction of the organization. When in place the strength and power of this is remarkable and gives any organization a capability they will value and need.

Major Chris Whip in *The Leadership Secret* (2013) provides a concise summary of both what this trust is and also of the power and effectiveness of it when used correctly by leaders. The strength of trusting a team is seen in the military approach called 'mission command' which focuses on 'what' and 'why' but then leaves and trusts, the 'how' to the team. Whip describes this as 'mission trust' and he comments, 'explain what is required and why, rather than how, and be amazed by the creativity'. The simple answer to how to get the best out of a team, he continues, is to trust them.

Within this sits a vital characteristic of a leader which is self-awareness, in particular being able to know truthfully what they don't know or are not the best at. The trust in a team to deliver an important outcome and for the leader not to get involved is one of the hardest things for many senior executives in organizations. Failing to do it, however, can be taken as a strong indication of a lack of trust in a team and that in turn can have the effect of disempowering and even disabling a team just at the time when you need them to be at their best.

This can be as simple as moving to a support and resource-securing role once the initial direction is explained and the reason for it. In 2011 at the Open University (the United Kingdom's largest higher education institution), one of the largest and most significant changes in the University's history (and the history of modern higher education in England) took place. Major changes to many systems, processes and practices were needed at breakneck speed. Universities were moving to set significantly higher fees for tuition and the Open University, as part of that process, needed to make changes to university entrance processes and a range of other core activities.

The Vice-Chancellor of the Open University in the United Kingdom, Martin Bean, made an observation about leadership and these changes at a small lunch meeting for senior staff, which was as essential in its simplicity as its importance. He said, 'Sometimes the most important thing for a leader to do is get out of the way.' His role, and that of other leaders at the Open University, was to support, motivate, inspire, secure resources when needed and to ensure recognition. The one thing they had to be careful to avoid was actually getting involved or seeking to direct or command on a task-by-task basis. The transformation project for the Open University was achieved on target: had it not been, the consequences would have been serious. Mission command works.

To move away from military examples, this same point is beautifully articulated by Simon Sinek in his book *Start with Why* (and is also supported by his many TED and YouTube videos). Sinek (2009) shows how trust is a fundamental human survival tool and how, by explaining 'why' a certain direction or course of action is the right and necessary one, you develop deep trust and motivation. People who trust and who are trusted work harder and better as they feel they are working for something bigger than themselves.

Trust is a fundamental part of society and it is a fundamental part of all organizations. When we are in high-trust organizations we are happier and so perform better as we are less worried and concerned. When we work, or live, in a low-trust environment our instinctive survival responses kick in. We become worried and concerned about things other than the job we do or the role. If you work on building and developing trust then performance as well as engagement will improve. Trust teams with the mission, with the 'why', and you consistently see amazing things.

Cineworld did just that and, as shown below, the results were remarkable. They provide an excellent example of how a focus on and development of internal trust can allow an organization to deliver its vision and strategy, in particular when it is that strategy's success which will allow the organization to compete against new and complex market conditions.

CASE STUDY Cineworld – building trust to meet the competitive challenge

Cineworld is one of the United Kingdom's largest cinema owners, with over £350 million in annual revenues and over 46 million admissions to their 80 sites (figures from 2012) – most of them multiplex theatres. As a business their strategy is clear, simple and focused: 'to create welcoming, contemporary cinemas that movie-goers will want to come back to time and time again... We want the whole Cineworld experience to be smooth, memorable and exciting.'

Cineworld lives in a world of complex competition, not only from other cinemas but also from television, internet broadband services, the DVD and Blu-ray markets and downloads to tablet computers which enable viewing on the move. As their strategy and mission highlights, it is the whole experience of going to the cinema that is critical, not just the watching of a film, and this underpins their success.

To see how well this part of their strategy was working, Cineworld undertook research into what their customers thought of them in 2011. Critical to the strategy's success is not only the overall experience of viewing of a film but also the willingness to return to the theatre as well as to recommend the experience to others. This made 'net promoter score' (NPS) a critical indicator for the business in giving a measure of the overall experience for customers.

What they discovered from the research prompted action and significant reflection. Although customers were very happy with the films and the auditoria, the overall experience of being a Cineworld customer was not scoring highly and, importantly, the NPS was not at a satisfactory level. The issue was not inside the auditoria or the quality of the films. What was affecting the customer experience was what was happening before and, to a lesser extent, after the viewing of the film. It was the speed, efficiency of service and empowerment of the staff to respond to customers which was the issue.

Many of the processes and systems in place in the movie theatres were based on previous concerns about access to and theft of money from the tills and stock from the stock rooms. Additionally, many of Cineworld's staff were young and there was a fairly high turnover of staff, which meant that there was a feeling from cinema managers that a high degree of command and control was necessary to ensure things were done properly. This had resulted in a policy and practice of very restricted access to tills – with only one person permitted to use each till. Keys to the stock rooms for replacement stock were also only in the hands of a manager, which meant that if they were busy customers either had to wait until they were free or go without if an item they wanted ran out. Additionally, authorization for giving replacement drinks and popcorn when these were dropped or spilt (which they always gave as part of the overall policy to create a good experience) was also only in the hands of managers.

The consequence of this was that although there may have been a lot of serving staff the payment process was highly restricted and customers had to wait to be served. This slowed down service and gave the impression of staff standing around doing nothing while queues built up.

Customers were frustrated by the wait, frustrated by the fact they could see plenty of staff but none of the staff could serve them and frustrated that the approach seemed far too controlling. Staff too reflected this lack of trust through lack of engagement – it was 'not their problem'. This, obviously, also adds to the lack of a good experience for customers.

The diagnosis came down to there being a low level of trust from the cinema managers of the serving staff, which was reinforced by policy and procedure. This was leading to blockages in customer service, delay and customer frustration.

Cineworld did two things. First, it trained its managers and serving staff in trust using Covey's Speed of Trust model and method (Covey, 2006). It made sure everyone was focused on the need for a great customer experience right the way through their time at Cineworld, on what that might look like and on the need for teams to take collective responsibility, including for the tills being right at the end of any shift.

Second, vitally, they changed a large number of policies and practices to match that investment in trust and show the staff they meant what they said when developing the idea of trust. Tills became multi-user for all team members on a shift. Staff could authorize and supply replacements from spilt or dropped drinks or food without referring to a manager. Keys to the stock rooms were held by teams serving and sharing a till, allowing them to re-stock quickly as needed.

Although there was nervousness in both the head office senior management and the cinema managers, the investment had startling results. In the cinemas where it was first applied, Cineworld started to see a drop in queues, far faster customer resolutions and a drop in the number of tills that were incorrect. Losses of stock (often attributed to staff) also declined. Teams, once trusted, and managers, once focused on trusting teams to both monitor themselves and act in a trustworthy way, transformed the customer experience. The NPS started to increase. Trust is reciprocal and by being trusted the staff in the cinemas also took ownership of the experience and of the decisions made for customers. The investment in trust in Cineworld continues.

Essential to the development programme is the focus on the 'why' behind the business – the desire to give all customers a wonderful experience from start to finish. This is a vision all the staff connect with. By including all the staff in that focus on 'why' and 'what' and then trusting them to deliver it, Cineworld improved the customer experience, delivered to their strategy and made the cinemas a much better and nicer place to work.

Stuart Holdsworth, Head of Learning at Cineworld, who led the development of the training and development in trust commented:

It is one of the most effective programmes we have run and we have seen the very significant impact it has had in those cinemas where it has been run and the changes implemented. We continue to roll it out. Trust, awareness of trust and active development of trust both in understanding of it and actions which support it has had a significant impact on our business.

Trust between team members in the same team or group

Of the dynamics of internal trust, the final one of great significance is the relationship between team members to trust each other. Depending on the nature and size of the team this will have plenty of variables. However, when you have a team that is not aligned on the objectives of the organization and has low or damaged trust within it you run the risk of a greater focus being placed on issues between individuals than on the requirements of the organization. Working on and building trust within teams is just as important as the trust flowing towards and from a leader.

The features and characteristics of a low trust organization are usually fairly easy to spot, particularly when coming in from the outside. There is little sharing of all the facts, information may be manipulated or withheld, assumptions are made about people's motives and intentions, blame turns up together with 'covering' e-mails, issues and concerns are voiced outside meetings but not in them. Two of the most obvious characteristics are low energy and low enthusiasm. Lack of trust within teams is very demoralizing.

High-trust teams display a far greater level of energy but also share information, views and options openly and with a feeling of safety and security. You see people actively take on projects, accept accountability and support colleagues even when they are absent. Innovation happens in high-trust teams, not because it is asked for but because it is the environment that enables it.

It is that thinking capability, that innovative thinking and freedom to think that will find and implement the solution to the unexpected event which may derail an organization. If an organization does not have it, combined with the other types of trust, then the very thing needed to survive will not be there when you need it most. You cannot build team trust after the storm hits you.

Building and maintaining trust within a team (the leader is also part of a team) is one of the central features of any team that excels in what they do, regardless of field. The methods and techniques which do or claim to do this run into the thousands and there is not an organization in existence that has not devoted time and money to team-building activities of one form or another. A team that does not have high trust is not really a team.

Internal trust – summary

The three dynamics of internal trust – to and from the leader and between team members – form a web of trust within and across any organization. Leaders and managers need and rely on that trust if they are going to give themselves the best tools to engage with new circumstances and challenges for their organizations. Internal trust reflects external trust, as trusted and engaged teams both trust and are trusted more by customers and suppliers. Almost everyone in the workplace has encountered a deeply dysfunctional organization as well as, hopefully, a highly functional one. The essential difference between the two will be the levels of trust across that internal web.

Combine the trust in a leader by those led with the trust of the leader in those they lead, then add into the mix deep trust between team members, and you will have created a fantastically strong and resilient platform from which your organization can address those unexpected events that are sure to come its way. It will enable the thinking, honesty, action and responsiveness that is needed. If, in addition to this internal state of high trust and a trust-centred approach to leadership, you also have an organization that actively addresses other issues such as mental toughness and keeps its employees trained and up to date, you have an organization with considerable resilience.

Nothing is perfect and organizations with all of these may still not be resilient enough, but it certainly moves the odds in favour of the organization.

Trust is a serious issue and organizations in the 21st century would be wise to really appreciate its enormous value and the significance it has in terms of their survival.

At the apex of the concept of trust are those in charge of the company and the leaders within it, in particular the senior leaders. They 'set the tone' and 'model the way'. If a leader trusts then a culture of trust builds inside an organization; if the leader does not trust then that will be copied and trust levels will drop. With low internal trust, external trust will suffer as the two are deeply connected, hence the importance of trust-based leadership. If trust is not at the core of your leadership, are you leading at all?

Suggestions on developing trust

The purpose of this chapter is to illustrate the significant role trust, in its many forms, plays in building and running organizations and how developing it will equip organizations to be better able to cope with the challenges they face in the future. It is not a 'how to' guide to developing and sustaining trust within an organization, although the work of the authors mentioned would be a very good place to start. There are, however, some initial steps and actions that any organization can take which will help start the process of using trust to support and drive the organization.

Get trust on the organizational agenda. Agree a trust framework or model and ensure people at every level of the organization are talking about it. If the simple method of splitting trust into external and internal and then further dividing within those two works for your organization, then use it. Covey's model is another which has proved its effectiveness. Organizations and change consultancies use models of their own construction to evaluate levels of trust and then improve them. Whichever model you use, make trust part of your organizational conversation. For every area of a business to thrive a level of attention and focus is required to be placed on it. If ignored then other activities and actions step in and start to absorb the space it once occupied. Leaders need to ensure there is a clear space for trust in the organization and that once it is on the agenda to make sure it stays there. Discussion must be combined with action, so identify the practices (as in Cineworld) which get in the way of a trusting environment and address them.

If you discover you have a low-trust organization, don't panic; at least you are able to work on it and change it. Explore the issues of trust in one-to-one meetings, feedback programmes such as 360° or employee surveys. When working on improving the levels of trust it is important to focus on the fact that it is something that leaders have to do first and have to 'be' much more than 'do'. Start at the top – model the way from your most senior people. Ensure that everyone in the organization realizes that trust is not a project: it is a way of being.

Final comments

A high level of trust is one of the most valuable assets any organization can have. Trust is both fabulously resilient and amazingly delicate. It can survive amid extraordinary difficulties and challenges and can come out stronger rather than weaker because of it. It can also be shattered in an instant by what might be a small but well-aimed blow. Trust is the corporate diamond: uniquely valuable, not as rare or as hard to find as you might think, amazingly resilient but can be shattered with one incorrect tap of a hammer.

Organizations and the people within them face and will continue to face challenges and opportunities that require great resilience. Leadership and within that leadership genuine trust plays a central role. Any organization that wants to build up its resilience must, among other things, take the issue of trust very seriously and ensure it is being actively examined, understood and developed.

In addition to this trust-centred approach to leadership there are many other characteristics that organizations (and the people within them) need in order to be able to resist the impact of the 'events' which will hit them. Trust is not sufficient on its own and will not alone provide an answer. It is, however, a necessary component and its absence will severely inhibit or even prevent an organization from being able to survive the challenges and demands it needs to deal with despite what other actions it takes or attributes it has.

Organizations with the highest chance of surviving whatever the world throws at them in the years to come will be the ones that understand the importance of placing trust at the heart of their management and leadership practice and development. You could almost say, if you want your organization to survive the events that will hit it the same way humans have been able to survive events in our history, then get to grips with trust and make your organization 'human' by building trust and real, not virtual, relationships and shared beliefs. This development of internal trust – the building of a community with a common purpose, or 'why' to use Sinek's word – is essential in equipping an organization to enable it to be resilient.

It is important to make sure trust is on the agenda throughout an organization and implement ways of evaluating and measuring it. Look at operational behaviours that indicate low trust and see if they really are needed. Focus on mission trust and ensure everyone in the organization is reminded why they are there and the purpose they fulfil. Finally, leaders go first and trust will only grow and develop in an organization if the leaders not only know about it, but do it and believe in it. We talk about 'being trusted' not about 'doing trust' or 'knowing trust'. For trust to truly exist as part of an organization's make up and bring with it the amazing benefits it does, it has to be part of what the leaders or the organization are, not what they say they are or think they are.

Trust is a very human need and something that has been a feature of human survival strategies throughout our existence. The statement 'but… I trusted him' is a plea against the sin of betraying a trust and that goes to the heart of the emotional importance of trust and how we, as humans, feel about it. Trust is very personal and leaders wishing to use its strength to support their organizations need to ensure they never lose sight of that. To trust is human, it is a human need and a social need contained deep within our make up. It has formed the basis for our survival as a species and plays a central role also in the survival of our organizations too. Trust-centred leadership helps give organizations resilience in the 21st century, and they are going to need it.

What will define the exemplary leaders of the 21st century? It will be the capability to lead in extreme complexity through and with technologies, practices and events that have not yet been thought of and to address problems which were impossible to imagine only a few years previously. How will they do this? How will they cope and rise to the challenges? Through placing trust at the centre of their approach to leadership and understanding what a powerful force it is – both to enable success and to avoid disaster. Leaders will have to be agile, be adaptive, have to think and respond quickly to totally new challenges but, above all, they are going to need to trust their teams, trust those who supply them and supply those they trust.

About the Institute of Leadership and Management

The Institute of Leadership and Management (**www.i-l-m.com**) is the largest leadership and management qualification awarding body in the United Kingdom as well as a professional institute representing over 30,000 members and a research organization. As a self-funding charity it is dedicated to advancing leadership and management excellence and in so doing driving social and economic prosperity.

Measuring trust – the Institute of Leadership and Management Index of Leadership Trust

A tool to assess internal trust of a leader by those that they lead

One element of building and developing trust is to be able to take a picture of the state of certain forms of trust at any particular time in an organization. The Institute of Leadership and Management has developed a tool which will enable organizations to do just that to a greater level of detail, looking at the trust that people within an organization place in their leaders.

This is a leading-edge instrument which meets an important need in the leader's or consultant's armoury. If something is important it is always best if we can measure it reliably and with validity. If we can do that we have the ability to assess and diagnose, and if we do something about what we find, we can measure whether (and sometimes to what extent) it worked.

With three years of data from over 7,500 employees, the Institute of Leadership and Management has built a highly robust benchmark of trust levels in UK organizations from every industry and sector, of all sizes and types. Using this as a starting point, and with the proven integrity of the six dimensions of trust as a mechanism for measuring trust levels, the Institute of Leadership and Management will be offering organizations the opportunity to assess their own leadership trust through the Index of Leadership Trust.

This is an organizational assessment tool which gathers views about trust from staff at all levels and processes the data into a set of Indices which act both to assess levels of certain types of trust at a point in time and assesses changes in underlying trust factors and in the levels of trust over time.

Why should an organization choose to measure trust in its leadership? Leadership is one of those qualities that is hard to define and even harder to assess, but there is common agreement that trust is an essential and highly significant factor in shaping leadership capability and equally strong agreement about the factors that determine trust.

The Institute of Leadership and Management's Index of Leadership Trust reflects the extensive research into trust carried out over the period 2010–2013. The Index has been found to be reliable. Employees have no problem rating their leaders – their line managers and their CEOs – on each of the six dimensions (ability, understanding, openness, fairness, integrity and

FIGURE 4.1 The six dimensions of leadership trust

Ability	You have confidence in their ability to do their job
Understanding	They understand your role and what is involved in performing it effectively
Openness	They encourage you to put forward your ideas and opinions
Fairness	They treat everyone equally and show concern about them
Integrity	They are honest and principled
Consistency	You are able to know what they will do or how they will behave

Respondents first assess the relative importance of each dimension as far as they are concerned.

This is aggregated into an overall weighting for each dimension representing the views of all people in the organization.

Respondents then assess their leaders in terms of this framework. These responses are converted through the weightings to give an Index of Leadership Trust.

consistency) nor do they struggle to express the relative significance of each dimension in their assessment of leadership performance (see Figure 4.1).

It is this combination of detailed assessment that enables the Index of Leadership Trust to be used as an effective diagnostic tool – any good diagnosis should enable effective prescription. Because of its level of detail, the Index of Leadership Trust makes it possible to identify where any deficiencies in leadership behaviour might exist, what needs to be examined further and ultimately shapes thinking about what changes are needed to bring about the biggest improvement in trust.

By combining assessments of leaders' performance on each dimension with a clear indication of which aspects are more or less important, the analysis offered by the Index of Leadership Trust enables priorities for improvement to be established.

An important element of the Index of Leadership Trust is the capability to create norms. Data from usage will calculate norms for the six dimensions as well as for the Index. Where possible and where sufficient data is provided, it is planned that there will be norms for sub-groups established – by sector and by geographical region. This will provide a measure of how trust is developing and changing over time. It will also enable individual organizations to benchmark themselves and their progress against their peers and against the general overall trend.

It will also be possible to monitor and report regularly (perhaps through an annual update) on movements in the relative weighting of the six dimensions of Leadership Trust.

The Institute of Leadership and Management, as the United Kingdom's leading leadership and management development organization, provides the prescription as well as the diagnosis. We know how to bring about improvements across all six dimensions, and have a network of 2,000+ training and development organizations worldwide able to provide the specialist support required.

This isn't just about offering training programmes either. Improving leadership performance on some of the dimensions may require training, but others may be better addressed through coaching or mentoring programmes, organizational development or culture change programmes to enable leaders to demonstrate the necessary behaviours.

The Index of Leadership Trust operates at two levels. First, it measures trust in line managers generally, which provides a picture of the general level of trust across the organization. Second, it also provides a specific measure of CEO trust, which provides chief executives with a detailed insight into how employees generally perceive their trust levels.

While line managers and CEOs may feel challenged by the idea of having employees' specific trust in them measured, one of the characteristics of effective leaders is the willingness to invite and listen to such feedback, reflect on it and plan how to change behaviour to bring about real improvements in performance. A reluctance to invite such feedback demonstrates a significant weakness in leadership capability and a lack of mental toughness on the part of managers. Those who cannot accept feedback are also likely to struggle to cope with any other challenges.

In fact, the Index of Leadership Trust is designed to operate in two ways as far as line managers are concerned. Large or even moderately-sized organizations will have several (sometimes hundreds) of staff who can be identified as line managers. The Index can ask employees to rate their line managers generally without identifying anyone in particular. This produces a general organizational perspective on the extent to which line managers are trusted. It can ask the same questions about specific line managers or groups of line managers (usually grouped by function – all the managers in the accounts department for example).

It might be that some organizations will start in the more anonymized format and migrate to the more specific format. Both will provide valuable information.

For the CEO (or even if it is a small leadership team being assessed at the top) there is really no such anonymity.

Importantly, the willingness to trust employees to make honest and objective appraisals is part of the process of building high-trust organizations. Trust is a reciprocated phenomenon – leaders who want to be trusted need to demonstrate trust in their followers. People trust those who trust them, and high-trust organizations benefit from this through more efficient working and lower absenteeism and labour turnover. The ability to have an accurate assessment of leadership trust is a valuable first step to creating a high-trust organization.

The Index of Leadership Trust is published and available from July 2014.

References

Adair, J (2013) multiple publications, personal communications

Bean, M (2011) The Open University – personal communications

Collins, J (2001) *Good To Great: Why some companies make the leap... and others don't*, Random House Business, London

Covey, S M R (2006) *The Speed of Trust*, Simon and Schuster, New York

Harford, T, (2011) *Adapt*, Little, Brown, London

Kouzes, J and Posner, B Z (2012) *The Leadership Challenge, 5th Edition*, Jossey-Bass, San Francisco

Sinek, S (2009) *Start with Why*, Portfolio Penguin, USA

Whip, M C (2013) *The Leadership Secret*, Matador, UK

Leadership, resilience and the 21st-century organization

05

**PROFESSOR SHARON TURNBULL
AND ROB NOBLE**

What is changing in the 21st century and why?

Every year at The Leadership Trust we meet several hundred managers from all sectors and parts of the world. They all tell us the same thing – that the demands on their leadership capabilities are being tested more than ever today as they position their organizations to meet the fast-moving demands of the 21st century. As we have seen in other chapters in this book, globalization, the war for talent, digital communications, societal changes, the changing shape of organizations and the aspirations of the next generation are all challenging 21st century leaders in new ways.

The quest for more sustainable and ethical organizations prompted by the many recent business scandals and the growing realization that we cannot continue to raid our world's natural resources without considering the future is also putting extraordinary pressures on today's leaders to perform against a range of criteria which go far beyond those of short-term business performance.

There are an increasing number of commentators who argue convincingly that measuring leadership success should increasingly include questions of the longer term common good socially, ethically and globally, at the same time as responding to the pace of change in a world where today's ideas might already be doomed to obsolescence.

The Leadership Trust was founded in 1975 as an educational charitable trust with a mission to influence leadership and develop inspirational leaders across all aspects of society for public benefit. It works both in the United Kingdom and internationally and has welcomed some 40,000 delegates on its programmes from all sectors of commerce, industry and society. Formerly focused on leadership development for directors and senior managers, it has recently extended its footprint to walking beside the delegate over the length of their leadership journey, from foundation to board leadership.

The Leadership Trust offers high-impact leadership development for directors and managers as well as for those individuals just setting out on their leadership journeys. Together with our global reach, this provides us with a range of useful and valuable perspectives. We are recognized as a leader in the field of specialist experiential learning. This is particularly valuable. As we will see, one of the more interesting observations about the future of leadership development is the increasing attention being given to experiential learning.

We support individuals and teams to rise to the complex challenges that face them as they seek to contribute to deep-rooted and lasting changes for the better in their organizations – where our research and experience tell us that developing leaders without addressing the culture in which they operate reduces the effectiveness of our interventions significantly.

This is echoed in the work carried out by Professor Peter Clough and Doug Strycharczyk in developing the ILM72 model and measure. They found that that they were able to assess *adopted* leadership style. They found that many leaders didn't apply their preferred leadership style but tended to adopt the prevailing leadership style (culture) prevalent in the organization. They too concluded that it appears to be nigh on impossible to develop leadership styles in an individual if they clash with the organization's preferences. Or to put it another way, to develop leadership most effectively probably means working simultaneously at the organizational, team and individual levels.

As the type of people who enter our organizations begins to change in terms of attitudes, beliefs, aspirations and abilities, we need to ask how leadership and culture will need to develop in the future. Will there be a preparedness to 'conform' to a prevailing culture or will there be a need for a new kind of diversity where organizations learn to accommodate those who wish to apply their preferred style rather than their adopted style?

Underpinning everything the Trust does is the simple belief that 'leadership is simple but not easy'. The intellectual journey is quite straightforward, but putting the theory into practice is the tough part. Leadership is undoubtedly going to become more challenging as the 21st century progresses, and preparing and supporting leaders for these challenges lies at the heart of our mission.

The Chartered Management Institute's white paper (Overell, 2013) on the top challenges facing UK-based CEOs indicates a range of preoccupations for CEOs, with customer relationships being their top strategic challenge, followed by operational excellence, human capital, government regulation and corporate brand and reputation.

So how can such multi-dimensional leadership be developed for these 21st-century challenges?

What *additional* capabilities do 21st-century leaders now need to help them and their organizations to cope with the speed of change ahead? And how can today's organizations develop leadership development strategies that will prepare them for these future challenges?

The 21st century has brought with it many additional challenges for leaders. The 'credit crunch', volatile oil prices, recession and climate change all remind us how interconnected our globe has become. Sustainability, energy security, food and water security, poverty, health and wealth distribution need to be urgently addressed and these global problems can no longer be ignored by business. Furthermore, businesses are confronted with a new global landscape of rapidly-growing markets in the developing world and increasing competition from areas which hitherto would not have been expected to provide this. In the last 10 years we have seen the so-called BRIC (Brazil, Russia, India and China) countries emerging as significant players the global economy. Even that is already changing. Almost unnoticed, the fastest growing economies most recently are emerging from African countries. The old order is certainly changing.

Faced with such competition, many leaders have had to entirely rethink their business strategies and continue to scan the competitive environment for new opportunities. New communication technologies, social networking, faster and more accessible mobile communications have all added to the fast pace of our global world.

Futurologists tell us that this pace of technological and global change will continue exponentially and that the changes they foresee are even more radical than those we have seen in the last 30 years. The introduction to this book gives a flavour of this but even this is just the tip of an exponentially-growing iceberg.

Our communication technologies, they say, will soon be even more inter-connected, and our lives will be run for us by smartphone technologies that can already monitor our sleep, order our groceries, plan our route to work in real time to avoid traffic congestion, schedule our diaries on our behalf and enable our health to be monitored in the process! Our businesses will also be similarly driven by these 'knowledge-creating' communications. 3D printing is set to revolutionize many of our businesses – by 2020 this is likely to be routine, everyday technology.

All this may inevitably demand new and critical dimensions of leadership in order to be a successful 21st century leader. Some of these dimensions are already becoming important, whereas other capabilities may only come to prominence as a result of the challenges ahead. Equally, this might mean that some aspects of leadership development which have hitherto received less attention now become more important.

This chapter is based on the countless conversations we have had with leaders in the United Kingdom and around the world. One of the authors' leadership research has taken her to China, India, Japan, Korea, Brazil, Canada and Europe in pursuit of leadership knowledge. The ideas in this chapter are based on her conversations with managers in these and many other countries, in global organizations such as LG, Panasonic, Fujitsu and Lufthansa as well as in many smaller entrepreneurial and family businesses across the globe.

What kind of leadership might be needed for the 21st century?

Vision

The leaders we meet tell us that it is no longer enough to stimulate follow-ers through heroic gestures and charisma alone. It might be argued that this was never the case anyway. Jim Collins makes a telling observation when he notes that 10 out of 11 CEOs for the most sustainably successful organiza-tions in North America turned out to be introverts.

Twenty-first century visionary leaders will probably need to focus on growing deep organizational engagement among their followers and on generating a shared and common understanding of a dynamic and evolving vision for the future. This kind of engagement has always been needed. A challenge here might be that the workforce of the future is a transient work-force, particularly if we accept the premise that the Gen Y/Z employee does not expect an employer to provide sustained employment. Engagement may have a different meaning in the future to that understood in the past.

Visioning today is no longer the static or solitary activity it once was. No longer is it the sole prerogative of the top team. Looking beyond the organization's immediate environment into the world, helping people to imagine the future and then converting this image into an exciting destination means developing a climate in which ideas are shared and co-created.

It also means using all available antennae and tapping into networks to continually create new knowledge inside the organization. This knowledge may include understanding trends and shifts in society, technology, markets and people, looking for tipping points and spotting them early, assessing the speed and destination of these changes and then of course interpreting these to determine how they will affect the organization and its purpose over time. Visioning alone though is not enough. It must be combined with inspiration and action.

Responsibility

The examples over the last few years of fraud, embezzlement and other financial misdemeanours have raised the profile of the need for 'good' or 'ethical' behaviour among our leaders. It has also led to a view that putting responsibility and authority for a business in the hands of a single, potentially fallible individual or small group of individuals, however capable or indeed charismatic, can sometimes lead to failure and even to organizational ruin.

Fortunately, a turn away from such unprincipled behaviour and a rejection of the 'win at any cost' cultures that damaged our economy and leadership credibility so badly is starting to increase in a number of sectors. The question is: can this be sustained and developed further? The sporting world, for example, has recently been vocal about the need to develop more principled integrity. Whether this can be achieved without regulation remains to be seen. Maak and Pless (2006), who have written extensively on responsible leadership, argue that we are now in a stakeholder society and an interconnected world which means that a leader is at various times:

> ... a servant to others, a steward and as such a custodian of values and resources, an architect of inclusive systems and processes and a moral infrastructure, a change agent by being a transforming leader, a coach by supporting and nurturing followers, and a story-teller and creator of moral experience and shared systems of meaning.
>
> (Maak and Pless, 2006, p 44)

Leaders must, therefore, focus on building trust relationships, and on making followers partners in a leadership journey.

Jim Collins in *Good to Great* (2001) makes the same observation that the best leaders (he calls them 'Level 5 leaders') are the leaders with 1,000 helpers.

This focus on responsible leadership through building networked relationships is also advocated by Chopra (2011). Against the backdrop of the mounting struggle by people across the globe to overthrow abusive and dictatorial regimes that have long oppressed many in the name of leadership, Chopra's book challenges the abusive use of power associated with old definitions of leadership. Instead he envisions a new form of 21st-century leadership founded on vision, creativity and a sense of unity.

Responsible leadership and applied ethics have only recently entered the mainstream leadership development debate, fuelled by the many leadership scandals to hit the media across the corporate and public sectors, the health service, the political world and of course the banking sector.

Responsible leadership that considers the impact of leadership on society is a critical element of leadership action, as summarized below:

> Leadership is inextricably linked to business and society. Without responsible leadership we will have a moral vacuum in business and society, and without stewardship we will be unable to address the imminent challenges that threaten our society and sustainability of resource. If we cannot break our attachment to the idea of the heroic leader, we are destined to experience the continuous failure of leaders to live up to the pedestals that society has built for them – and the inevitable breaches of trust, uncertainty and upheaval that follow such disappointment.
>
> We are all aware of the impact that high profile cases of poor 'leadership' have had on society, but the importance of businesses in stimulating the economy and creating jobs is greater than ever. Our belief is that a drive for more effective leadership will enable businesses to have a much greater positive impact on society, and reduce the cases of poor and unethical leadership.
>
> (Leadership Trust, Think Tank Report, 2013)

Humility and common purpose

Humility enables leaders to recognize and unlock the value and potential of those around them, and make use of all of their talents. To listen to others is one of the most important elements of leadership.

Egocentric leaders do not do this. Their own opinion is the only one that really counts and they pay lip service only to the opinions of others.

Humility is a trait that is much loved by followers. It motivates, energizes and builds self-esteem in followers with its explicit recognition of their value.

Humility enables a leader to direct his or her attention on a purpose and outside themselves. Leaders with humility are more likely to follow an ethical path than those driven primarily by the need for personal success. Humble leaders value the importance of society. We are critically in need of leaders who can see the big global picture and then act for the benefit of sustainable business for future generations. In the wise words of Benjamin Franklin: 'A man wrapped up in himself makes a very small bundle'.

Kaipa and Radjou's recent book *From Smart to Wise: Acting and leading with wisdom* (2013) argues that leaders cannot simply rely on 'smartness' to solve complex issues in today's fast-changing world. 'Wise leaders' go beyond 'smart leaders' by applying smartness wisely for *mutual* and not just personal benefit. Wise leaders act authentically, achieve clarity about their roles and purpose, are discerning in their decision-making, are flexible but tough and act with courage as well as enlightened self-interest. For Kaipa and Radjou, therefore, wise leadership blends practical and smart action with responsible and networked practice, a view of leadership that blends eastern with western leadership thinking and focuses on common purpose.

Authenticity

Authenticity has been argued as being a key element of wise leadership, but it is a construct that is relatively new to the mainstream study of leadership, although interest in it is growing fast. At The Leadership Trust we focus directly on helping leaders to know and control themselves. We see this as an essential starting point for successful leadership and also the first step towards authentic leadership. To be truly authentic, however, also requires a deep understanding of how our identity has been shaped by the societal norms around us, a rejection of the pressures to act as others want us to and a refusal to display feelings we do not really feel. Those of us who have lived through the faddish workplaces of the 1908s and 1990s, often exemplified by characters like David Brent in the BBC's 'The Office' series, will recognize these pressures. Fortunately our appetite for filling our workplaces with cultish rituals to be followed blindly and evangelistically has waned. The happy backlash is a return to authenticity.

Goffee and Jones have written extensively about the need for authentic leadership in organizations today. For them, 'knowing yourself, being yourself, and disclosing yourself are vital ingredients of effective leadership'. This is an important message, but in a world where organizations are continually forming alliances, partnerships and networks that are fluid and dynamic and often span the globe, it is a challenge. Organizations today can be pulled in so many directions, responding to the needs of so many stakeholders that leaders can start to lose touch with their true identity and purpose.

Achieving authenticity requires leaders to develop courage, self-knowledge, compassion and strong personal conviction. Those who work towards this goal confirm that they find themselves happier in their working relationships, more successful as leaders and more able to engage and inspire their followers. For the 21st-century leader this is one of the most challenging but also one of the most important qualities a leader can aspire to. As Goffee and Jones (2000) advocate in their seminal *Harvard Business Review* article 'Why should anyone be led by you?', authentic leaders should learn to 'be yourselves – more – with skill'.

Organizations, like people, can act authentically. And authentic organizational leadership is crucial for organizations as their networks become more extensive and diverse. It is this dispersed and values-based leadership that will provide the inspiration and goals that bind people together through a common pursuit, and retain a shared sense of organization across geographic and cultural divides.

Integrity

Warren Bennis, a professor at the University of Southern California, and Robert Thomas, a former MIT professor, now Associate Partner and Senior Fellow with Accenture, partnered in a research project focusing on different generations of leaders and their development (2002). They interviewed 'geezers', their label for leaders over 70, and 'geeks', leaders under 35, to discover how era and values shape those who lead. Their findings are revealing. While they found interesting and significant differences in the world-views of the two groups, they were also surprised to find more that bound them together across the generation gap. The geeks and geezers demonstrated four common leadership competencies needed for today's world, irrespective of their age or background. These were:

- adaptive capacity (including applied creativity and the ability to thrive on ambiguity);

- engaging others by creating shared meaning;
- a compelling voice; and
- *a sense of integrity.*

Integrity has arguably only recently reappeared as a leadership priority, following the many leadership scandals that typified the end of the 20th century. Richard Sennett (1998) then argued that 'impatient capitalism' was 'corroding character' and Mangham, in a chapter entitled 'Leadership and Integrity' in Storey (2004), feared that:

> Leaders will continue to bend the rules and will be richly rewarded for it... In the pursuit of higher returns for their investors, it is hardly surprising that some have lied, cheated and manipulated information whilst others have looked on with barely suppressed admiration.

A growing backlash to these behaviours and norms is now calling for a refocus on leadership integrity and for leadership development programmes to include the teaching of ethics.

Perhaps one of the most marked shifts in thinking about leadership for the 21st century is the renewed emphasis we are now placing on team development, as well as on growing the next generation of leaders. We are beginning to see some of the more forward-thinking universities and business schools creating opportunities to learn and work in teams during an academic programme. Indeed, part of a student's academic attainment can be dependent on working with others. The Hult International Business School has pioneered exactly this. Students on MBA programmes are expected to do some of their work in teams. Most academic programmes are based on individual attainment but it is rarely the case that the newly-employed graduate is expected to work on their own in any organization. Work readiness has to include the capability to work with others.

In team working and team building we are also beginning to sense a change in emphasis. Many programmes look at team dynamics and pay a lot of attention to that. That is important. However, working in a team is also supposed to be productive and there is a growing emphasis on team working which delivers important outcomes even where the team dynamics might be less than perfect.

It is here that work on resilience and mental toughness is beginning to make a contribution.

Many 21st-century leaders aim to try and spend more time with their teams in order to understand their aspirations and to identify the areas in which they need intervention, mentoring and direction. Others see their leadership roles as being about unlocking the potential of their followers and helping them deliver without micromanaging.

Resilience and adaptability

In order to build resilient organizations, leaders must first build their personal resilience in the face of change and adapt to alternative futures.

Our understanding of building resilience has been shaped by AQR's extensive work on resilience and mental toughness, which includes control, challenge, commitment and confidence. This is described more fully in Chapter 3 of this book.

What is especially interesting is the work now emerging which indicates that mental toughness is also a factor in the way we develop relationships with one another. The mentally-tough individual is less sensitive to what others say and do in the sense that they are aware of it but they can take it in their stride. What this might mean is that when teams have to perform and the team members might not always see eye-to-eye, developing this kind of resilience and confidence could produce teams that perform well in circumstances that the more sensitive might find trying.

The research of Robertson Cooper similarly found that resilience is a blend of confidence, social support, adaptability and purposefulness. Heifetz *et al* (2009) also argue for adaptability as critical for 21st-century leadership. In their *Harvard Business Review* article they argue:

> ... only adaptive leadership can use the turbulence of the present to build on and bring closure to the past. In the process, they change key rules of the game, reshape parts of the organization, and redefine the work people do... The art of leadership in today's world involves orchestrating the inevitable conflict, chaos, and confusion of change so that the disturbance is productive rather than destructive.

Professor Mary Uhl-Bien (2007) and her colleagues' work on complexity leadership theory makes a radical shift from seeing the leader as the person at the top to an understanding of leadership as an emergent event, a complex adaptive process that emerges through the interactions of actors. Others have also suggested that more dispersed or collective forms of leadership are now needed to meet 21st-century challenges.

In complexity leadership:

- The role of the formal leader is to enable the conditions within which the leadership process occurs.

- Top leaders focus on creating the conditions in which relationships and interactions can occur to produce adaptive and creative organizational responses.

- Leadership becomes less person-centric, more process or event focused, less fixed and more emergent, and more adaptive to today's leadership challenges.

- All organizational members are encouraged to be a leader in each interaction.

- Responsibility is therefore driven down the organization.

New forms of leadership require new forms of leadership development

Our research into the qualities now required for 21st-century leadership lead us to three key points upon which we base our recommendations for 21st-century leadership development.

Our research has found that the key leadership qualities for building resilient organizations today are:

- vision;
- responsibility;
- humility and common purpose;
- authenticity;
- resilience and adaptability.

Many of these qualities that we have identified as being essential for the 21st-century leader are age-old qualities, but we believe that they are now required more than ever and have often been overlooked by today's leadership development programmes.

Most leadership development programmes have until recently been aimed exclusively at individual 'leader development', in other words, at the creation of 'human capital' inside organizations. New thinking on building resilient organizations is now focusing on leadership development in addition to leader development, in other words, on creating social capital through leadership behaviours across all levels of the organization in order to produce more adaptive organizations able to respond to complexity (Day *et al*, 2000).

Much of what we have found involves a change in mindset, attitude, belief and behaviours in order to respond to the leadership challenges ahead. These combined changes will need to take place at individual, team, *and* organizational levels and this integrated multi-layered approach will, we believe, need to be the focus of effective leadership development in the future. This aligns with the findings outlined in the chapter on mental toughness and again supports the notion that resilience, however described, is of increasing importance.

What does existing research tell us about leadership development for resilient organizations?

Raelin (2004) suggests that most leadership development provision starts with a list of desired attributes:

> Most investment in leadership training subscribes to a list approach. What I mean is that the provider of training typically has either an explicit or tacit list in mind of what attributes it takes to be a good leader.

> (2004, p 131)

This reflects the dominance in recent years of the competency movement, which often starts with a job analysis to determine the skills, competences and behaviours that will be required to do a job. The design of leadership development programmes has tended to follow this trend, thus many programmes include in their aims and objectives the development of a range of leadership behaviours, competencies or skills.

As noted above, most conventional leadership programmes are designed around individual and internal mental processes and are based on the notion that ideas are transferred from one mind to another. However, many now argue that leadership learning is essentially a social process. Raelin (2004), for example, points to the importance of the social relations embedded in an organization or 'community of practice' within which learning takes place, and the essential role of context for learning about leadership. He suggests that instead of focusing exclusively on learning skills and competences, context-based learning using real work issues enables the learning of situation-specific principles.

Thorpe, Gold and Mumford (2010) have argued that good leadership 'is not simply the ability to read situations; it also requires leaders to understand fully the organizations in which they work' (p 21). They suggest that leaders must do more than just acquire competencies. They must also become 'reflective practitioners' and 'practical authors'. As reflective practitioners, organizational development is seen as inextricably linked to an individual's personal development as well as to the context of both the individual and organization. As practical authors, they suggest, leaders must also help others to make sense of situations and develop connections between perspectives (Thorpe *et al*, 2010, p 21). They argue, therefore, that what has been missing from leadership (and consequently leadership development) is 'imagination, judgment and vision'.

Gosling and Mintzberg (2003) criticized conventional business school management education for leaders, especially traditional MBA programmes which organize learning around functional knowledge and overlook leadership qualities or mindsets. Their research pointed to the need for five key managerial mindsets for leaders in today's world: reflection, analysis, collaboration, worldliness, and action. These mindsets have now formed the basis of a number of global leadership and management education programmes, and resonate strongly with our own list of leadership qualities discussed above (and derived from our own research).

Learning to lead is both planned and emergent and a blend of multiple opportunities

A few years ago, we surveyed leaders on how they had learned to lead (Bentley and Turnbull, 2005). Until then, little research had been conducted into how the learning taken from leadership development programmes interplays with the learning taken from other sources such as work-based learning, books, conferences and networking opportunities, and which of the many experiences open to leaders, including leadership development programmes, have most impact.

Our analysis revealed the ten major triggers for developing leadership capability are:

- a significant leadership challenge at an early age;
- observing positive role models;
- being 'thrown in the deep end';
- mentoring, coaching and consultant relationships;
- experiential leadership development courses;
- impact of negative role models;

- MBAs and other professional qualifications;
- international or multicultural experience;
- voluntary and community work;
- team sports.

All are experiential to an extent, which is often significant. Interestingly all link in some way to the 4 Cs (and the 8 subscales) described earlier as components of mental toughness. They all require or cultivate developing a sense of:

- can do (control);
- getting things done for self and for others (commitment);
- pushing back boundaries and learning from that experience – whatever the outcome (challenge);
- self-belief (confidence in my abilities and dealing with others).

Resilience or more likely mental toughness will underpin all of these triggers. If they are important for future success, then developing some form of resilince is essential.

We found that leaders take advantage of both planned and opportunistic leadership development opportunities. Ninety-nine per cent of the leaders said that they are 'aware of what aspects I need to improve in terms of my leadership capacity', and the same number said that they 'proactively look for appropriate ways to develop my leadership capability'.

Only half of these leaders, however, said that they do this to a 'great' or 'very great' extent. The leaders said that they 'take chances and opportunities as they turn up' for their development as a leader, and half of them said that they do this to a 'great or very great extent'. Ninety-seven per cent of the leaders in our survey acknowledged that adverse circumstances make them aware of the need to improve their leadership capability, but again only half of them said that this was true to a 'great extent'.

The triggers listed above were invariably interconnected, and the leaders' stories often revealed a number of these triggers operating simultaneously. The way that these triggers combined to support their leadership development and to act as a catalyst for their learning varied from leader to leader. This depended on a combination of factors which included the leaders' backgrounds, the nature of their organizations, the contexts and circumstances in which they found themselves, the challenges they were facing at the time, the stage they were at in their careers, and the responsibilities that they held.

An age-old debate in the leadership field has asked whether leaders are born or made. Our findings suggest that most people have the capacity to learn the ability to lead, but that desire to lead needs to be combined with a number of triggers for this to happen.

We were intrigued to find that time and again the same 10 triggers were embedded in our leaders' stories. For some leaders, these were described as positive learning experiences. For others, these had been quite painful, although most felt that they were much stronger leaders as a result. This of course is a feature of experiential learning. It is rarely comfortable. It also requires a degree of tolerance of pain and discomfort – again a characteristic of the resilient leader.

Some triggers were described as being the results of a clear plan. Others were the results of an unexpected turn of events or serendipity. Despite these differences, however, the leaders were unanimous in their certainty that it was these events and circumstances that had been the turning points for them and the catalysts that they had needed to learn about leadership.

The future will of course bring with it a number of additional leadership challenges, not least of which will be the growing requirement to lead people from a distance, a phenomenon sometimes called 'virtual leadership'. Losing the face-to-face cues that leaders take from being alongside their followers will mean that new forms of leadership development may be needed. Understanding the subtleties of people's responses and feelings across a geographical divide will increasingly call for more sophisticated leadership antennae and mental toughness, and new forms of leadership development that will employ electronic or virtual communications to enable leaders to develop these antennae.

Again, this will challenge leaders at all levels. It takes many into an area where they have to develop skills and attitudes which are based on trust and their confidence in themselves and others.

Leadership development has three key elements: work-based learning, ideas and concepts, and social interaction

As well as containing a balance of both planned and opportunistic learning, we found that the leadership learning process invariably contains three critical elements: work-based learning, learning new ideas and concepts, and social interaction.

Experiential leadership development training courses, which replicate or use work-based leadership challenges, were cited as having been of great value and in some cases life changing. These courses blend work-based learning either directly or through replicating work-based experiences, offer new ideas and concepts, and enable social interaction. They are not perceived by the leaders (or by us) as teaching leaders to lead. Instead, the courses stimulate reflection and create spaces to reflect on and practise different approaches to leadership, and *act as catalysts* for changing leaders' behaviour at work as illustrated in the quote from a delegate:

> I attended a Leadership in Management course at The Leadership Trust. The biggest thing I learned was to trust other people, to trust the members of the team. I had always felt that I needed to know every single aspect of the job in great detail. When I attended the course I realized that I simply needed to take an overview and trust the specialists within our company more. The course gave me the confidence to follow my gut instinct. It taught me that our team and collective knowledge is the most important asset we have. I learned to communicate what I feel and how I think, so that other members of the team are able to understand me more.

Our study demonstrated that leaders learn leadership as a result of a wide range of experiences throughout their lives. Leadership cannot be learned through a single activity. Training courses and education act as important catalysts for reflecting on leadership and provide ideas and concepts to stimulate important changes in leadership behaviour, but they cannot teach leadership in isolation.

In most organizations there is considerable investment in leadership development, but many leadership development initiatives and programmes fail to hit the mark and thousands of pounds are thrown away on unproven, uninspiring and out-of-date approaches to leadership development.

Bolden, Petrov and Gosling (2010) have noted a number of trends in leadership development for 21st-century organizations:

- A shift in provision from standardized leadership development courses to customized interventions based on real-life challenges.

- A trend away from one-off courses towards ongoing and continuous development journeys. The growth of coaching and mentoring as a valuable development approach would appear to endorse this.

- A move away from classroom-style lectures towards ways of learning that involve hands-on, practical group work focusing on real leadership challenges. Again we see a growth in action learning sets as a resonating development here.

- Recognition that leadership learning can be work-based or blended as well as offsite.

- A move from purely individual learning towards a focus on groups.
- A desire by organizations to change the relationship with outside providers from supplier to partner. This means that the nature of the support built into a programme is now more extensive with inbuilt coaching and relationship focus.

These trends have all been very evident to us at The Leadership Trust. Ten years ago our provision was predominantly focused on individual 'leader' development (human capital). Today, tailored provision of organization-focused leader*ship* development (social capital) developed in partnership with our clients will soon reach 80 per cent of our total business.

What are the essential elements of effective leadership development for resilient 21st-century organizations?

We see leadership development as a learning pipeline that starts on entering an organization and continues to the highest levels of governance, with each level of responsibility and experience requiring a different balance of leading self, leading team and strategic leadership of the organization.

We believe that leadership development needs to focus on more than just the top team, and that leaders are needed at all levels of the organization.

Research has suggested that the most effective leadership development works at a number of levels and here we will argue for three key levels of focus and analysis.

We believe that the most effective leadership development for creating resilient organizations will be leadership development that simultaneously achieves individual, team and organizational impact, so that the personal learning taken away by individuals transfers smoothly and seamlessly to the individual's team and ultimately to multiple teams and to the workplace as a whole. This will therefore make a real difference at all levels over the short, medium and long term, and building a culture of vision, responsibility, humility and common purpose, authenticity, resilience and adaptability.

Each level is discussed below:

Level A: leading self

Effective leadership development makes significant space for self-reflection and challenges the leader to reflect on their own behaviours, style, values and their impact on others. A growing range of tools is of course available to assess these. For example, 360-degree feedback and tools such as the MTQ48 and the ILM72 that have been outlined in Chapter 2 of this book have become an important part of a leadership developer's repertoire. Used on their own, such tools are unlikely to produce more self-aware or more resilient and adaptive leaders. They are tools and are in part dependent upon the skill of the user. But there is a new generation of normative measures emerging which are focused closely on the needs of people and team developers. They do add elements which have not always been there before, such as the ability to benchmark individuals and teams and to measure progress across specific and relevant parameters. Also to understand better what might be happening within an individual or a team. Ultimately, they are most likely to support learning when part of a rigorous learning process that follows Kolb's cycle of experiencing, reflecting, conceptualizing and testing.

We have discovered that the most effective leader development subscribes to the following 'golden rules':

- **The delegate must want to learn to be a leader.** (This sounds self-evident and yet many organizations send delegates onto leadership courses who clearly do not want to lead!) There are many barriers to successful leadership development at the level of the individual, but lack of desire features at the top. Lack of desire to lead may stem from low self-confidence or fear of failure, but it may also be a genuine choice by those oriented to more technical professional challenges. It is important for organizations to differentiate between these barriers and help those who may simply need to build greater self-confidence and awareness to recognize their own potential.

- **Setting and agreeing the learning agenda is important.** Agreeing objectives with a line manager or a more senior leader in the organization prior to embarking on a leadership course can reduce doubt, remove fear or cynicism, increase self-confidence and dramatically increase the motivation of the individual to learn and become a more effective leader. This again may sound self-evident, but our frequent experience has shown that many organizations skip this step and cause themselves big problems as a result.

- **Safe opportunities for delegates to practise and reflect on new behaviours should be provided.** The best experiential leadership development courses are designed to create a safe environment for new behaviours to be practised and for feedback to be given and received. Practising new ways of behaving, developing sensitivity to others' motivations by strengthening emotional intelligence and giving and receiving ongoing feedback are essential elements for effective individual leadership development.

- **Post-course follow up and evaluation should be built into the design.** Many courses end with a basic evaluation of the delegates' responses to the course itself. Often referred to as Kirkpatrick's Level 1, or the 'happy sheet', this does not evaluate the impact and outcomes of a leadership course in terms of the leader's behavioural change, nor their impact on others.

Evaluating the true impact of leadership development can only be achieved by adopting more rigorous evaluation techniques over a longer time period in order to ascertain how well the learning is being sustained by the individual, whether their improved self-awareness is becoming embedded over the long term in their behaviours, and how this is manifesting itself in their work and well-being as a leader. This ongoing evaluation needs to be accompanied by ongoing support within the organization. This support is discussed below.

Incidentally, this is also where the use of the new generation of valid and reliable personality-based competency measures which assess aspects of mindset can make a contribution, MTQ48 being an example. You can measure that at the start and at the completion of an intervention – if you haven't got a shift in mindset you probably won't get the outcomes you seek in due course.

Level B: leading the team

Individual leadership development is too often conducted in a vacuum that ignores the learner's real-world leadership context and the specific challenges that they will face when they return to work. For real transfer of leadership development to a leader's team to be effective, the leader must understand how to go about transferring the new behaviours learned in the safety of the other delegates on the course to the more complex challenges of leading their real-world teams. Culture, history, individual differences in the team and the leader's own reputation in the organization can each affect the transfer of leadership learning back into the team.

For a leadership development course to be effective at the level of the team, as many of the following factors as possible should be present:

- The individual must leave the course feeling confident enough on his or her return to try out the newly learned behaviours back in the workplace.

- The individual must also feel confident enough to authentically share their learning with their team in order to cascade learning and build a spirit of knowledge-sharing.
- The individual should feel encouraged to seek regular feedback on the impact of their changed behaviours from their team members by displaying an ongoing desire to learn.

Coaching opportunities following leadership development can often aid individuals returning to the workplace to think about how to deal with difficult situations or team members, and how to better understand the different needs of their own team.

Action learning sets can also be a useful alternative for leaders dealing with the ongoing challenges of leading their teams. Some leadership courses offer the opportunity for learning sets to continue within the peer group with whom they have built trust on the course. Others offer such opportunities within their organization. Both add value by offering the essential post-course support that is needed.

Level C: leading the organization

Too often this essential element of leadership development is overlooked. Individuals nominated for leadership development often return from a course or programme dramatically changed, but they return to an unchanged organization. Quite quickly, disillusionment can set in when their new skills and behaviours are disregarded or underutilized. It is very important that organizations offer support to these changed individuals who return with a desire to impact positively on their organizations but are too often met with unresponsive line managers, or bosses who feel threatened by their new self-confidence.

For a leadership course to be effective at the level of leading the organization, and to enable resilience building to go beyond the level of the individual or group of individuals to become embedded in the organization's culture, a number of conditions should be present:

- There needs to be active and authentic top-down support for an organizational leadership programme and a genuine interest in its impact and outcomes for the organization.
- A leadership development pipeline should be in place for leadership development that starts on entry into the organization and continues up to board and governance levels.

- The most successful organizational leadership programmes are based on a model of distributed, shared or complexity leadership, and build leadership capability across hierarchical levels, by creating the space for adaptive and creative action.

- Organizational projects embedded in a leadership development course that operate cross-functionally and cross-departmentally can often help to sustain energy and the desire for change beyond the end of the formal element of an organizational leadership course, and produce real organizational benefits.

- Alumni networks in place for those who have been through an organizational leadership course offer an opportunity to share experiences and use the common language built by the course. Organizations that take these seriously often offer master-classes and leadership events for their alumni.

- Opportunities post-course for leaders to step up to challenging assignments that enable them to draw on their new knowledge and behaviours are imperative for sustaining momentum and reinforcing learning and self-confidence.

- Continually monitoring and measuring outcomes from the programme. This will ensure that the budget for such training is sustained. Sound arguments for continuity are often found in either the financial savings produced as a result of the course or new innovations that have emerged as a direct result of the programme.

Unfortunately, we have found that it is all too rare for all of the 'essential elements' for effective leadership development to be in place. However, we firmly believe that an integrative approach to leadership development that blends leadership development at all levels to generate a leadership development pipeline is essential for building resilient organizations.

A summary checklist is provided below for leadership developers:

- Develop a leadership development pipeline inside the organization that enables leadership to be developed early.

- Enable leaders at all levels to balance their learning to include work-based learning, learning of new ideas and concepts, and social interaction.

- Balance experiential learning with work-based learning in order to trigger cycles of reflection and practice.

- Include opportunities for leaders to coach and be coached formally or informally and to give and receive feedback.
- Offer access to role models and opportunities to learn from other leaders' approaches.
- Provide opportunities to generate and apply new ideas and concepts.
- Facilitate opportunities at all levels for people to engage with new leadership challenges.
- Promote access to new contexts and cultures for people to develop themselves and be stretched as leaders.
- Create a culture of distributed leadership in which opportunities to contribute to leadership activity are open to all.
- Include an evaluation process for understanding the effects of the learning on the leaders' capabilities, self-confidence, self-awareness and impact.

Conclusions

Vision, responsibility, humility and common purpose, authenticity, personal resilience and adaptability are emerging as essential dimensions of 21st-century leadership. We have argued in this chapter that organizations today are facing ever more complex challenges in a turbulent and fast-changing global and technological world, and it is these five qualities that will make the difference in enabling effective resilient leadership at all levels. We have also shown that leadership development strategies have not kept pace with the changing nature of the leadership needed to build resilient organizations for the 21st century.

We subscribe to Uhl-Bien, Heifetz and others' arguments that developing distributed, adaptive and complexity leadership will be key to success in the 21st century and will enable the building of resilient organizations. This will mean finding new ways to develop more adaptive leadership capability across individual, team and organizational levels simultaneously. The second part of this chapter offered practical suggestions for doing this.

We believe that leadership development cannot continue to focus on top leaders alone. Resilient organizations will only be built by extending the focus of leadership development to all corners of the organization, focusing on leadership by the many, and on the development of social capital that will enable adaptive change through fast, responsive, complexity leadership.

Chopra has argued that leadership is enacted everywhere and that leadership that arises from ordinary lives is the type of leadership most needed to fill the chronic 'leadership vacuum' of modern society. This is also true in organizations. We agree with Chopra that through effective and wise leadership development 'countless leaders can rise to the highest levels of greatness'. We would add that it is through these countless leaders that resilient organizations will be built.

The pace of change that we have described in this chapter is unlikely to reduce. Indeed, the turbulence of the early 21st century may even increase as globalization and technological change accelerate. Leadership capacity and mental toughness will become increasingly important as this century brings unforeseen new challenges. Indeed, it is highly likely that only the most agile and flexible organizations will survive and thrive in the long term.

Leadership development programmes will, therefore, need to adapt to meet this need. Resilience, both personal and organizational, will increasingly become a core element of leadership development courses. This resilience will include the ability to scan and understand the competitive global landscape, the ability to adapt to change as well as to lead change, the ability to build leadership capacity across the whole organization and to embrace new technologies. In short, leadership is likely to require greater agility and mental toughness, but it will also require vision, responsibility and humility. We should start preparing the next generation of leaders now.

References

Bennis, W and Thomas, R J (2002) *Geeks and Geezers: How era, values, and defining moments shape leaders*, Harvard Business School Publishing, Boston

Bentley, J and Turnbull, S (2005) *Stimulating Leaders: Developing manufacturing leadership skills*, Manufacturing Foundation, Birmingham

Bolden, R, Petrov, G and Gosling, J (2010) *Developing Collective Leadership in Higher Education*, University of Edinburgh, Edinburgh

Chopra, D (2011) *The Soul of Leadership*, Rider, London

Collins, J (2001) *Good To Great: Why some companies make the leap... and others don't*, Random House Business, London

Day, C, Harris, A, Hadfield, M, Tolley, H and Beresford, J (2000) *Leading Schools in Times of Change*, Open University Press, Buckingham

Goffee, R and Jones, G (2000) Why should anyone be led by you? *Harvard Business Review*, 78(5), pp 62–70

Gosling, J and Mintzberg, H (2003) The five minds of the manager, *Harvard Business Review*, 81(11), pp 54–63

Heifetz, R, Grashow, A and Linsky, M (2009) Leadership in a (permanent) crisis, *Harvard Business Review*, 87(7/8), pp 62–69

Kaipa, P and Radjou, N (2013) *From Smart to Wise: Acting and leading with wisdom*, Jossey-Bass, San Francisco

Leadership Trust (2013) Think Tank Report, Leadership Trust

Maak, T and Pless, N (2006) *Responsible Leadership*, Routledge, Oxford

Mangham, I (2004) Leadership and integrity, in *Leadership in Organisations: Key issues and trends* ed Storey, Routledge, Oxford

Overell, S, Chartered Management Institute (2013) *The Conference Board CEO Challenge 2013: The UK* Challenge (white paper)

Raelin, J (2004) Preparing for leaderful practice, *Training and Development*, 58(3), pp 64–70

Sennett, R (1998) *The Corrosion of Character: The personal consequences of work in the new capitalism*, W. W. Norton, London

Thorpe, R, Gold, J and Mumford, A (2010) *Leadership and Management Development*, CIPD Enterprises Limited, London

Uhl-Bien, M (2007) Complexity leadership theory: shifting leadership from the industrial age to the knowledge era, *The Leadership Quarterly*, 18(4), pp 298–318

PART TWO
Practitioner perspectives

Leadership and the BP grit in the oyster – developing mental toughness

06

Case study: How can developing mental toughness help forward-thinking organizations grow outstanding leaders?

JO SHUTTLEWOOD AND RACHEL BILLINGTON

This chapter explores BP's talent development programme, Spotlight. The programme was devised in response to its determination to grow and retain its high-potential middle managers and secure its long-term capacity to remain resilient to changing economic times and market challenges. Mental toughness sits at the heart of the Spotlight programme, with its focus on confidence, challenge, control and commitment. Here we will examine how the programme brought these elements to life and how richly it impacted on participants' thinking and behaviours, specifically their confidence, which increased significantly.

BP recognized that we live in an energizing period of complexity and change. However, that is not always the default response of many. Some see complexity and change as debilitating and to be feared. Some organizations which, in the past, ran on a traditional directive model of leadership, are now examining and embracing the opportunity to explore more human, negotiated routes to success. Those seeking to attract the creativity and commitment of new generations of leaders will need to offer more than just money or promotion – opportunities for continued learning, experiences which engage the imagination, emotionally intelligent relationships which support, challenge and nurture are what the 21st century's emerging talent will look for in their careers.

More than anything, individuals will want to be recognized and valued for their unique contribution to the mission of an organization, rather than just to fill a certain role or slot or attend to a delegated task list. Systemically and specifically, organizations will engage with their employees as whole people with minds, spirits and hearts on offer, working together in living networks rather than fixed constructs.

Trust will be the defining attribute of the relationship between management and teams: emotionally intelligent, motivated workers, all focused on delivering the best possible outcomes for business. An emerging leader in a trusting organization such as this is like grit in the oyster – a beautiful irritant, creating layers of learning for the whole organization, building up new leaders like pearls to be sought out and treasured, 'cultured' in the corporate environment.

Trust is explored more fully elsewhere in this book in Chapter 4. It resonates strongly with what we find in our work. Trust is important and is becoming increasingly so.

Do we recognize this view of the modern workplace? Or is it more likely that we see just glimpses of the human in the machine, and have to learn to fill the emotional gap between what we need and what we routinely get? If so, mental toughness offers us a bridge to fill that gap.

Neuroscientists are beginning to tell us that every event that stimulates the brain triggers an emotional response first. It is the amygdala, the process centre of the brain's limbic system that enables us to register the mainly energizing emotions of pleasure, joy, love, as well as the largely survival emotions fear, disgust and aggression. All of us are emotional beings: the degree to which we regulate our emotions is important in determining how we respond to change and to challenge of all types. This is a learned process, and one which we can control. Mental toughness gives us a framework within which to develop and practise this control. For many, this provides a hugely helpful resource for those whose emotional responses to the challenges they face might otherwise prevent them from fulfilling their potential.

This case study looks at what happened when Perform-in-Business (PiB) was commissioned by BP (Fuel Value Chain UK) to create a programme to develop highly effective leaders in a shortened timeframe to ensure future leadership talent. A review highlighted the opportunity for the company to find a creative solution to the issue of medium-term succession. HR Manager Jo Donovan believed a bold, bespoke intervention could offer the way forward. She determined to find a reliable solution, capable of making a difference in the long term, with a strong evidence base of delivering results.

The commission was based on some shared values:

- Leaders who are mentally tough and emotionally intelligent will excel in coping with the present and in shaping the future.

- Outstanding leaders know themselves: what drives outstanding performance is authenticity and ease, present when people are able to regulate their emotional hijacks and suspend their ego in order to think well and act decisively.

- Leadership is primarily about emotionally engaging others to deliver the right outstanding results – it exists in the relationship between self and others, between people and systems, between needs and results.

What was the idea?

The challenge was to engage the participants in a transformational programme that would challenge them on a professional and personal level, and would deliver the measurable business results that BP were looking for.

PiB began to weave together a comprehensive and properly-integrated programme, a cloth if you like, strong enough to hold all these aspirations. Jo Shuttlewood is the founder of PiB and the lead practitioner working with BP on delivering the Spotlight Programme. Drawing on PiB's experience in industry and learning and development, and her psychological training, Shuttlewood worked closely with Donovan to develop an approach that would:

- empower the learner;
- create a safe environment for thinking well;
- offer creative and emotionally-engaging learning opportunities;
- courageously model authenticity;
- insist on seeing action as a result of learning.

Looking at these in turn, each was carefully defined using practical, down-to-earth terminology. The goal was to use language and definitions which were clear and understood in the same way by both facilitators and learners. This also applied to the way desired outcomes were described – especially where we were describing new behaviours and habits.

Empower the learner

Learners in this programme would be aware of their own capacity for making change. This programme would not embody a deficit model of learning that sees the participant as an empty vessel to be filled with knowledge by the teacher, but rather would enable the learner to discover the skills and insight that they need to drive forward their own learning journey. This included learning how to transfer skills developed in other areas that were wholly transferable to their roles at BP – current and future.

In turn, this would require learners to be active participants rather than passive recipients. This contrasted with other training experiences they had known, but their input would be rewarded by a clear sense of being valued as an individual, heard, seen and treasured.

Create a safe environment for thinking well

Key to the success of the programme would be the skill of the facilitators in holding the space for the learners and nurturing a sense of trust in the group. Thinking well requires the brain to still the shouting voices of the amygdala and its emotional hijacks – not to shut them up, but to hear them, note them and regulate them so we can make the right choice for the challenge at hand. This would be a collaboration of brains thinking well, rather than egos struggling for their position in the group. Thinking well is the genesis of all positive action, and creating the right environment for this function would be a crucial skill for the group to master so they could really get to grips with their *mental toughness*.

Offer creative and emotionally-engaging learning opportunities – being bold, brave and beautiful

Fuelled by the use of metaphor and imagination, the programme would be unapologetic about asking learners to boldly tell their stories, bravely share their histories and beautifully design their dreams.

We find the brain gets more flexible in the presence of metaphor, more able to toggle between different options, more able to deal with divergent ideas before coming to rest on the chosen pathway.

Learning in this way is 'sticky' – it impacts on our understanding at a deeper level and is thus more likely to lead to behaviour change. Programme design would also stimulate the learning agility and progress of each learner, with significant investment in reflection and analysis by the facilitators to ensure as far as possible that each learner would experience a learning pathway bespoke to their needs.

Courageously model authenticity

The facilitators would value the role of attendees as co-learners on the programme and would genuinely seek to position themselves as equals in the group dynamic. The imperative is clear – emerging leaders need to establish their own authentic leadership brand, rather than seek to copy that of another, no matter how charismatic or successful or appealing. They need to focus on their own mental toughness, rather than lean on someone else's.

The facilitators would need to model a different kind of leadership that would engender safety and trust while making space for learners to plot their own course – so-called 'egoless leadership'. This would be characterized by a sense of ease with self and others, not needing to jockey for position, regulating emotional responses to allow for crisp thinking and positive choices for the good of the 'system' rather than the individual.

Peter Senge, in his book *The Fifth Discipline* (1990), explores 'systems thinking', a view of how strategy, action and reflection fit together for optimum business performance. He recognizes the imperative for personal mastery and personal growth if systems are to achieve their potential. Senge also suggests 'an organization's competitive edge lies in its ability to learn faster than its competitors' – a salient idea in the context of the Spotlight programme.

Easy! In attempting to model this ideal set of behaviours throughout the programme, the facilitators would actually need to model the value of authenticity, not being afraid to share finding things hard, getting things wrong, having to try again, all the time learning and building on that learning.

The research of Carol Dweck (*Mindset: The New Psychology of Success*, 2007) points to the benefits of a having a growth mindset – one that values the opportunity to learn and hard work over a reliance on a fixed mindset – with a heavy reliance on talent. Typically, a fixed mindset is threatened by the perceived failure of not knowing the 'right' answer and will often give up. Those with a growth mindset know the answer is there somewhere and needs perseverance and learning to get to it.

Dweck's discourse reflects time and again how a growth mindset can be valuable in all aspects of human performance and can be developed by modelling attitudes and language which celebrate the process of learning, trying, growing and dogged persistence rather than already knowing or succeeding without effort.

This calm recognition of successes and failures would require an almost ruthless commitment to reflection and honest feedback to self and others, that in other circumstances could be hard to deliver and to take – hence the value of a safely held space. Participants in this process would become used to challenge, offered in a spirit of optimum learning and genuine belief in the learners' potential to think for themselves and build their own unique success.

Insist on seeing action as a result of learning, with learners accountable for their own progress

Built into the process would be the requirement for learners to link their learning to their real-life work projects, both to demonstrate the impact of their learning to line managers and other stakeholders and to provide rich seams of experience to mine as the learning journey continued.

Once the expectations were clearly laid out for learners, they would be expected to deliver with minimal hand-holding. They would also be expected to appreciate the privilege of having been selected for the programme, and as a consequence be more likely to respond positively to the inspirational opportunities offered to them through the programme design.

Facilitators would support progress towards targets with determination, challenging any limiting beliefs that emerged and exposing perceived barriers. If progress stalled, alternative strategies would be agreed until the learner found a pathway that worked for them.

From the start, the programme would be framed as rigorous, pragmatic and delivering tangible results for the business – dealing with the emotional would not equate to touchy-feely introspection, it would be keenly practical and robustly evidence-based.

Again this reflects some of the thinking which emerges elsewhere in this book. There is an increasing focus on achievement.

The Spotlight Programme emerged as the response to these aspirations. Mental toughness would become the cornerstone of the programme, with the 4 Cs – challenge, control, commitment and confidence – forming the building blocks of syllabus. The MTQ48 psychometric measure, designed both to measure mental toughness and to offer developmental strategies to improve it, would play a vital part in providing a baseline measure of each individual's starting point and in shining a light on where improvements could be made.

Because it is also a normative measure, it would also deliver valuable evidence of progress made to positive changes in mindset by the end of the programme.

What happened?

BP is a global leader in oil, gas and petrochemicals. It operates in 80 countries, employing around 80,000 people worldwide. It fuels the productivity of many, in more ways than one. BP (Fuel Value Chain UK) drives the fuel business on the forecourts of Britain, making sure there is petrol in the pumps and that customers recognize the quality and value of the BP brand throughout its chain of outlets, whether they are own brand, partnerships or franchises.

Leaders in this part of the business have a diverse and complex range of stakeholders, and manage an ever-changing set of circumstances in order to deliver results. To achieve this, BP leaders need to demonstrate agility, resilience and the ability to make good decisions in tough situations. In addition, they need to be able to lead their teams to do the same. In essence, they need to be emotionally intelligent and mentally tough.

An annual talent review in 2010 highlighted an issue with medium-term succession for senior leadership roles. With low employee turnover and few external new joiners, the challenge was on to find an internal solution. A number of high-potential individuals were identified who had intellectual capacity and were assessed by BP as high achievers, but didn't necessarily demonstrate the attributes of mental toughness considered to be necessary to be leaders in the medium term.

The Spotlight programme was commissioned and designed to meet this need. Over two years, the participants would work together and individually, with the carefully prepared and focused support of the facilitators, through a range of challenges and tasks that would invite them into new layers of learning and growth. Returning to the oyster metaphor, the grit of their potential would become pearls of capability as outstanding leaders for BP.

It's not what you do, it's the way that you do it

Structurally, there is little that is particularly groundbreaking or unique about Spotlight: it is crisp, simple and based on recognizable professional learning models and theory (this is described in Table 6.1).

So what is special about the programme?

This lies in the extent to which its development is based upon the progress and needs of the individual learner, and the investment made in genuinely

TABLE 6.1 The Spotlight Programme structure

In summary, how the programme was structured and what the core elements of each stage were
MTQ48 baseline measurement and individual feedback sessions
Introductory Knowledge event – building rapport with fellow learners and the PiB team, establishing shared language and understanding of concepts, introducing reflection tools
Six mental toughness modules introducing 21 techniques to build positive thinking, attentional control, anxiety control, goal setting and visualization designed to respond to the learners' needs. Each module consists of: <ul><li>Pre-work: text/research to explore, materials to prepare, practice to report back on.</li><li>Delivery: a group day facilitated by PiB to introduce, model and practice techniques.</li><li>Review and action setting: how the learning was impacting on thinking, behaviour and action in the business setting.</li><li>Learning support: individual coaching sessions for each learner to address any blocks or identify any breakthroughs.</li><li>Thinking pairs activity with programme buddy.</li><li>Line manager session – to share new learning and seek support for new practices</li><li>Mentor session – with BP colleague</li></ul>
MTQ48 progress measurement and individual feedback sessions
Commitment event – sharing evidence of progress and increased leadership capability with senior leadership

meeting those needs. It is the sincere commitment to emotionally engaging with the learner in order to achieve the right results.

Yes, but what do you do?

Twenty-one techniques are introduced over a programme of six modules. The learners practise these both in the facilitated sessions and back in the workplace – purposeful practice being the key to behavioural change, as new neuro-pathways develop that form new habits. Purposeful practice being repeated practice which at each iteration seeks to make a small advance. It combines repeatability with incremental development.

The techniques relate to the areas identified by mental toughness development experts as being most effective – positive thinking, visualization, anxiety control, attentional control and goal setting. The MTQ48 measure helps users and facilitators to identify which areas might be most appropriate for a particular individual. Again, the attention is given to the individual's needs and their engagement in their own development. For example, the more the learners were able to practise their positive-thinking techniques, the more habitual their positive thinking became, the less energy they had to commit to challenging negativity, all leading to improved performance. This flow between learning, practice, reflection and support is hugely helpful in transforming theory into practice.

There's little point in learning a raft of leadership theory if it stays in your head and never makes it into practice – Spotlight is a programme entirely about learning it, doing it, thinking about it and then doing it more, and better, until you are performing at your peak.

The content and delivery of each intervention is designed only after the impact of the previous module has been reviewed and analysed. This requires a greater commitment of resource (and skill) from the facilitators but results in a far more responsive programme which values the learners, both empowering them and making them more accountable for the success of their own learning. It is more resource intensive but, as is often the case, 'you get what you pay for'. This is a clear case of seeing this kind of support as an investment and not just as a cost.

The participants genuinely drive the programme and recognize their own role within it, underlining their perception of themselves as leaders. For instance, a clear theme emerged from the group around fear of failure, so in response, practice time was allocated in the following sessions to techniques to build confidence through positive thinking. As a direct result of this, one of the learners used his new-found resilience to face the challenge of a very tough business goal when all the market odds were against him. He found that he was able to exceed his target against a backdrop of managing costs in decline and flat revenues.

Each delivery session is facilitated by two professionals from the PiB team to make sure that there is capacity to facilitate sensitively, to observe precisely and to model authentically. The professional expertise of the facilitators in holding the space, judging the style and pace of delivery, offering the right balance of challenge and support and accurately surmizing what is really going on for participants adds significant value to the programme, while offering great return on investment.

What do we mean by 'holding the space'? This is a key concept. There is a dynamic tension between the thinker and the listener when there is an explicit agreement that the space they both inhabit is:

- exclusively available for the thinker;
- free of judgement;
- characterized by positive regard;
- safe and supported.

This means the thinker can be comfortable with potentially difficult or challenging trains of thought.

Each session is carefully planned as a Thinking Environment, with the ten components key to thinking well at the heart of the delivery model. Nancy Kline, in her book *Time to Think: Listening to Ignite the Human Mind* (1998) describes a set of principles that best support the thinker: Attention, Equality, Ease, Appreciation, Encouragement, Feelings, Information, Diversity, Incisive Questions and Place. Spotlight sessions adopt these principles rigorously, ensuring that learners have the best opportunity for quality thinking, which is a necessary precursor to quality action.

Again, the apparent simplicity of the model belied its power to unlock potential and proved one of the most effective techniques for the learners and one which they would put into practice in the workplace both during and after the programme. It was the delivery of the modules and the challenge and support of the facilitators that was cited in evaluation as being the most effective element of the programme.

Many of the techniques address the idea of the desired future state – what do I want and how do I get it? All help to develop the mental toughness needed to work out the answer to these questions.

Simple techniques for goal setting to achieve business objectives include: turning self talk from negative to positive; mental rehearsal leading to more conceptual, exploratory exercises around the individual's leadership brand, and compelling vision. Learners are empowered to think beyond the confines of 'SMART' objectives and strive for something more satisfying than that – an intrinsic motivation to perform and deliver against a set of targets which flex to respond to business needs, informed by values embraced by organization and leader alike in pursuit of a compelling vision of success.

The Hero's Journey

This is an example of an exercise used in Spotlight to help craft and communicate a compelling vision.

Joseph Campbell's work in describing the myth of the Hero's Journey (Campbell, 1949) is seminal in the fields of storytelling, ritual and psychology. The basic pattern of the Jungian archetype of the Hero, who sets out on a perilous adventure to bring back a great treasure for the ultimate benefit of the community, has been common to all cultures and times and has been reflected in great storytelling from Greek myths to *Star Wars*.

In Spotlight, learners were asked to reflect on their own Hero's Journey – recognizing their reality, trusting their call to adventure, seeking out their trusted allies and mentors, testing their commitment to the journey, celebrating their victories and confirming the change that the journey has wrought in them.

In an act of risky creative exposure, they were encouraged to present their stories to each other, either written, spoken, animated or represented in some other format of their choosing. Figures 6.1 and 6.2 below track the emotional journey this exercise covers and shows how relevant it is for the emergent leader.

FIGURE 6.1   The CM Brand Hero's Journey

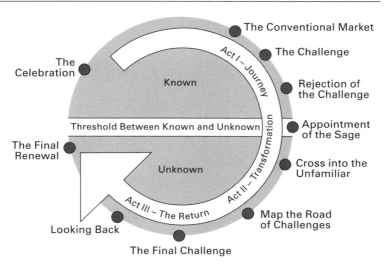

SOURCE Taken from Robert Rose (www.contentmarketinginstitute.com) and Christopher Vogler (www.thewritersjourney.com)

FIGURE 6.2 The Hero's Inner Journey

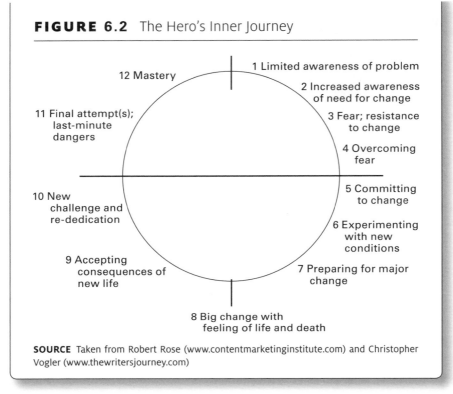

12 Mastery

1 Limited awareness of problem

2 Increased awareness
of need for change

11 Final attempt(s);
last-minute
dangers

3 Fear; resistance
to change

4 Overcoming
fear

10 New
challenge and
re-dedication

5 Committing
to change

6 Experimenting
with new
conditions

9 Accepting
consequences of
new life

7 Preparing for major
change

8 Big change with
feeling of life and death

SOURCE Taken from Robert Rose (www.contentmarketinginstitute.com) and Christopher Vogler (www.thewritersjourney.com)

What changed?

For the first cohort of Spotlight participants, results have been both transformational and exceptional.

We tested participants with the MTQ48 measure at the start and at the end of the programme. The measure assesses mindset. If the programme is doing its job, we should be able to see evidence of a change in mindset.

Analysis of the repeated MTQ48 questionnaire showed a 20 per cent increase in confidence, with confidence in abilities improving by 25 per cent.

Was this reflected in any way in terms of important outcomes for the programme? In fact this correlated strongly with excellent achievement on high profile projects: three people were promoted, two changed roles, one took on extra responsibilities and three used their new-found confidence to facilitate leadership team meetings.

Donovan reports that the leaders:

... now use their skills to coach and mentor [subsequent] cohorts two and
three, their motivation and engagement with BP and the business is admirable

and they actively practise what they have learnt with their teams, creating an environment which is driving cultural change around the way people lead.

Other feedback from BP includes this from Neale Smither, BP (Fuel Value Chain UK) Manager and the senior business leader who is the main programme sponsor:

> The leaders on The Spotlight Programme have grown and matured in their leadership by five to ten years, exceeding the two-year programme length. At the graduation it felt like a leadership team had emerged, that the programme had created an environment of trust and the experience was clearly personally uplifting resulting in leaders who knew where they were heading and have a much clearer game plan.

Our experience has led us to believe strongly that the quality of leadership action is directly proportional to the quality of leadership thinking and that thinking will always precede behavioural change, so evaluation focused on two questions: how has your thinking changed and what are you doing now that you were not doing before?

Responses pointed to a huge increase in positive thinking among the group and an ability to successfully regulate the negative emotions which threaten to hijack performance. Many of the responses from the delegates make excellent testimonials:

> Using positive-thinking techniques every day. Using reflective practice. Focusing a lot more on what matters and getting faster and better results. I use empathetic listening techniques to allow people to come up with their own solutions. I am more in control, calmer and less stressed. I understand the importance of my relationship with my boss. I'm supporting colleagues by using the techniques I've learnt to help them improve performance. I stop myself from having emotional hijacks and am generally a lot more positive. I use empathetic listening techniques. I live my brand.

> I catch myself thinking negative thoughts and turn these into positive. I use quiet times to clear my mind and allow better creativity and focus. When in conversation with others I always consider how empathetic I am being. I constantly reflect on situations and consider how I could have done things better. I constantly ask myself if I am focusing on what's important. I recognize when I am being emotionally hijacked and stop and think before reacting.

> Sitting comfortable and confident in my own abilities. Paying more attention to my actions and the effect they can have on others around me. Feeling confident in my future. Drawing on different tools to approach different situations.

I am spending far more time reflecting both looking back and forward. Before it would be worry; now it is positive thinking – a completely different mindset!

Confidence is a big word. Understanding yourself, understanding leadership techniques and understanding you are respected. Mental toughness development really does work. I am amazed by how confident I can be.

So how can developing mental toughness help organizations grow outstanding leaders – particularly those suited to the challenges of the future?

We can see from this evidence that the increase in Mental Toughness, specifically in the confidence component, has led to a treasure trove of new leadership talent emerging at BP. These outstanding leaders perform more effectively, behave more positively and demonstrate ambition and well-being which inspire others towards even greater success. The authenticity of the delivery approach of The Spotlight Programme empowered these leaders to own their success and to develop a sense of ease with themselves and others which will mark them out as the senior leaders of the future.

What questions are we left with?

As any good researcher or practitioner will tell you, the moment you think you have 'cracked it' is the moment you should then look for the next generation of questions to answer. It is what genuine continuous improvement embraces.

How do we humanize leadership development?

If organizations want to flourish and benefit from the very best of the talent available to them, they will need to see that talent as people first. BP (Fuel Value Chain UK) saw the people that they had, trusted that they could become bigger and better in some way that mattered and empowered them to grow. The return on investment is mutual – organization and individual benefit and grow together, for the good of each other, and both become stronger as a result.

What do we need to do in order to help people fulfil their leadership potential?

We need to create the right environment for them to think well and in which they can harness all their resources of mental toughness to cope with the present challenge and to shape the future possibilities.

With all of their expertise, sophisticated analysis and in-depth knowledge, PiB's most effective contribution was not what was taught, but how it was learned – through authentic human connection.

How do we encourage organizations to grow?

Many organizations, large and small, from all kinds of sectors, struggle with the notion of empowered employees. They might be far too gritty and just serve to irritate, rather than develop into pearls! Undeniably, to make the change from command and control to empower and trust requires huge amounts of vision, trust, courage and commitment. Growing organizations, however, need to maximize the talent of every one of their people if they are going to reach their peak performance, and the return on investment will be worth it when they succeed.

What are the challenges for organizations as they seek to grow into the future?

Firstly, there's a need to attract the high-potential employees of the future. The Millennial generation with all their digital prowess, creativity and team working feel themselves entitled to work which is of value and makes a difference, where they are listened to and have some say about what they do, with exciting future opportunities to tempt them to stay loyal to the company. They would also like to earn well, be flexible and have a good work/

life balance. (See Ron Alsop's *The Trophy Kids Grow Up: How the Millennial Generation is Shaking Up the Workplace* (2008) for more on this.)

How much of this they can have, or indeed should be able to have, is debatable but it is clear that some organizations are reaching out across the generation gap to meet these aspirations. How is this done while maintaining adult relationships? Only by developing the emotional intelligence and emotional literacy of all involved.

Then how do we develop structures and practices that genuinely reflect the human culture we believe we want?

No matter how earnest a leader's desire to humanize their organization, if systems and structures don't change at all levels to bring this to life, change is unlikely to deliver the desired transformation. It is a matter of doing it as well as wanting it, with a robust attention to detail in matching processes to desired outcomes.

PiB's experience with BP (Fuel Value Chain UK) shows how leadership development can work at its best, delivering beautiful results for all and generating pearls of learning which will be of value for years to come.

References

Alsop, R (2008) *The Trophy Kids Grow Up: How the millennial generation is shaking up the workplace*, Jossey-Bass, San Francisco

Campbell, J (1949) *The Hero with a Thousand Faces*, Bollingen Foundation, Pantheon Books, New York

Dweck, C (2007) *Mindset: the New Psychology of Success*, Ballantine Books, New York

Kline, N (1998) *Time to Think: Listening to ignite the human mind*, Cassell Illustrated, London

Rose, R [accessed 26 March 2014] *Content Marketing Institute* [Online] www.contentmarketinginstitute.com

Senge, P. (1990) *The Fifth Discipline: The art and practice of the learning organization*, Random House Business, London

Vogler, C [accessed 26 March 2014] *The Writer's Journey* [Online] www.thewritersjourney.com

Changing times for the public sector

Case study: The response in Wales – how the Welsh public sector has seen and managed the challenge

ZOE SWEET AND JO CARRUTHERS

Mental toughness as both a concept and an aspect of professional practice had historically been most prominent in the world of sport. However, in recent years we have seen its emergence as a valuable concept in the organizational and occupational worlds, as evidenced by the increasing use of tools and diagnostics such as the MTQ 48 mental toughness questionnaire. Its use in the corporate arena was originally associated within the healthcare field, although it has theoretical roots in psychology through the notion of resilience. However, it is now much more commonly associated with performance or attainment and the adoption of positive behaviour. Its role in well-being continues to grow.

Resilience focuses on withstanding external forces and pressures and the ability to recover quickly from a change, a setback or misfortune. It is not specifically about winning but rather about enduring and surviving. Resilience is most commonly now understood as a process, rather than as a trait of an individual. Professor Peter Clough's chapter in this book provides a good introduction to the concept and where current thinking takes us.

In carrying out research on mental toughness and its meaning, much of what was reflected back did not have one definitive meaning. It did however make a connection with and specific reference to psychological resilience, a term sometimes used in relation or within the same discourse as mental toughness. A typical dictionary definition is as follows:

> Resilience: to rebound... ability to recover.
>
> (Urdang, 1991, p 395)

It is often the case that resilience and mental toughness have similarities and exist within the same discourse and practice in relation to the leadership development area.

Leadership

There are many definitions concerning leadership that not only go some way to describing what leadership is or is not but also outline the popular theories and styles of leadership.

> When they look at leadership many people begin by asking, 'What is it?'...
> for thousands of years philosophers and writers on leadership and latterly
> behavioural scientists have tried to answer this question. The result is a
> multitude of answers, each contributing to the debate in some way...
>
> (Owen *et al*, 2004, p 6)

The research and discussion that is ongoing for the characteristics and traits of great leaders is one of the earliest strands of leadership theory. In addition, much of the research into leadership theory and practice looks to define it in order for it to be taught as a method. Adair (1984) has gone some way to illuminating that leadership can be taught, with much of his case-study work for his method, 'action-centred leadership', being employed in developing leadership in the army. This chapter does not intend to rehearse the history of leadership theory, but notes here that this remains a contested topic, where labels such as 'transformational', 'transactional' and 'charismatic' leadership compete for attention. This chapter will touch on leadership development theories and practices being used in public service leadership specifically.

The changing role of the public sector in the 21st century

As society has developed, a number of services have emerged which society generally believes should be universally available to all. These are what are known as 'public services'. This has been subject to a range of interpretations which change over time. Sometimes that public service is thought to be applicable to all irrespective of income or status. Sometimes some form of rationing through price, etc is introduced to direct a public service provision to an area of greatest need or benefit and even this changes over time.

In many societies the term 'public services' will typically apply to:

- utilities such as water, electricity and gas;
- education;
- public transport;
- law and security;
- emergency services such as fire and ambulance;
- health care;
- housing;
- armed forces;
- environmental protection;
- postal services;
- broadcasting;
- social services;
- planning;
- waste management;
- telecoms.

The public sector developed steadily in many countries around the world before the Second World War and accelerated rapidly in the period immediately afterwards, when nationalization became a popular activity. As we approached the end of the 20th century, we began to see in many countries a trend back towards privatization, which occurred for a variety of reasons. Often the reason was political – it was driven by ideology. Sometimes it was economic – there was a need for cheaper and more efficient supply to make better use of often limited resources.

In 2014 in the United Kingdom generally, as in many countries, there is a publicly-stated determination to reduce the size of the public sector and, for the foreseeable future, this might be the goal for many central governments. However, there is no reason why a group of people who manage and provide a public service should perform better or worse per se just because they are public servants or private sector employees.

There is a need for more efficient and more effective provision of public services and the challenge is an economic one. As societies become used to the provision of public services the demand for them grows but the resources for their provision become scarcer. One part of the solution could be, and perhaps should be, improving the performance of the public sector. In Wales there has been a purposeful and highly-structured approach to do just that through developing the leadership capability of its leaders and managers.

PSMW/Academi Wales

Over the course of the last 10 years, since the Government of Wales Act devolved political power to the National Assembly for Wales, the Welsh Assembly Government (WAG) has focused on the continuous improvement of Welsh public services through an aggressive programme of citizen-centred delivery. One of the Welsh Assembly Government's first actions was to establish Public Service Management Wales (PSMW) as a key enabler. PSMW's initial remit was to build management and leadership capacity and capability across Welsh public services.

> Better leadership and management, including developing future leaders, able and committed to realizing the vision for public services.
>
> (WAG, 2004, p 35)

In October 2004, the Welsh Assembly Government released *Making the Connections: Delivering better services for Wales* (WAG, 2004). The report outlined the vision for the future of public services, providing a blueprint for the areas of focus, action and sustained investment. As a result many public services across Wales focused investment and resources accordingly, building innovative programmes of change that would transform the way they worked and their services to ultimately improve the lives of their citizens.

This also changed the management and leadership landscape within Wales significantly. In 2004 the styles of leadership within Welsh public services focused on the traditional models that produced services that were highly responsive to need and delivered by professionals who decided on behalf of others. These autocratic, prescriptive and authoritative models of leaderships had proved highly successful over the previous 20 years.

Devolution however brought a shift in the ethos of public service delivery. The citizens of Wales had decided that they wanted more input and say into the way public services were delivered and the politicians responded by driving a new collaborative agenda. What took place was a shift in leadership focus: leaders now needed to become transformational in nature, be able to engage with all stakeholder groups and lead organizations based on cooperation and a move away from compliance models of delivery to those of demonstrable and measurable commitment.

With this consideration, PSMW endeavoured to support public service leaders and managers attempting to bring to the forefront the use of new concepts and innovative learning interventions. PSMW invested in the creation of organizational and individual relationships across Welsh public services. This strategy resulted in the increase of individuals and organizations approaching PSMW for their service offering:

> ... has also become evident in the confidence with which individuals and organizations have approached PSMW to support them in the personal and professional challenges they face to deliver the improvement agenda.

> (Wooding, 2008, p 4)

This work continued until 2008 and although the collaborative agenda remained a key delivery factor, the global financial downturn meant leadership needed to yet again refocus. This brought about the need for leaders to be able to develop at pace the ability to influence with integrity, engender confidence and trust in employees and service users, be self assured and be willing to deal with difficult issues. This while developing and living the leadership qualities of innate curiosity, with an outward focus, building the ability to listen, remaining resilient when taking tough decisions and finding new ways to ask challenging questions.

In 2009, the Welsh Assembly Government released *Better outcomes for Tougher Times: The Next Phase of Public Service Improvement*. The paper set out seven areas for action that would deliver improved services and better outcomes for the people of Wales. The focus on collaboration, efficiency, innovation and outcome delivery was at the forefront of the focus for the public sector. Public services across Wales were again facing considerable challenge: with a change in the UK Government and the deficit between tax revenues and public expenditure at £170bn, there was a need for national transformation (Griffiths, 2010). In a recent report, the Institute of Leadership and Management (2010) evidenced that while public service leaders and managers felt that the future was uncertain and budgets would be constrained, they were up for the challenge:

> Our research shows a committed, experienced and talented cadre of management professionals who are highly motivated to make a difference in their roles.

> (Institute of Leadership and Management, 2010, p 10)

As a direct result, Wales now has a cadre of leaders that have learned through experience that what has got them to this point is not going to get them or

FIGURE 7.1 Great leadership through learning

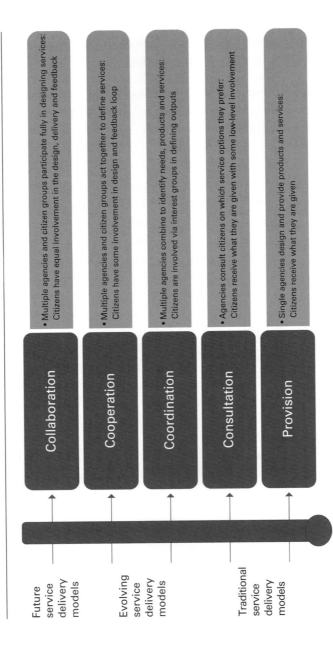

SOURCE Academi Wales (2013c) *Sowing Seeds – Collaboration: A new narrative for 21st century public service delivery*, Academi Wales, previously PSMW, Wales

their organizations to the next and that the traditional models of problem resolution and preconceived, habitual ways of doing things need to be replaced with the courage to change some of these practices and encourage new perspectives and insights that accompany more flexible and agile leadership.

So as public services in Wales focus on core business and learn to manage risk better, there will be an assumed impact on workforce development and jobs, both current and future. In Wales 210,000 people represent the 'squeezed middle', earning between £30,000 and £50,000 per annum, the 'squeezed middle' being the lower-middle class: many of those in leadership roles within public services. A recent report by YouGov suggests that 75 per cent of Britain's 'squeezed middle' fear for their jobs (Mills, 2010). In a period when pressure will be apparent in the workplace in terms of both delivering outcomes and managing increased workloads, many will be also driven by the fear of losing their jobs and livelihoods.

The transition of leadership within Wales is depicted in Figure 7.1 and Wales' public servants must now turn their attention to what qualities, behaviours and characteristics are going to get them ahead on the road to sustainable, collaborative, quality-led services.

How does Wales now build the leaders of the future?

The evidence suggests that the future will bring leadership that must focus on the whole system, leaders must be adaptive in their approaches and style, technical solutions will no longer be sufficient and building effective relationships will become the cornerstone of leadership success alongside the ability of leaders to influence without positional power, be resilient in the face of difficult decisions and be willing to potentially risk their own personal significance to deliver the changes needed. Adaptive leaders will need to recognize that it is attitude, values and behaviours that not only underpin the characteristics of high-performing individuals and organizations but also create and sustain improvements in the long term.

Meeting the challenge

This focus on building and developing leadership capability has remained constant through the changing policy landscape within Wales, the UK economic changes and the impact of globalization. In 2012, PSMW was renamed and relaunched as Academi Wales and the organization's position within the delivery context of Welsh public services has been strengthened through ministerial endorsement.

The challenges and difficulties facing managers and leaders in Wales have never been greater. Faced with financial constraints, political intervention and increasing stakeholder demands and expectations, managers across all sectors need to find a fresh approach to leading and managing change if they are to thrive and perform for now and into the future. Managers and leaders need to operate in difficult circumstances, under increasing pressure to deliver high-quality services to meet an expanding range of complex needs.

When delivering in these ferocious and complex times, leaders and managers need unprecedented levels of resilience, an ability to operate calmly and with confidence and to be able to recognize their own strengths and weaknesses. Leaders must be courageous in a manner that builds trust and inspires others such as colleagues, stakeholders and service users. Leadership here is often about management, the tensions between being agile and flexible enough to change one's mind but congruent in values and beliefs.

To be effective managers and leaders and to thrive in times of change, individuals must acquire the following skills:

- an understanding of change, its complexities and its effect upon organizations, teams and individuals;
- an ability to operate effectively, making sound decisions and exercising intuition, emotional intelligence and resilience;
- to manage the tensions and conflicts that often accompany contradiction and complexity;
- to lead in a deft and agile way while instilling confidence in others.

(Academi Wales, 2013a, p 3)

The preconditions for leadership to meet these challenges were identified by Heifitz, Grashow and Linsky in 2009.

Get rid of the broken system's illusion

There is a myth that drives many change initiatives into the ground: that the organization needs to change because it is broken. The reality is that any social system is the way it is because the people in that system want it that way. In that sense, on the whole, the system is working fine, even though it may appear to be 'dysfunctional' in some respects to some members and outside observers, and even though it faces danger just over the horizon.

As Jeff Lawrence (in Heifetz *et al* 2009) poignantly says, 'There is no such thing as a dysfunctional organization, because every organization is perfectly aligned to achieve the results it currently gets.' No one who tries to name or address the dysfunction in an organization will be popular. When you realize that what you see as dysfunctional works for others in the system, you begin focusing on how to mobilize and sustain people through the period of risk that often comes with change, rather than trying to convince them of the rightness of your cause.

Learn to live in the disequilibrium

To practise adaptive leadership, you have to help people navigate through a period of disturbance as they sift through what is essential and what is expendable, and as they experiment with solutions to the adaptive challenges at hand. You need to be able to do two things:

1 manage yourself in that environment; and
2 help people tolerate the discomfort they are experiencing.

Engage above and below the neck

If leadership involves will and skill, then it requires the engagement of what goes on both above and below the neck. Courage requires all of you: heart, mind, spirit and guts. And skill requires learning new competencies, with your brain training your body to become proficient at new techniques of diagnosis and action.

Connect to purpose

It makes little sense to practise leadership and put your own professional success and material gain at risk unless it is on behalf of some larger purpose that you find compelling. What might such a purpose look like? How can you tell whether a particular purpose is worth the risks involved in leading change in your organization? Clarifying the values that orient your life and work and identifying large purposes to which you might commit are courageous acts. You have to choose among competing, legitimate purposes, sacrificing many in the service of one or a few. In doing so, you make a statement about what you are willing to die for and therefore what you are willing to live for.

Responding to these strategic challenges and working within these preconditions is an ongoing and constant focus for public service leaders.

The challenge for Academi Wales is to ensure that development activity is focused on enabling organizations, teams and individuals to be effective and manage change in this context, working across Wales to reach a tipping point of leaders and managers working with a core set of knowledge, skills and behaviours to deliver the sustainable changes needed.

What follows are two working case studies that demonstrate how one particular intervention has been spreading virally through the public services in Wales in support of managing change at the heart of services and service delivery.

Managing Change Successfully

The Managing Change Successfully (MCS) programme, designed by Academi Wales, was born from a joint request from North Wales Local Authority chief executives to support their staff at all levels in understanding the concept of change collectively and to have a common language, set of principles and tools to use when driving improvements into their roles, daily responsibilities and ultimately service provision. The MCS programme has since grown in its use and breadth and is being used collaboratively across a number of public service organizations in Wales.

The strategic aim of the programme was to enable senior managers to be confident in driving programmes of cultural and structural change, engaging others in the process of transformation and delivering high-value outcomes.

The programme consists of three stages: pre-course preparation, two consecutive classroom-based learning days and a one-day follow up to evaluate impact, address any outstanding needs and measure success.

Prior to the programme, each participant completes a mental toughness questionnaire. This diagnostic enables participants to understand their own resilience and internal drivers, and how these relate to their performance, behaviour, well-being and aspirations. Each participant receives reports describing their mental toughness. Where appropriate, this is supported with guided feedback and coaching to enable participants to optimize self-awareness and to adopt effective development strategies. Each participant will assess their own contribution to delivering successful adaptive change using a delivery outcome they are responsible for in their role and their organization.

The learning outcomes for the programme focus on:

- identifying the key stages of the change process to anticipate and make the right intervention at the right time;

- influencing the way people think and act to deliver personal change both intrinsically and extrinsically;
- motivating and engaging others to manage the tensions and conflict associated with change in a positive and productive way;
- developing a culture of innovation and promoting a cycle of continuous improvement to underpin ongoing change;
- demonstrating a range of change tools and technologies to deliver greater efficiency and innovation;
- developing an agile, tough-minded and resilient approach to change;
- measuring personal change impact and developing a strategy for delivery.

(Academi Wales, 2013b)

Once participants have identified their own leadership style and personal reaction to change, they look at their individual traits and attributes as a leader of change. These include emotional intelligence and mental tough-ness, discovering the effective behaviours in the use of power and creating collaboration, and inspiring others through transformational conversations.

The final part of day two asks participants to review their delivery out-come and apply the skills and knowledge they have acquired to creating a 60-day action plan where they will put their learning into practice.

In the final session, a structured review process enables participants to measure their success to date and learn lessons, both from their own expe-rience and from the experiences of others. Furthermore, participants are encouraged to form a community of practice to share learning and provide ongoing support.

Case studies

CASE STUDY   Team case study

Issue

As part of a government-led restructure, three national public services organizations were to be merged. The initial focus of the changes would be on the senior executive teams and the establishment of one new leadership team, led by a newly appointed Chief Executive.

As it was a government-led merger, the senior responsible officer leading the changes would be a senior civil servant and it would be the external project team that would establish the processes for the recruitment of the new Chief Executive and leadership team. There were significant time pressures with the project and between November and April the new organization needed to be established and all senior appointments made.

Under the human resources policy used to support the mergers there was a three-part process to recruitment:

1 Matching and slotting in – based on a two-thirds match against the roles and responsibilities of the job, individuals would automatically take up the post, ie slot in.

2 Restricted competition – at this stage in the recruitment approach only those within the current organization would be those eligible to apply.

3 Open competition – the new posts would be advertised externally.

As part of the recruitment for the new leadership team, it was decided that slotting-in arrangements would not apply, as the new posts were significantly different, and that restricted competition would apply to all those within the existing executive teams. This decision instantly brought a significant amount of distrust, competition and relationship breakdown between the three teams and between the individuals involved. Up until this point, the executive teams had been working together alongside the government project team to set up the new organization. This decision meant that the levels of engagement, sharing of information and collaborative working instantly diminished.

Insight

The interim Workforce and Organizational Development Director who was working as part of the government team noticed the impact of the decision on the senior teams and the individuals involved and took immediate steps to put in place a support framework. The support at the start included attending a tailored version of the Managing Change Successfully programme with a specific focus on the personal aspects of mental toughness, resilience and emotional intelligence.

Key was the understanding of where the individual's resilience levels were currently and to use this evidence as a benchmark to be able to tailor support to ensure that regardless of the outcome of the recruitment processes individuals would be able to work through any necessary personal choices and the wider change process.

The four Cs, commitment, control, confidence and challenge, of the mental toughness tool MTQ48, became the basis of the crucial conversations between the Workforce Director and the individuals involved when discussing the reality of the new posts, potential opportunities and realistic discussions on whether there was a fit in the new organization for those who had led the organizations of past.

The supporting programme also included coaching support, career counselling and a 'living 360' undertaken with a trained facilitator in order to surface or bring to the forefront hopes and manage expectations.

The focus on developing resilience during a period of crisis had beneficial results. In the majority of cases, the challenging and honest conversations were made easier by individuals being supported to understand their personal levels of control and commitment, with a focus on being able to make decisions that would work for them and allow them to manage their emotions, specifically levels of happiness with the changes.

The unintended consequences included the robustness of the senior team that was appointed into the new roles, made up of individuals from the original three organizations. The team immediately demonstrated key strengths in the areas of commitment, challenge and confidence when taking up the new roles and delivering the executive function effectively from the outset.

The key learning points related to the use of resilience in this area have been:

1 Benchmarking and understanding individual and team openness and potential for change.

2 Underpinning skills and personal characteristics are useful to develop even during a period of rapid change.

3 The long-term effects on those taking up new roles or posts, having had a chance to focus on the development of resilience prior to appointment.

CASE STUDY Individual case study

Issue

The individual in this case study was a chief executive of a national public service organization in Wales between 2007 and 2013 in the field of equalities and diversity, with a staff population of 50 across a range of roles and an additional 40 volunteers operating on a pan-Wales basis at four regional bases.

In November 2010, the financial ramifications of the economy and changes to funding hit this particular organization. At this point in time, the organization had taken a 56 per cent cut from a government funder. In 2009, the chief executive had been told there was going to be a cut to funding. During this period, the chief executive engaged with the government funder to carry out scenario planning, working on a 30 per cent cut assumption over three years. The projected figure rose from 30 per cent to an actual figure of 56 per cent. All of the scenario planning, all of the redesigning of services using continuous improvement and lean had gone: essentially a year's work. Due to the lack of any significant reserves, the chief executive had to come up with a structure, consult with staff and agree on it within two months in order to ensure the validity of services. This was done without the benefit of an internal HR department, the organizational structure being one in which financial resources historically were focused on its frontline and volunteer staff rather than operating a corporate resources function (this is not uncommon in organizations of this nature).

The 56 per cent cut had to be achieved within a four-month period in order to accommodate any redundancies within the end of financial year timescale. The chief executive was already engaged with the National Audit Office carrying out some scenario planning for the future, which now changed to be based around this particular 'real-life' scenario. Within that one week, change had to involve making real decisions rather than hypothetical ones, ultimately aided by the provision of expertise.

Impact

The chief executive remembers going into a period of crisis:

> *Personally I remember it being a time of a high state of anxiety for me, how I was going to plan for this, I remember going back to a PSMW Sowing Seeds 'Leadership in Turbulent Times', reading over a weekend and it touched on slowing down the process, building alliances, how was I going to stand back and have a different way of looking at it?*

The chief executive felt the pressure at the time of having to issue redundancy notices, something they had not done in this organization or to this scale before. As the person in charge of managing resources overall with no direct HR support, this was a very challenging time. During October 2010, the chief executive had embarked on a doctoral programme of research. This meant a period of being busy personally, engaging in this important leadership development, writing the first chapter and dealing with a major organizational restructure in order to ensure the survival of the service. It was personally a really difficult time for the chief executive – having to talk to staff in the run up to Christmas that year about not spending much money and being verbally attacked for spoiling family Christmases:

> It was emotionally quite challenging, trying to do the day job, having people out there who were planning for the future in case it was a deeper cut than 56 per cent, managing staff, managing clients, managing the management team who were under pressure and stressed and turned inward on themselves, every area felt quite fragile, chaotic and unfocussed and I was just trying to hold it all together.

It was a really important experience for the chief executive: one that they felt was also personally quite painful. While the challenge with hindsight was one that can be reflected on as an important learning curve, the feeling was often one of imbalance.

Insight

In order to remain resilient, the chief executive looked around, relying on UK colleagues and senior mentors to provide guidance and respite. Another chief executive in the third sector was particularly supportive, providing experiential advice. Colleagues of the chief executive on his doctoral studies were also listening. Networks were an incredibly supportive part. Partners that were engaged with the changes assisted the chief executive in presentations of changes to the organization's board. Networks were both professionally and personally important, whether giving the opportunity to gain expert advice or to gain a different viewpoint or to unwind, the key insight was about balancing well-being in order to be resilient and able to succeed when things seemed to get tougher and tougher. This included changes to the day-to-day work: some of the business as usual had to be put to one side during this period:

> Some of our national reporting and monitoring for that period just did not happen and colleagues who would usually have put me under pressure to provide that information just understood or I was able to make them understand that it just wasn't doable and that was incredibly helpful.

Equally there were some extra things that the chief executive did during that period to cope, including shifting attention when required to take breaks during the day and do something different to refresh and change scenery, allowing them to come back into the work environment 30 minutes later able to refocus.

> I made sure I did some 'me' stuff; writing the first chapter of my doctorate was incredibly uplifting to my confidence and sense of self-assuredness

where in my professional sphere that was taking a knock. I would walk my dog twice a day before and after work to just prepare and unwind, to loosen some of my anxiety and concern through exercise and pleasure.

During this time the chief executive was meeting with client users in the community, staff, government organizations, partners and the organizational board across the country.

You draw on all of your experience, that of others too, all of your development and knowledge, considering your behaviours. I remember going back to the MCS programme and using that to map my networks, look at my emotional intelligence, remember my strengths, consider my weakness, think about what I knew about my levels of resilience and plan personally better for myself, in order to achieve what I was being asked to do for what I felt was the sake of the organization's surviving.

The key learning points related to the use of resilience in this area have been:

- mindfulness as a coping strategy and practice in work;

- that being an authentic leader is important;

- explaining what you can and can't deal with;

- understanding your emotional intelligence and how you use it is imperative;

- the balance of understanding how much challenge you can manage and what to do when you can't.

Conclusion

The complexities of exercising leadership within the public sector are present on a daily basis and how governments support their public services leaders is crucial to delivering the service changes and modernization needed for the future. Engaging with this idea of mental toughness and creating resilience in organizations will be based on the needs and future direction of public services in Wales and the key considerations will be:

- The increased demand and interest in understanding and developing mental toughness to improve individual and organizational resilience.

- The focus on development of talent and succession in organizations and the support this might offer.

- How organizational change evolves and the successful impact required for change inside and across systems.
- Understanding the balance needed in behaviour and degrees of excess in behaviours and understanding the impact these can have.
- The links with the characteristics of high-performing organizations and the future focus required for delivery and strategic success.

Wales has demonstrated through its attention to strategic leadership learning, identifying adaptive solutions to its development of leaders and focusing on the intrinsic characteristics of resilience, emotional intelligence and strength of purpose that it understands the conditions for future success and will give its leaders the support and development necessary to achieve this.

Looking ahead

Welsh public services are now looking into the future with a specific focus on Wales in 2025 and the establishment of a specific project focusing on four key areas:

- the long-term finances and budget options for Wales;
- demographic and other cost and demand pressures and possible responses;
- the state of public innovation in Wales;
- what we can learn from the experience of other small countries and states.

It is clear that public services in Wales now need a radical approach to delivering better outcomes for the people of Wales if they are to remain sustainable. This will depend on a substantial programme of change, innovation and efficiency consistently applied over time.

There are growing pressures, with the Welsh Assembly Government likely to have up to 17 per cent less to spend by 2018 than it had in 2011 and the funding gap for Wales having the potential to grow to £2.6 billion by 2025. The impact on the leadership of Welsh public service organizations means redesigning services, reducing waste and creating new capacity with:

- greater engagement of Welsh citizens;
- greater freedom for frontline professionals to innovate and meet citizen needs;

- a collaborative and co-productive approach to provision; early intervention.

This means a change in leadership behaviour requiring:

- a common set of values and shared outcomes across the whole public sector;
- a move to whole systems, methodologies and rigorous adaptive solutions;
- leadership and management styles that encourage initiative and innovation and that promote transfer of knowledge between services.

(Research Briefing, Wales 2025, 2013)

Academi Wales must continue to add value through the development of greater expertise, greater credibility, greater collaboration and greater value for money, by focusing on bringing together the best leadership programmes and leadership themes from across the globe to ensure a consistently high-calibre offering of learning and development opportunities. They will also do this by setting the quality standards and raising the bar for public service leaders in the future, ensuring a future-focused work programme and enabling the creation of smart, cross-sector leadership networks that have leadership adaptability and collective capacity.

Academi Wales must also maximize opportunities for those working in Welsh public services to learn together, share experiences and create new networks for delivery and strategic partnerships for combining resources.

Academi Wales is currently at work on setting the future direction of leadership for Wales and from its research and development believes that in order to deliver the future agenda, leaders within Wales must focus on systems leadership and the adaptive skills required to be able to deliver across established and perceived boundaries.

References

Academi Wales (2013a) *Sowing Seeds. Leadership in turbulent times: Developing a personal strategy to deal with difficult circumstances*, Academi Wales, Wales

Academi Wales (2013b) *Managing Change Successfully*, Academi Wales, Wales

Academi Wales (2013c) *Sowing Seeds – Collaboration: A new narrative for 21st century public service delivery*, Academi Wales, previously PSMW, Wales

Adair, J (1984) *The Skills of Leadership*, Gower Publishing Limited, Aldershot

Griffiths, P (2010) Taking the public sector through the massive financial hurricane, *Review*, the magazine of the Bevan Foundation

Heifetz, R, Grashow, A and Linsky, M (2009) *The Practice of Adaptive Leadership*, Cambridge Leadership Associates, Cambridge

Institute of Leadership and Management (2010) *Leading Change in the Public Sector*, Institute of Leadership and Management, London

Mills, E (2010) Middle class and the taxed off, *Report: Tightening the Belt*, *The Sunday Times*, London

Owen, H, Hodgson, V and Gazzard, N (2004) *The Leadership Manual: Your complete practical guide to effective leadership*, Pearson Education Limited, London

Urdang, L (1991) *The Oxford Thesaurus: An A–Z dictionary of synonyms*, Oxford University Press, Oxford

Wales Public Services 2025 (2013) *Research Briefing*, Wales 2025, Wales

Welsh Assembly Government (2004) *Making the Connections: Delivering better services for Wales*, WAG Report

Welsh Assembly Government (2009) *Better outcomes for tougher times: The next phase of public services improvement*, WAG Report

Welsh Assembly Government (2011) *Sowing Seeds. Leadership in turbulent times: Developing a personal strategy to deal with difficult circumstances*, WAG Report

Wooding, N (2008) *Public Service Management Wales*, Annual report 2008

New realities: Personal growth for an uncertain future

How to be a resilient leader in a challenging world

**SUE PINDER, RAYMOND ROBERTSON
AND CRAIG THOMSON**

O ur perspective in presenting this chapter is both personal and professional. Our focus is on what senior figures in the private and public sectors need to know and to learn to work effectively and successfully in a changing world of new realities. We write as three individuals with lengthy experience of the professional territory in focus.

Collectively, we draw on a depth of experience at senior level in the public and private sectors. We draw on local, national and international experience and on political badges and bruises at local, national and ministerial levels. As individuals, we build on the foundation of our life experience and the points at which this has interrelated, overlapped, interacted and been fundamentally affected by our professional and business lives.

Change is a complex concept that is understood differently in different contexts and in different ways by different people. The introductory chapter in this volume highlights the multi-layered and multi-dimensional changes that have shaped current times. Even then it only hints at some of the complexity of change as this arises in the 21st century. Change is constant and it is pervasive. It comes in layers and in waves. It affects us individually, corporately and collectively.

We, the authors, know how it feels to be at the epicentre of radical, fundamental change and we have first-hand experience of its impact on the personal and professional standings of individuals as well as their financial and personal security.

We write from a practical and experiential standpoint and recognize that we verge on the heretical in that we leave the terms 'leadership' and 'management' entangled, opting for language such as 'senior figures' or 'individuals in senior posts' to define the group in focus in our work. However, this is more than a convenience in that we do not feel that a firm distinction between management and leadership is particularly necessary or helpful in our work and tend toward the view of Mintzberg (2004) that 'management without leadership is sterile; leadership without management is disconnected and encourages hubris'.

Elsewhere in this volume, the concepts and practicalities of leadership are disentangled and considered comprehensively by other authors. We recognize and value the depth of their insight and leave this task to them.

The individuals in our minds as we write are those who get up on a daily basis and face the challenge of guiding institutions or companies or departments and the people in them to achieve a set of objectives. In this, they have to inspire, direct, plan, question, reflect and calculate. They have to operate in a complex web of alliances and affiliations. They have to work effectively with and through their colleagues and they have to recognize themselves as accountable. In all of this they have to dig deep every day to remain self-motivating and to maintain their integrity.

Our joint work at present relates to the extended range of skills, abilities and attributes required by managers and leaders who are already able and skilful and now need to grow to face the new realities of a future which includes uncertainty, challenge and opportunity.

We endeavour to consider the ways in which learning has developed and needs to develop continuously to equip those in senior roles with the personal and professional skills and emotional resilience that they require. To this end, the remainder of this chapter is organized around five sections.

In the first of these, we briefly reflect on the types of programme that have tended to be available for this group and consider how understanding of the skills, knowledge and behaviours required has changed. We then move on to a section in which we suggest a re-orientation of this understanding to highlight the new attributes and abilities required in today's changing world. In the third of the five sections, we reflect further on the changed and changing world in which senior staff will work in the future and the harsh realities that will face them. The fourth section is concerned with the ways in which these realities will impact on the professional and private lives of our focal group. Finally, we consider the learning that will be required by the robust senior figure of the future and the attributes and abilities that will shape their personal growth and will form the essence of their success.

Learning for life at the top

An ever-growing array of programmes and qualifications is available to individuals to help them prepare for or to grow into a developing role in middle or senior level management. At the centre of these is the Master of Business Administration (MBA), which has enjoyed a very lengthy period as market leader in the world of high-level management qualifications. A wide range of other shorter or lower level programmes has tended to be shaped significantly by the content and assumptions that lie behind this offering.

Throughout much of its history, since the first programme was launched by Harvard Graduate School of Business Administration in 1908, the core of the MBA has focused on a set of key higher-order technical skills and knowledge. 'Received wisdom' has tended to frame these as the ability to evidence proficiency in managing finance, operations and business development. Indeed, these could be viewed in the traditional MBA (and the many programmes influenced by it) as having formed the 'essence' of the set of skills and knowledge required by the aspirant or active senior manager or leader (See Figure 8.1).

What has happened is that providers of the majority of traditional MBAs have limited their programmes to this narrow range of learning. These programmes appeared to exist in a space that was distant from that inhabited by their students, offering what Mintzberg (2004) dismissed as 'specialised training in the functions of business, not general educating in the practice of managing'.

It is the practice of managing and leading that concerns us in this chapter and in our work. Together we have a range of direct experience of 'the MBA', including teaching on various programmes as well as organizing MBAs in our own institutions. We acknowledge that the caricature of 'only technical

FIGURE 8.1 The traditional essence

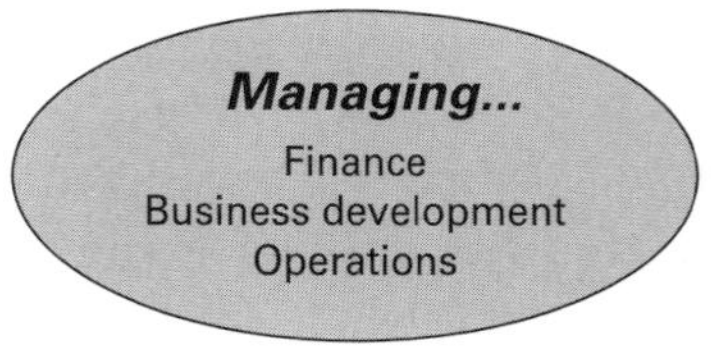

Managing...
Finance
Business development
Operations

skills and nothing else' is generally harsh but would argue that it is not very wide of the mark in a significant proportion of programmes.

Perhaps this is not surprising in one sense. There are those who argue that MBAs don't exist to teach people to lead or manage organizations but to teach students how to administrate. It is also harsh in another sense in that some of the more progressive business schools have recognized these shortcomings and have widened their offers. As part of this they have moved to include components that attend to what are traditionally called the 'soft skills' but (as is argued elsewhere in this chapter and more widely in the book) these are anything but soft.

The Hult International Business School offers an example of this more progressive standpoint. Hult course planners have been active in introducing two significant changes to their programmes. The first of these has involved embracing assessment of mental toughness and the second focuses on the introduction of coaching and mentoring skills.

In 2013, assessment of mental toughness was introduced for every student along with follow-through support (coaching and counselling) for those who it was judged would benefit from this. The reasons behind this development were simple and very much to the point. First, Hult take the view that the more mentally tough their students are, the more likely they are to be able to gain maximum benefit from their learning. Second, they recognize the importance of developing the employability of their learners and are able to build on the clear correlation between mental toughness and employability.

In 2014, Hult plan to break further new ground as they take the unique step of introducing a coaching and mentoring skills elective. In addition to contributing to the overall MBA, this is capable of independent accreditation through the Institute of Leadership and Management.

Setting progressive changes such as those at Hult to one side for the time being, we return to the general criticism of more traditional MBAs noted above. This more traditional caricature is used as an initial reference point as we begin our reflection on how the development of managers and leaders has changed and now needs to change further in the future.

In this, our focus rests firmly on 'the practice of managing' and we locate management and leadership development as informed and underwritten by technical skills and knowledge but as shaped and brought to life by experiential and reflective activity.

Rudyard Kipling wrote: 'I keep six honest serving men (they taught me all I knew); their names are what and why and when and how and where and who'. The development of the 'whole' leader requires an understanding, for example, of 'what' they need to know, 'how' they can best apply their learning and, most importantly, of 'who' they are.

As an increasing pace of change has impacted on business, industry and the public sector, management programmes including the MBA have taken action to widen their perspectives from the narrow one suggested in Figure 8.1 (See p. 171). The 'knowing' and 'doing' associated with the 'traditional essence' illustrated above have been recognized as necessary but insufficient components of the programmes required by managers and leaders.

'Being' has begun to find its place beside them. This leads us into the territory that is our primary concern and which we explore in more detail as the chapter progresses. In this context, 'being' can be defined generally using the work of Datar and Garvin (2011) as based on 'the values, attitudes, and beliefs that form managers' world views and professional identities' and as reflected in behaviour exemplifying integrity, honesty, fairness, self-awareness and the balanced treatment of others. We believe that it is important to extend and enrich this understanding of 'being' to encompass 'strength of being' and to embrace aspects of inner strength and mental toughness.

We introduce the concept with some caution. Our current work is informed by experience of how those moving through middle management into senior positions can experience a range of challenges and an element of confusion in developing their sense of 'being'. For those entering a new organization, there is a need to establish a working understanding of interpersonal dynamics quickly and to locate themselves positively within these. Individuals involved in transition into a senior role following an internal promotion have to be particularly sensitive and aware in reconciling issues resulting from the pattern of relationships that they have developed. There is a need for them to recognize the opportunities and understand the challenges presented by established loyalties, links and affiliations (See p. 174).

The identification of need for specific awareness and learning at this initial point of entry into a senior role raises questions about whether other stages can also be distinguished. We recognize three closely interconnected stages in the life cycle of a senior leader/manager: the transition, formative and mature stages (See Figure 8.2 on p. 175).

Our experience has led us firmly to the view that each of these stages is part of a continuous process but needs to be recognized by and requires a different form of reflection and learning to each of the others.

In the transition stage, each individual will fulfil their new role based on a complex mix of visible and invisible subjectivity; informed and ill-informed assumption; and appropriate and inappropriate skills, abilities

Loyalties, links and affiliations

The challenges that individuals may experience at the point of transition to a senior role in their own organization have been evident for two of us in our work in chief executive roles in further and higher education. For the third of us, observations of this journey have included close experience of individuals making progress within the structures of the UK Government at Westminster. It also includes experience of those progressing through structures in the private corporate world in public relations and public affairs.

In further and higher education, the internal route to senior positions is often a challenging one. A member of staff may begin in a non-promoted teaching or lecturing position prior to moving on to a coordinating and middle management role. For some, the journey will continue as they move into a senior position. Areas of responsibility will include those in which friends and close former colleagues work and relationships will be re-cast and re-defined. We have seen this being handled extremely well with trust and loyalty being established as a result. We have also seen it handled very badly with hostility and mistrust being generated.

These points can also be understood with reference to the UK Government at Westminster, where the obligations associated with existing links, loyalties and affiliations tend to be much more overt. Those elected as UK MPs may aspire to move through the ranks as Private Secretaries and in other roles prior to being elevated to ministerial office at various levels.

The loyalties, links and affiliations that they develop on their journey are critical in achieving and sustaining these positions. The cases we have witnessed in this domain also include the successful and the fundamentally unsuccessful. These are also evident in the private corporate world. All organizations are organic and inherently political.

Relationships are complex and, whatever the sector, there is no single recipe for success. However, the cases that we have witnessed make it clear that the ingredients for sustained success include sensitivity, openness and a willingness to listen while the ingredients `for failure include remoteness and an excessive recourse to structural authority.

FIGURE 8.2 Stages of development

Transition Stage   Formative Stage   Mature Stage

and attributes. Following this transition, the formative stage can be argued as being characterized by higher levels of self-awareness and confidence where the individual begins to form a picture of how they believe they function. The third stage, maturity, can continue the process of self-development as where aware, adaptive and experienced individuals develop (dare we use the word) wisdom while remaining open and receptive in their outlook. Alternatively, maturity can be a period of inertia in which an individual's standpoint becomes more closed and complacent and where learning and change are resisted.

The short road from isolation to resignation

The importance of being open to learning and a willingness to draw on the experience of others can be most evident where they are absent. Our first-hand experience of individuals arriving at the top in education includes a wide range of positive stories of those who looked to experienced colleagues for support and guidance, assessed their own assumptions critically and carefully, identified role models and engaged positively with a wide range of learning. Our experience also extends to less positive episodes, some of which are incorporated into the brief description below.

An experienced senior manager with a good understanding of the technical side of college operations, 'Lynn Martin' was appointed as Principal of 'Fulwood' College. The college was well regarded in its community and was perceived to be a 'good college' by funding bodies and inspectors alike.

Early in her tenure, the new principal recognized that the numbers did not add up and there was a need for radical change in the college's business model. Costs would need to be trimmed back and efficiency gains made in the ways the college delivered its courses and retained its students.

Analysis of business levels and trends and of the overall financial position of the college also made it clear that the changes required to secure the college's future stability would be significant and would impact on jobs and the terms and conditions of teaching and support staff. The college was highly unionized and the new principal could see that these changes would stimulate strong resistance, especially from the teaching unions.

This was a time of wider change in post-school education and training. A strong network of principals had developed in her region and a supportive and informative continuous professional development programme was in place, providing coaching and development. This had been embraced by principals, especially those newly appointed to their posts.

Lynn decided not to take part in the programme or to engage in the network. Experienced principals recognized the challenges that she faced and offered advice and support. They also pointed out that by exempting herself from the programme and the network she was missing out on a range of opportunities to acquire key skills such as negotiating skills and, most importantly, was not able to take advantage of the knowledge and experience of others and their willingness to reflect on their own successes and failures.

Several colleagues continued to attempt to give support to Lynn over a period of months as she resolutely ploughed her own furrow and became increasingly isolated, overwhelmed by the detail and worn down by staff resistance.

The problems of Fulwood College crystallized and she faced a whole array of issues which became insuperable: industrial action, academic failure, severe financial deficits, loss of public support, management failure and a breakdown in trust at board level which ultimately resulted in her departure from the organization.

In addition to reflecting on *what* needs to be learned for life at the top, it is important to consider the *how* of learning. As the pace of change has quickened, the value of experiential learning and strong contextualization have become increasingly evident.

The New Realities programmes described later in this chapter reflect these points. They aim to be relevant to the circumstances in which individuals might find themselves and to foster and develop individual creativity and innovation. They emphasize the importance of the adoption or development of a positive mindset which is open and receptive to the learning offered by all of life's experiences. Failures and disappointments on the one hand and successes and triumphs on the other are recognized as equally valid in the development of confidence and self belief.

Extending and reshaping the essence

As life has become more complex and demanding and as the mismatch between what is on offer and what is required has become more apparent, the shape and content of many internal and external management and leadership development programmes have changed. The traditional essence has been recognized as insufficient and has been joined by a large number of other elements that reflect the 'being' and align with the work of contemporary thinkers such as Hamel (2012).

In considering the main aspects of change which are of significance to business leaders, Hamel identifies five paramount elements or foundations for success: values, innovation, adaptability, passion and ideology. Figure 8.3 extends the simple essence diagram presented earlier in Figure 8.1 to include a range of abilities and attributes that reflect the 'being' characteristics of leaders and managers. These reflect the shift of management and leadership from analytical or scientific activities to a wider footprint including elements of art and practical craft (Mintzberg, 2004).

FIGURE 8.3 The wider landscape

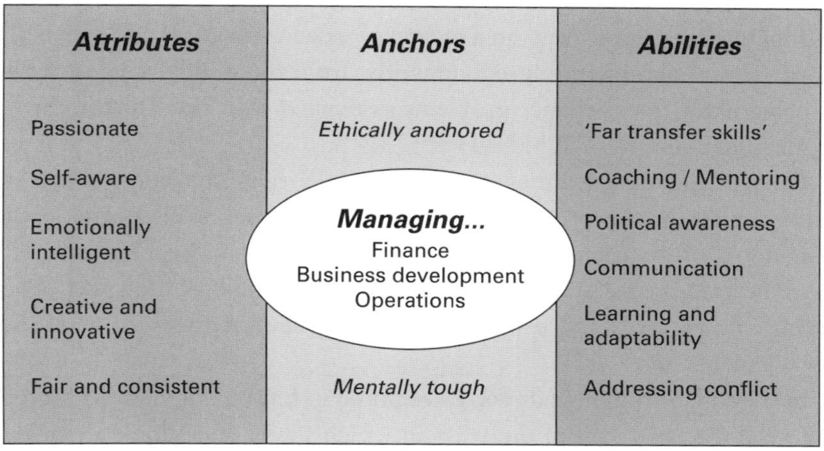

Attributes	*Anchors*	*Abilities*
Passionate	*Ethically anchored*	'Far transfer skills'
Self-aware		Coaching / Mentoring
Emotionally intelligent	*Managing...* Finance Business development Operations	Political awareness
		Communication
Creative and innovative		Learning and adaptability
Fair and consistent	*Mentally tough*	Addressing conflict

It is this wider landscape and the deeper understanding that lies behind it that create a foundation on which to build an understanding of what will be required by managers and leaders in the future. However, Figure 8.3 itself remains problematic in that it continues to suggest an essence that is dominated by technical knowledge and skills. We present it simply as a stepping stone in constructing a new view of the relationship between the 'doing' and the 'being' elements of successful and ambitious individuals in senior roles. This is presented in Figure 8.4 later in this chapter.

Prior to describing this, it is worth pausing to reflect on the apparent effectiveness of current management and leadership. Looking briefly at the situation in the United Kingdom suggests that all is not well. Despite significant progress being made in understanding the complex sets of skills, abilities and attributes required by today's managers and leaders, studies of management and leadership in the United Kingdom indicate that their effectiveness remains problematic.

In considering the 'quality of working life', Cooper and Worrall (2012) highlighted poor management styles with a consequential negative impact on managers' job satisfaction, well-being and working relationships.

Work carried out by the Department of Business Innovation and Skills (BIS; 2012) found that, from those covered by their surveys, 43 per cent of employees rated their line managers as ineffective and 75 per cent of UK-based organizations reported a deficit of management and leadership skills. Their analysis suggested that incompetence or bad management on the part of company directors had caused 56 per cent of corporate failures in 2012.

These failures and the problems of business or public sector effectiveness resulting from them can be argued (with reference to Figure 8.3) as resulting, in part at least, from CEOs and managers being 'stuck in the middle' and falling back excessively on a technical 'essence' to guide and shape their work. Those who operate predominantly 'from the middle' can be viewed as being likely to experience problems associated with operating in the low or medium columns of Table 8.1.

Recognizing new realities and meeting the new challenges that these will bring requires a rethink about how the attributes, skillsets and learned behaviours of managers and leaders interrelate. It is not enough simply to move beyond the technical and to surround traditional skillsets with a peppering of new skills and behaviours, nor is it enough to know what these new elements are.

In thinking through what will be required in future, our view is that there is a need for a reversal of the ways in which senior staff think about their

TABLE 8.1 Moving beyond the technical

Ability to:	Low	Medium	High
Communicate vision and a sense of common purpose			
Anticipate change			
Interpret political, economic and social trends			
Manage expectations			
Engage empathetically			
Use interpersonal skills imaginatively			
Use coaching and mentoring appropriately			
Acknowledge and/or manage conflict			
Draw on experience of stakeholder engagement			

roles and the ways in which they address them. Rather than starting from an 'essence' made up of fewer technical, financial, business development and organizational skills, it is a different set of abilities that needs to move to the middle and now be recognized as the 'essence'.

These can be argued to be the greatest and most useful set of attributes and abilities that a senior manager or leader can acquire. They are found most in those who put service before self, have a rich and ethical belief system, and respect and nurture people. They exhibit higher purposes and principles and are authentic, wise and humane. Developing and adopting this new essence requires individuals to understand the nature of power and influence and to be able to use each appropriately.

These are the core points that have shaped and driven our thinking as we have reconfigured our views of the skills, abilities and attributes required to

FIGURE 8.4 The new essence

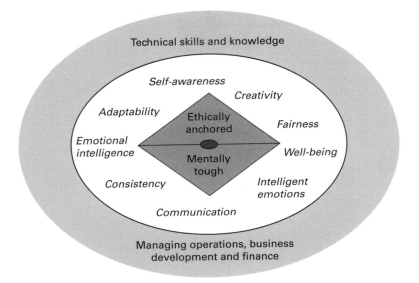

work effectively in a world of new realities. They have firmed up our commitment to enabling existing and new managers and leaders to synthesize and 'own' such a profile and to achieve personal growth.

In the final section of this chapter, we look in further detail at both the learning processes and the range of fields making up that profile. Before moving on to do that, we consider a few of the critical elements of the new realities that these individuals will have to face.

The harsh realities of the 21st century – a changed and changing world

Elsewhere in this volume the huge changes that are shaping our lives are set out in some detail. Financial crises, shifting patterns of world power, recessions and depressions provide a backdrop for a bewildering range of technical, social, economic and political changes.

Senior managers and leaders find themselves in a landscape in which they have to reconfigure their assumptions about how they can do well personally and professionally. In the future that they face, they will work in increasingly competitive environments in which previous norms and certainties break down. The new environment will have new 'winners and losers'. For example, it is argued (Cowen, 2013) that certain groups can be viewed as more likely to do well. At the present time this seems likely to include women, marketers, coaches, generalists, those who embrace the full potential of the computer, the conscientious and immigrants.

Managers and leaders will also experience a tectonic shift in the personal and professional environments in which they operate, as new realities created by information and communication technologies impact on their roles. Two broad sets of points can be used to illustrate the future that they will face.

First, senior staff of the future, operating in what Cowen (2013) terms the 'hypermeritocracy', will do well to ensure that their skillset allows them to harness the continuing rise in the power and impact of computers. Cowen predicts that over the next two decades those who can embrace and harness technology, ie the top 15 per cent, will reap rich rewards. Cowen argues that we are about to enter 'the age of genius machines and it will be the people who can work with them that will rise'.

However, rather than seeing this as dependent on a technical skill (that is, the ability to use the technology) we see it as critically linked to the ability to understand *potential* uses of, and limits to, the use of data. We are entering a world of exceptional granular detail and big data sets covering the present and the past and fuelling predictive analytics which will create more detailed and reliable pictures of the future.

Television and satellite TV offer further examples from the recent past of radically different perspectives in the exploitation of technology. Viewers can now have access to hundreds of channels covering every subject and every interest. These can be streamed into their lives through increasingly sophisticated receivers, using wafer-thin flat screens and 3D technology. On the one hand, these developments are driven by the skills and understanding of the technicians involved. On the other, they are critically dependent on the business people who recognize the applications and opportunities involved and understand complex issues to do with market trends and scalability. It is unlikely that the CEO for Sky Broadcasting would be able to fit a satellite system at his or her own home. However, they will understand at a deep level the opportunities opened up by systems being installed in millions of homes.

Second, the interface with computers and with communication and information technologies will locate them in the realm of pervasive and often intrusive communication. Increasingly it will prove difficult for senior figures in business, politics and the public sector to separate their personal and professional lives.

Living and working in a networked society that is significantly, and often scarily, shaped by social media and in a landscape characterized by massive economic, social and technological change will require a different understanding of how the suite of skills available to them can be used to best effect. Central to this is a change of perspective and an acceptance that lines or distinctions between the working self and the personal self are gone for ever.

This time it's personal

We view the weakening of the distinction between private and working lives as a critical development. The networked society is deeply intrusive. More is being demanded and increasingly will be demanded of managers and leaders surrounded by an increasingly sophisticated and informed audience of stakeholders and critics. Scrutiny of public bodies and public leaders is already intense and is rising.

This is equally true for the private sector. In boardrooms, governance and leadership have taken on a new meaning as once-revered institutions fail and ethical standards are revealed to be low or absent. There is little that any organization can provide to any stakeholder that does not become subject to some form of scrutiny or regulation. On some occasions, this might be driven by mistrust of providers. Increasingly it is also about raising standards and about consistency of provision.

In Chapter 1, Strycharczyk highlights the importance of recognizing less visible changes in the world around us. He cites the global financial crisis as an example of a development that has been allowed to overshadow a number of changes that will have an equally profound impact on the ways in which we live and work in the future.

Among these changes, we would argue that the impact of information and communications technologies on the lives of senior figures in the workplace is recognized but has been seriously underestimated. As electronic communication reaches into every corner of life and the use of social media continues to grow exponentially, previous assumptions about how work and life can interrelate positively need to be revisited. Senior figures will need to draw on deep reserves of mental toughness as they experience the reduction of the personal and private space available to them.

Increasingly there will be more stakeholder and customer engagement through social media. The first generation of leading social media sites such as Facebook, Twitter, LinkedIn and Pinterest will be replaced by increasingly sophisticated and differentiated incomers. Already, social media sites have challenged governments, created a new kind of consumer and are forming the backbone of advanced corporate marketing strategies. Social media will shape societies, influence elections and define much more of our personal and working lives in the decades to come.

However, as the law of unintended consequences comes firmly into play, norms and limits remain dangerously ill-defined or unenforced/unenforceable. Developments in technology that open up huge opportunities for positive communication, business development and for increases in the reach of art, education and culture are also being used for unsavoury applications such as child abuse, pornography and exploitation. Webstreams and messages from parliamentary chambers and boardrooms excite the press and influence the markets. As the focus becomes finer, so individuals will potentially find themselves open to constant scrutiny and question and potentially vulnerable to threats.

From positive scrutiny to negative intrusion

As former CEOs, we are used to seeing declarations of interest and expense claims on business websites. This transparency can be viewed as fair and reasonable. Our view is that in future this will be considered to be 'light touch' and that legitimate public scrutiny of the behaviours and activity of senior leaders will reach much further.

We have experienced social media and related forms of communication allowing diaries and day-to-day business and personal activities to be made more freely available and have felt the tide line of personal privacy receding. The often humdrum detail of everyday work situations has become shared or public property thanks to the internet and the content being made available through increasingly sophisticated and intrusive technologies.

Alongside this, our experience is also of wider and less well-motivated scrutiny, with the increase in public knowledge of individuals' private lives raising issues of personal risk and job security.

We have used social media positively and constructively to communicate with staff, to increase the reach and effectiveness of education and training and to enrich and extend contact with customers. We have also experienced it being used as a vexatious tool to undermine and disrupt. In this dimension, truth can slip from view as anonymity gives licence to the mischievous or malicious.

Our experience is that, in its negative and furtive form, social media can pose significant and serious challenges to an organization. These can stretch from often quite transparent planting of comments on product and service review sites to much more sinister, troll-like, vexatious campaigns. The latter has the potential to combine intrusion and invention in ways that expose organizations to damage and, when they focus on individuals, leave senior figures open to attack and to serious personal and professional harm.

Shareholder involvement in setting salaries is already a fact of boardroom life and the packages of senior staff in the public sector are now routinely listed on websites. Fast forward a few years and we may find that all senior posts in business and the public sector are appointed consensually and publicly using web technology.

Instead of being interviewed in private by a recruitment panel of board members and peers, appointment processes are more likely to begin with a thorough screening of an individual's web presence. In a world where the concept of a private life is increasingly difficult to sustain, this scrutiny is likely to reach out to include details of private affairs, personal finances and lifestyle before skills and expertise are even considered.

Cowen (2013) warns that employers will use computers with 'oppressive precision' to evaluate performance, judge individual and team commitment, promote and retain the conscientious and part company with those who are less committed and able.

In this new world, the CEO and other senior staff will be accountable in public and in real time for every action or inaction. In addition to drawing on the abilities, attributes and anchor points of the 'new essence' to ensure that they are fair and effective in their treatment of others, they will need to focus on how they protect and ensure fair treatment for themselves.

We are concerned that future leaders and senior managers may often be unaware of the extent of this intrusion and as a result be unprepared for the 'price tag' they might have to pay. Hence our interest in developing a robust and comprehensive programme in which participants can test themselves against many of these new challenges in a safe and supportive environment.

Learning for a world of new realities

We have spent time in this chapter giving thought to and describing key points relevant to the successful development of tomorrow's leaders and senior managers. We have drawn on our own knowledge and have set this against insights from prominent academic thinkers.

In this section, we briefly describe our thinking around the New Realities programmes that we have developed. We accept as critical the financial and other technical skills and knowledge associated with the traditional essence. Indeed, we take mastery of these as given in those with whom we work. Our focus is on the new essence illustrated in Figure 8.4 (See p. 180) and our start point is the individual.

New Realities programmes recognize that the single biggest resource available to those in senior positions is who they are: their value base, their empathic skills, their ability to connect with people and their skill at joining the dots between competing pieces of information, knowledge, intuition and opinion.

The programmes are designed to help individuals to develop greater confidence in 'how they do what they do because of who they are'. Individuals are challenged to celebrate and build on the person they have become as a result of the integration of their personal experience, faith in themselves and professional skills.

Rather than being skills developers, we aim to operate as 'people growers' and to develop in each outstanding individual a more comprehensive and eclectic set of coping strategies that will enable them to face the known and unknown challenges of an uncertain future.

We highlight and develop an individual's mental toughness and actively encourage them to understand and question their ethical base. We aim to open minds to deep learning and to encourage a willingness to unlearn what is no longer useful or usable in the new reality.

Each individual is unique. Our view is that each New Realities programme has to be personal and specific and, while its development is guided, the detail has to come from within and be self-defined.

This type of 'development from within' can be illustrated with reference to how an individual might pursue physical fitness. While fitness programmes may help and exposure to role models may inform and inspire, the essential components in achieving physical fitness are internal strength, commitment and belief. Understanding development from within with reference to a fitness model also highlights the importance of paying close attention to issues of personal well-being.

Jo Shuttlewood's chapter on BP's talent development programme and the principles upon which it is founded also touches on this area. As a large, well-resourced company involved in exploration and the development of new energy-producing technologies, BP operates in a more risk-laden sector than most organizations. Considering the future and taking a view about it is recognized as central to BP's success and, increasingly, is understood to be critical in shaping the destiny of all organizations as they move into the riskier, uncertain world of the future.

Culturally, companies such as BP could be viewed as better suited than most to a future where challenges will come thick and fast and where confidence in one's abilities will be a key factor in success. This will be a future in which organizations and individuals may fail more than ever before. BP has had its fair share of dry wells. However, such failures need to be seen as learning opportunities and as steps on an uncertain path to future success.

New Realities programmes recognize and take as given high levels of competence in those taking part. In considering 'why' they wish to do so, they need to be able to commit to personal growth and extending their skills and competences into new areas, as the programmes provide them with a set of experiences, tools and resources that will enable them to excel in the turbulent and challenging times ahead.

Three simple questions help to orientate and tailor the programmes:

- Who? – Generating an insight into an individual's understanding of self.

- What? – Identifying key elements of learning that are of most relevance to the individual.

- How? – Creating a practical understanding of the ways in which learning will be applied.

Who?

As described above, we use the two anchor points illustrated in Figure 8.4 to generate (and subsequently to re-assess and reflect on) an understanding of self. Programmes involve an initial (and ongoing) review of the intrinsic characteristics that make individuals more or less robust or resilient, with tried and tested instruments used to assess mental toughness.

Those taking part are also encouraged to develop and build on deeper personal insight and awareness of self. This emphasizes the importance of individuals looking within themselves and to role models and developing a clearer set of understandings and aspirations in relation to their *ethical anchor points*.

What?

The programmes identify and address the key elements of learning that are of most relevance to the individual. What has to be understood and learned is personal and specific to each individual and is based, among other things, on the development of emotional intelligence and intelligent emotions, awareness of self, ability to communicate effectively and deeply, the fine tuning of personal antennae to heighten external awareness (of past, present and future events) and the ability to recognize and address conflict or dissonance.

How?

The programmes draw a distinction between what is learned by an individual (what is known and understood) and how this learning is applied (actions and behaviours). Learning about the *how* is fundamentally dependent on practical insight gained through observation and engagement with others.

Across each of the who, what and how fields, New Realities programmes create the opportunity for individuals to benefit from the 'experience, reflection, learning' cycle illustrated in Figure 8.5 and the power that comes from learning from each other, building learning relationships, creating learning organizations and strengthening their own resilience and performance.

Our work has focused on the development of a programme that can support the creation of rare and unstoppable individuals who can weather the

FIGURE 8.5 The 'experience, reflection, learning' cycle

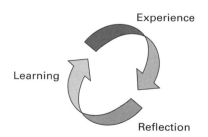

Experience

Learning

Reflection

new realities of a changing and uncertain future. In this, we endeavour to build on exposure to effective role models and real-life scenarios to deepen individuals' understanding of themselves and to make what lies ahead more familiar.

The programmes aim to develop the whole individual. As 'total programmes', they encompass the development of strategies to manage the relationship between the working self and the private self.

Time spent on programmes is variable and programmes are delivered using a tailored set of instruments and activities such as:

- the use of diagnostic tools to enable the individual to gain a better understanding of their mental toughness (in addressing this, we turn to the methodology and instruments developed by AQR. The methodology behind this is described in Chapter 3);
- exposure to accurate and up-to-date information on key changes in policies and legislation;
- masterclass sessions designed to challenge thinking, values and personal ethics;
- facilitated visits and workshops which illustrate corporate and social responsibility;
- tools that provide insights into individual relationships and interactions;
- engagement in an online supportive network of like-minded individuals;
- group activities in which strengths are shared and solutions to complex challenges are offered;
- case studies relating to cultural shift as the key to organizational change;
- confidential executive coaching and monitoring;
- practical guidance and support on strategic leadership;
- in-depth guidance on addressing the use and misuse of social media;
- workshops on professional and personal well-being including sessions on positive thinking, creativity, attentional control, mindfulness as well as traditional anxiety control programmes such as stress management and harnessing techniques.

Finally, in considering how learning takes place through these and other activities, we emphasize that learning happens every day and in a whole variety of ways. All deep learning has to be contextualized and transferable and all that needs to be learned is not easily taught. Earlier in the chapter we highlighted the importance of experiential and contextualized learning. We view this as the basis on which to:

- provide insights that enable and encourage reflection rather than giving 'instruction';
- create space to take every experience and ask 'what did I learn from that?';
- build confidence to know 'what is known' and 'what is not known' and to assume that much of what is experienced will be unknown;
- approach the unknown with confidence and for individuals to develop the ability and humility to recognize what they know themselves and what they have witnessed in others;
- create inner strength and confidence;
- develop a hunger to seek the wisdom of others and never be too proud to ask the stupid question.

Through reflection and learning, New Realities programmes aim to create transformative pathways and positive journeys to a mature stage of development for senior managers and leaders, recognizing that:

The most powerfully transformative executives possess a paradoxical mixture of personal humility and professional will. They are timid and ferocious. Shy and fearless. They are rare and unstoppable...

(Covey, 2004)

... and the journey never ends.

References

Cooper, C and Worrall, L (2012) *The Quality of Working Life 2012*, Chartered Management Institute, London

Covey, S R (2004) *The 8th Habit: From effectiveness to greatness*, Simon and Schuster, London

Cowen, T (2013) *Average is Over: Powering America beyond the age of the great stagnation*, Penguin, New York

Datar, S M, and Garvin D A (2011) *The Changing MBA Marketplace and Approaches to MBA Curriculum Redesign*, presentation to AACSB – The Association to Advance Collegiate Schools of Business

Department of Business, Innovation and Skills (2012) *Leadership and management skills development: Benefits of investment*, BIS, London

Hamel, G (2012) *What Matters Now: How to win in a world of relentless change, ferocious competition, and unstoppable innovation*, San Fransisco, Jossey-Bass.

Mintzberg, H (2004) *Managers, Not MBAs: A hard look at the soft practice of managing and management development*, Berrett Koehler Publishers Incorporated, San Francisco

Ethics, ethical practice and their growing importance in developing sustainably performing organizations in the 21st century

RICHARD CRESSWELL AND MURRAY CLARK

Introduction

We feel ethics drive everything we choose to do and not to do and in this chapter we will look at four key interrelated themes. The first three are: ethics and ethical behaviour; key ethical theories; and business challenges and leadership behaviour. We then turn to look at the relationship between ethics, resilience and sustainability in the final theme. Through looking at these themes some of the issues we explore will include:

- how media coverage affects our perception of 'unethical organizations';
- why organizations can neither be ethical or unethical;
- what some of the core ethical models and theories propose;
- real-life leadership dilemmas;
- perhaps the greatest threat to resilience and sustainability – environmental mismanagement.

Topics such as the advance of globalization are covered in brief so as not to repeat what other contributors have included. We touch on some of the many ethical issues related to globalization such as outsourcing, with a brief, narrow focus on consumer attitudes, supply chain management, public relations, child labour and financial penalties. Some may find the issues raised, especially child labour, emotive and distasteful. We try to take a balanced view and include information about what some may say is 'best practice'.

A chapter on ethics would not be complete without looking at the development of the topic area. Therefore theories have been included and we have also included a pictorial framework you may wish to refer to if you wish to study ethics in general later.

Leaders and managers are tasked, among other things, with balancing the needs of stakeholder groups, business objectives and society as a whole. As we will see, this is not an easy path to follow and the pressure, at times, can be unbearable. In this chapter we share metrics on studies showing just how bad this pressure can be. This is just one area we briefly look at that shows how unethical behaviour reduces the ability to be resilient.

In closing this chapter we will propose a framework of essential ethical factors which we feel must exist for any organization to become resilient and, when resilience has been achieved, maintain resilience. These factors also help to achieve sustainability.

Several references to supportive media and other work have been included throughout the chapter. Like most other authors, we have endeavoured to ensure they are correct, but internet-based sources have a habit of being moved around and therefore referenced websites may be subject to change. If you want to look up the references contained in this chapter and experience difficulty, please do not hesitate to contact us and we can direct you to them.

Theme 1: Ethics and ethical behaviour

The term 'ethics' is taken from two ancient Greek terms: *ethos*, meaning personal characteristics, and *ta ethika*, which means to enquire into the nature of good and bad in a philosophical way. *Ethics* are related to *values* and *morals* but they are not the same things.

For example, *values* are the deep-rooted principles that people feel are important. Some of the more frequently-heard ones are: compassion, responsibility, honesty, integrity, respect and fairness. When a group of people ascribe to a number of similar or identical values you have a belief system, from which rules are developed. These rules are often referred to as *codes of behaviour* or *conduct (morals)*, but only if those rules are good rules – by that we mean there is little or no desire to cause harm in them. *Ethics* is about applying or implementing these codes. It also means looking at the language used, theories about what makes people take certain actions and also the outcomes of ethical behaviour.

Ethics is a branch of philosophy and early scholars include Plato, Socrates and Aristotle. These scholars would identify important ethical issues, analyse any ethical dilemmas that existed and offer insight into how to create a better way to work and live together. Once the preserve of classical ethical academics, we now see academics, politicians, theologians, doctors, scientists and others learning and applying ethics.

Some people may say, 'ethics in business – it's the latest management fashion'. To this we would say, 'then why did Confucius and Aristotle talk about it centuries ago?'

What does 'being ethical' mean? To look into this, take a moment to complete this brief exercise consisting of two questions:

1 If we asked you to list five organizations from any sector located anywhere in the world that have been or might be considered to be unethical, who would you choose?

2 Are there any particular sectors you would focus on and what is it specifically they have done to warrant your choice?

Partly because of media coverage, it is highly likely that at least one organization from the financial services sector will be on your list. You might also choose an organization that adversely affects our environment or has the potential to severely harm the environment. An organization that outsources work to companies that use child labour might be there too.

It is relatively easy to take a moralistic stance and criticize an organization for being unethical, isn't it? Yet there can be a duality – call it hypocrisy – in those quick to point out unethical action taken by organizations who do not consider their own ethical behaviour. This, arguably, is supported by Jackson (2013), who says 'as long as you leave money in accounts with banks you are, to an extent, complicit in (any of) their actions'. So, as an example, those of you who feel it is right that businesses in developing economies deserve financial support at low rates yet deposit savings at an institution profiteering from high-interest loans – aren't you unethical? Some may even argue you are more unethical because you are not following one of your own ethical beliefs.

This is an example of an ethical dilemma that is affecting many people at this moment in time as economies are depressed, causing wages and other ways to earn income to be suppressed. One of the things this example serves to show is the cause of ethical dilemmas. To show what we mean by this:

1 Ethical issues are *actions and activities that might give rise to an ethical dilemma*. Examples of ethical issues include:

- breaking the law;
- investing ethically;
- managing people fairly in a place of work.

2 A standard is some measure or model that facilitates comparative evaluations and an ethical standard can be said to be one relating to ethical issues. By generating ethical standards *we are able to see if ethical issues are being conformed with, exceeded or met*. Examples of ethical standards can often be seen in professional codes of conduct, an example being the standards of conduct, performance and ethics for nurses and midwives (Nursing and Midwives Council, 2008). At an organizational level we can see ethical standards incorporated (sometimes vaguely, sometimes not) into corporate social responsibility statements.

3 An ethical dilemma can be said to exist when *at least two ethical standards associated or related to the same ethical issue conflict with one another*. Therefore an ethical dilemma cannot exist if:

- an ethical issue has not been identified; and/or
- an ethical standard has not been set.

An organization is not a sentient being. Therefore unlike individuals it has no power to feel, no ability to think or reason by itself. It cannot identify issues nor develop ethical standards. In essence it is a lifeless entity. It can be argued, therefore, that only through its people can an organization be seen to be and thought of as ethical and to do this people must:

- develop values that apply to internal and external stakeholders;
- ensure these values are shared;
- develop codes of conduct governing behaviour; and
- attempt to ensure everything done is (and is perceived to be) 'just'.

If an organization has the propensity through its people to act in a moralistic way, does it follow that moral behaviour will occur? If we look at what the media has to say, we could conclude 'no'. Some of the unethical actions by organizations (and individuals) claiming an interest in ethics include:

- a weapons manufacturer knowingly selling weapons to a government that uses them to suppress civil protest from its own peoples;
- city traders committing insider dealing which artificially increases the market capitalization of a company;
- situating a new chemical factory in the middle of a Third World community and when an explosion occurs failing to help rebuild the community;
- journalists illegally accessing private voicemail messages;
- politicians submitting false claims for expenses;
- banks refusing to loan contingency funds to a small company – then just before it liquidates buying shares at a very low cost (followed by releasing contingency funds).

What we would like to move on to now are behaviours that occur every day, because it is important to understand that unethical behaviour is not the preserve of the corporate world. For example situations such as:

- an individual stealing stationery from an employer;
- people throwing away waste that can be recycled because it saves them walking to the recycling facilities;
- someone being wrongfully terminated from work;
- an employee deliberately damaging machinery or office equipment because they were not given a bonus they felt they deserved;
- managers favouring 'friends' when it comes to accessing development opportunities;
- people being kept at work by their managers after normal working hours and not remunerated or thanked for their efforts.

There are of course many circumstances where highly ethical actions have occurred, yet here in the United Kingdom we seem to see less media coverage of 'good news'. Is this because 'bad news' sells more copy? Is it because it is in our culture to feast on negativity and failure?

There are good news stories out there and these real-life examples of good ethical behaviour that have created positive results serve to illustrate this.

- A major UK steel manufacturer chose to implement the international standard for environmental management (ISO14001, 2004).
  This resulted in better use of resources and less natural resources being mined. Apart from significantly reducing their operating costs, it has almost ensured their business future.

- An investment company aligned a mutual investment society with a range of charities. Being a mutual society, no preferential, ordinary or other type of share dividend is payable to investors.

  The outcome was investors being able to make wider investment choices and reducing their risks to volatile markets.

- A global food retailer funded research into farming practices targeted at helping the producers and community without harming the local environment. It also offered producers 'fairer rates' for their produce.

  Two of the benefits were knowledge and technology transfer – contributing to economic self-sustainability.

If we look at the history surrounding ethics, it could be assumed that it is a westernized phenomenon. But nothing is further from the truth. For example, Confucius (from China) was one of the earliest recorded philosophers and ethicists. Before him, Indian, Arabian and other pre-ancient Greek civilizations all had moral codes of behaviour and embraced ethical practices.

Ethics is not some stoical, stable topic where the total sum of knowledge has already been gained. Future ethical questions will emerge from many areas and three of the more recent ethical questions come from:

- mankind exploring beyond the known universe (eg is it right that people from earth may damage the geology and ecology of another planet?);

- mining resources from the Arctic Ocean and Antarctica (eg should companies be permitted to extract minerals from perhaps the last two places on earth that mankind has not polluted?);

- the age at which people must retire (eg as people live longer, shouldn't they have the ability to enjoy extra 'free time' as opposed to working longer?).

For those with an interest in how ethics can be studied as a subject in itself, take a look at Figure 9.1.

This original diagram has been developed from the joint works of Bowie and Frye (2008) and Rachels and Rachels (2009) alongside our own views. It shows how we could look at ethics in a systematic way. For example, after looking at how values, morals and ethics are related we could move on to look at what are often called the three main areas of ethics. We could then go on to look at four main sub-branches of normative ethics and then theories (which come from meta-ethics and normative ethics).

FIGURE 9.1   A framework to study ethics

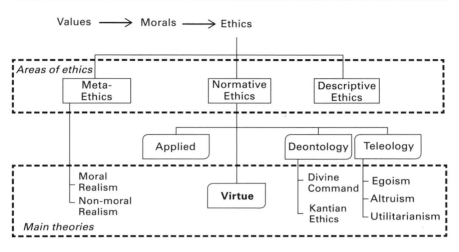

Let's look at what we mean by 'areas of ethics':

- Meta-ethics – the language used in relation to ethical statements and judgements.
- Normative ethics – how people ought to or should act in general.
- Descriptive ethics – the empirical study of what people have done or would do as a result of their beliefs.

Meta-ethics, unlike normative ethics, does not prescribe or propose what someone probably should do about some ethical issue. It encourages people to think about ethical principles (or judgements) such as 'it is wrong to steal from an employer', the language used (eg 'wrong') and what it all means. Unlike meta-ethics, normative ethics deals with what people ought to do or should do in general. In part it looks at what drives someone to act. Broadly speaking, normative ethics can be divided into the sub-disciplines of:

- virtue ethics (the inherent characteristics of a person driving them to act);
- deontological ethics (a sense of duty, what is right or the individual's responsibilities are the key drivers to action);
- teleological ethics (morally right actions are driven by the action's probable outcome).

Virtue ethics, while a branch in its own right, is also a theory in its own right. Applied ethics can mislead some people because normative ethics is about applying ethics. However, applied ethics is a branch of normative ethics dealing with specific aspects of *applying normative ethics*. For example, all of these topics can be described as 'applied ethics':

- medical ethics;
- business ethics;
- environmental ethics;
- informational ethics;
- bioethics;
- political ethics;
- media ethics;
- legal ethics.

Business ethics is sometimes referred to as *corporate ethics*. It looks mainly at the conduct of internal organizational stakeholders and how an organization is perceived to have acted (or not to have acted). The area that business ethics is often associated with is an organization's financial matters. But business ethics also involves looking at HR practices, corporate social responsibility, how the organization sells and markets its products (and services), ownership of intellectual property and international trade.

The third area of ethics is called *descriptive ethics*. This refers to the empirical study of what people have done or would do as a result of their beliefs. It is sometimes referred to as *comparative ethics* and people from other disciplines are often involved in uncovering beliefs and characteristics. These people may include anthropologists, psychologists, neuro-biologists and sociologists.

No study on ethics would be complete without an overview of key ethical theories. These can be found in the next theme.

Theme 2: Key ethical theories

There is a range of ethical theories: two of those mentioned relate to meta-ethics (language, judgement and meaning) and eight relate to normative ethics (what we ought to or should do). There are others, but let's look at the main ones here.

Meta-ethical theories

These can broadly be divided into two main areas and these are *moral realism* and *moral anti-realism*. Moral realism (also referred to as *moral objectivism*) takes the view that all language is based on holding values that are not dependent on emotions and other attitudes. Rather, everything is based on objective fact for which objective evidence exists. Conversely, moral anti-realism takes the opposite stance.

Normative theories

Normative theories fall into one of the three main categories: virtue ethics, deontological ethics (of which there are two main sub-categories) and teleological ethics (of which there are three main sub-categories).

Virtue-ethical theories

This is both a branch and a theory. People associated with virtue ethics include Aristotle, St Thomas Aquinas and more recently Annette Baier along with Michael Slote. It is an approach that supports the view that a person's character is the most important driver of their ethical thinking, rather than what the consequence(s) of ethical actions may be or of 'ethical actions' themselves. It can be said that there are three main approaches to virtue ethics and these are:

- *Agent-based theories*
  A more modern approach, this theory takes the view that action is driven by a desire to be a good person and to live a 'good life'. This may involve looking around for people who may be family, friends, people we work with, in the public eye or elsewhere who have character traits they find admirable. Typical admirable traits include compassion and kindness.

- *The ethics of care*
  Many reference books, along with overviews of materials available on the internet (Sander-Staudt), propose that this approach came through the belief that males think predominantly in terms of autonomy and justice but females think differently, specifically in respect of caring. It also holds that society does not truly value the benefits of female-orientated virtues derived from a sense of care. These include patience, looking after others, solidarity and having the ability to nurture others.

- *Eudaimonism*

  This approach, of which Aristotle is possibly the most widely-known proponent, is derived from the Greek word *eudaimonia* which loosely translated means 'happiness' and it is something people can strive for. Some of you may be thinking 'what do you mean by happiness?' Let's look at an example.

  You may be sat in an airport lounge reading this book. By reading this chapter you will (hopefully) gain a greater understanding of a highly important topic area (ethics) – but according to Aristotle this isn't happiness as it is 'a subordinate aim'. By reading the other chapters you will finish reading the book. Again according to Aristotle this isn't happiness – it is another subordinate aim. But if you read this chapter, the rest of this book and you compare the ideas and views in here you might see a less stressful way to work and for your organization to be stronger. This, according to Aristotle, is the 'superior aim' and by achieving this you will be 'happy'. So eudaimonia can be thought of as the end goal or purpose behind everything we do. Aristotle goes on to say that eudaimonia occurs from having moral virtues, intellectual virtues and cardinal virtues:

  - Moral virtues – which include generosity, patience, truthfulness, modesty and friendliness. These are grown through practice. For example, 'to be more truthful I must practise being truthful'.

  - Intellectual virtues – which include knowledge, common sense, practical capability and understanding. These are grown through instruction.

  - Cardinal virtues – temperance, a sense of justice, courage and wisdom. According to Aristotle an individual must possess all four of them.

  Aristotle believed that holding a virtue entails keeping a balance between two extremes called 'excess' and 'deficiency'. Irrespective of the virtue, this was called the 'mean' and is symbolized in Figure 9.2.

  So according to Aristotle, in this circumstance a person who is too cowardly to have courage needs to be more reckless in order to re-balance things. This could be what we may call today 'calculated risks'?

Deontological ethics

This approach takes the view that people act ethically because it is right to do so and for no other reason. It doesn't factor in the consequences of an

FIGURE 9.2 Holding a virtue through balance

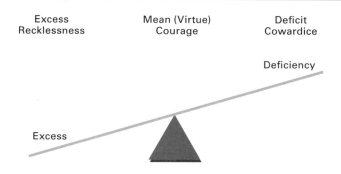

ethical action (what will happen as a result of doing something), nor the character of the person acting ethically (the agent – are they doing the best they can to be and do right?). Some people, therefore, refer to deontological ethics as rule-based ethics. Two types of deontological theory are the divine command theory and Immanuel Kant's categorical imperative.

- *Divine command theory (DCT)*
  DCT dictates that people will act ethically if God says it is right to do so. For example, should God command that Sunday working is right, it follows that people will be ethical if they work on a Sunday. It goes therefore that what God forbids, if done, will be unethical.

- *Kant's categorical imperative*
  The German philosopher Immanuel Kant developed a theory in the 18th century known as the categorical (absolute) imperative (command). Kant perhaps more than any other philosopher or ethicist made people think in a radically new way about how people act. He emphasized the centrality of *duty* in our actions. He was a rationalist, that is, someone who sought to find a rational basis for everything we do. Allegedly he had no interest in arguments for God's existence. Something of interest, perhaps, is that he was brought up in a very strict religious household and one of the cornerstones of his theory is that people must always act, not as if they were just individuals, but, as law-abiding members 'of moral ends'. Kant rejected favouritism (there is no place for it in being ethical) and by 'duty' felt it did not mean 'my duty is to follow orders'. He proposed that people can rationalize and impose duty on themselves freely. The categorical imperative theory holds that people self-impose rules that bind them to always act the same way.

For example, if someone internalizes the categorical imperative of 'it is my absolute duty to be kind to animals', that absolute duty – to be kind – is transferred to children, adults and the environment also. However, Kant recognized that there can be exceptions to categorical imperatives and introduced the term 'hypothetical imperatives'. For example, to Kant, 'to be happy, I will take exercise' would be a weak command because 'happy' is contingent on 'taking exercise'. So if someone adopts this hypothetical imperative, in this example, they cannot be happy if they do not take exercise.

Kant believed freedom to be highly important: freedom from control through emotion and from what he termed 'unthinking tradition'. He supported the principles of the French Revolution (liberty, equality and fraternity) but became shocked when the revolution, for some, turned into a terror campaign.

Teleological ethics

We have seen that deontological theories can be described as rule-based moral theories and virtue ethics are related to someone having good moral characteristics. Teleological ethics can be exemplified by someone taking an ethical action which is dependent (or contingent) upon an action's outcome.

- *Ethical egoism*
  This theory argues that humans act out of 'self interest'. Self interest should not be confused with selfishness. In this context, self interest does not mean people should not support or help others. Say Person A does something to help Person B. In return, Person B might help Person A to meet the self interest of Person A.

- *Ethical altruism*
  This is an approach that argues people can feel obliged to help others, if necessary, at all costs. To illustrate this, take the case of a soldier on patrol with their comrades when a grenade is thrown at them. If the soldier jumps on top of the grenade to limit harm to their colleagues and dies, that soldier is acting out of being ethically altruistic.

- *Utilitarianism*
  Developed by the English social reformer Jeremy Bentham, this theory consists of three sections:
  - All people are motivated by pleasure and pain, the actual motivation being to avoid pain and seek pleasure. Bentham called this, not surprisingly, 'the motivation of human beings'.

- Right or wrong is determined by the usefulness of an action. Bentham called this 'the principle of utility'.

- The pain and pleasure are weighed up to see how painful an act is, see if it will be long- or short-lasting and what the likelihood of pleasure is. Bentham called this 'the hedonistic calculus'. Utilitarianism takes the perspective that people behave in order to create the greatest good for the greatest number.

There are other theories such as those of St Thomas Aquinas, Friedrich Nietzsche and David Lewis. Aquinas, who lived in the Middle Ages, is associated with natural law and divine right. Nietzsche, a more recent contributor, looked at several ethically-related issues. Perhaps one of particular note is what he termed the *will to power*. Nietzsche held that each and every human strives to force their will upon others. It is a primal act that seeks to show his or her determination, spirit and strength of character. Lewis is another recent contributor to many aspects of ethics, perhaps most notably in respect of meta-ethics and decision theory.

We said earlier that ethics is not some stoic 'all knowledge is already known' topic. It is an emergent discipline and a timeline of some of the notable theorists is shown in Figure 9.3.

Given the length of the chapter we are unable to cover all of the ethical areas, theories and associated topics in great detail. But we hope to have given you some useful insights. If you are interested in learning more about

FIGURE 9.3 Some prominent ethical theorists

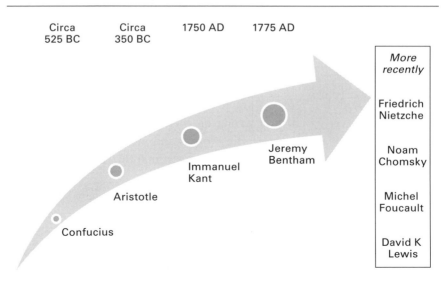

this, we suggest a good place to start is to obtain a concise handbook for you to refer to in your own time. An example of this might be the *Oxford Handbook of Ethical Theory* (Copp, 2007).

Theme 3: Business challenges and leadership behaviour

In this section we turn to the notion of applying normative ethics principles (discussed in Theme 1) to the field of business ethics and in particular to discussing ethical leadership dilemmas.

At some stage in most discussions about leadership, the question of what makes a good leader is asked. In this case, 'good' is usually used to mean 'effective', rather than in its moral sense. It highlights, as Ciulla (2003) suggests, the fact that 'in leadership, one is often tempted to put what is effective before what is ethical' and this leads to what she calls 'the Hitler problem'. If a good leader is someone who is effective at getting others to perform a task successfully, then 'yes' they are. However, if the leader uses immoral means to be successful, then the answer is a resounding 'no'.

So what actually constitutes an ethical or moral issue in leadership? The distinction between ethical problems and moral problems might be regarded as confusing especially when contemplating what might be a leadership dilemma. The nature of ethical problems that leaders and managers encounter in their work might in fact be problematic in ensuring that their work endeavours are compatible with their personal moral values and goals.

So the question of 'Is there a difference between ethical and moral behaviour?' seems a pertinent one to consider. Both ethics and morality derive their origins from terms that relate to customary or usual practice (Kimmel, 1998). As discussed earlier, *ethics* is derived from the Greek *ethos* and is concerned with a person's character, nature or disposition. It relates to distinctions between right and wrong or good and evil. Morality on the other hand is derived from the Latin *moralis* and means 'custom, manners or character'. Thus the etymology would suggest that they are synonyms for usual or normal behaviour.

Ethics might thus be defined as dealing with moral problems and judgements of what is taken to be proper conduct. When a manager questions whether an individual's actions are consistent with accepted societal notions of right or wrong, this is a moral concern, whereas 'ethical' pertains to rules for behaviour or conformity to a set of principles. For leaders and managers an ethical dilemma thus arises where their action or behaviour might be viewed as proper or ethical according to the 'rules' or principles of the organization (eg the HR department's procedures) but unethical in terms of broader moral principles (eg society might see as right or wrong).

For example, as a manager you have real concerns about the recent performance of one of your team. The individual is not delivering on key projects and as a result the whole of your team and your department are under review. Reward is based on team performance and pay and even job losses are being considered.

You know that the individual's poor work ethic is due to some serious personal issues. So do you sack them? This is the proper thing to do according to the organization's 'rules'. However, your personal moral principles might suggest this is unethical.

An organization might draw up a protocol or code of conduct on how to behave with respect to fellow workers. So you might say that an employee who followed this protocol might be regarded as acting ethically, in the sense of not violating the rules for proper behaviour (as dictated by the organization). However, from a personal perspective an individual might find this code of conduct conflicts with their broader moral concerns, such as when following organizational rules is against your moral values.

Consider for example the case of a British Airways employee who lost her appeal to wear a symbol of her faith on her uniform. Other ethical dilemmas reside within the notion of 'whistleblowing'. By considering whether to 'blow the whistle' on what might be considered dangerous and even life-threatening practices within an organization, as has been the case in the UK's NHS in recent times, the potential whistleblower faces an ethical dilemma. Do they turn a blind eye to the problem and learn to live with the consequences or do they go public with their concerns and risk the careers and livelihoods of their colleagues?

Or what about the case of the manager whose organization needs to cut costs due to the economic downturn and is told by the head of HR that she needs to make redundancies based on seniority (ie higher up the pay scales). She knows this strategy, to get rid of experienced employees, would have potentially devastating effects on her department's performance. Also, she is aware that those made redundant will be older workers whose probability of gaining new employment and pensions is low. Should she tamely accept company policy?

So what are ethics in a leadership sense? Some would argue (for example Ciulla, 2003) that ethics is about what we should do and what we should be.

If ethics is about right and wrong and the relationships of human beings to each other and other living things, then the relevance of ethics in the understanding of leadership should be clear.

Ethics are often thought of as a set of rules that define right from wrong, or as John dalla Costa comments:

> Ethics are often presumed to be a rigid set of self-standing rules that, like a business balance sheet, clearly delineate right from wrong, asset from liability. Although they do provide guidance, ethics work more as a living, shifting, dynamic process of reflection for expressing the morality of the community in everyday acts.
>
> (dalla Costa, 1998)

Of course it might be a little naïve to presume that everyone shares the same definition of right or wrong as individuals experience different economic, social and religious beliefs. But it is the case that people everywhere can discern the distinction between the concepts, act with regard for others and what is right will eventually emerge and what is wrong will usually be avoided.

The terms 'ethical' and 'moral' are inevitably linked with behaviours about which society holds certain values. An ethical (or moral) dilemma thus occurs when managers face uncertainty about how to balance competing values and each value suggests a different decision or action that cannot be easily reconciled.

Leadership and ethics

The study of leadership has posed many problems and raised many issues for scholars of leadership, most notably through the search for normative or prescriptive models based on developing knowledge that is in some way superior to the models it replaces. Writers approaching leadership from an ethics perspective tend to emphasize the view that a greater understanding of the part of ethics in leadership will improve leadership studies – principally by focusing on the question of what is good leadership.

As with the concept of trust and leadership, many authors imply the importance of ethics and morality in the understanding of leadership and as Ciulla (1995) notes, somewhere in almost every book devoted to leadership there are references (ranging from a few sentences to chapters) to strong ethical values being critical to the practice of leadership. Yet Ciulla states, 'given the central role of ethics on the practice of leadership, it's remarkable that there has been little in the way of sustained and systematic treatment of the subject'.

In the work of the many authors who offer a chapter in their texts on ethical leadership, there is a common theme where the authors talk of a few scholars (in most cases the same three) who have influenced current thinking about leadership from a broader perspective than many other researchers. In this way the role of ethics in leadership has been discerned, that is, the authors start to answer the question of where theories on leadership locate ethics. Leadership is seen as a process of influence and the leader has an impact on the lives of those they lead, which implies huge ethical responsibility.

The three works often cited as examples of work by prominent scholars who have addressed, albeit perhaps implicitly, issues related to ethics and leadership are briefly discussed now.

Ronald Heifetz's approach (1994) emphasizes how leaders help followers to confront conflict and effect changes from conflict. It is an ethical approach as it deals with the values of workers, organizations and communities. Leaders must use authority to mobilize people to face tough issues. The leader provides a 'holding environment' in which there is trust, nurturance and empathy. Within such a supportive context followers can feel safe in confronting hard problems.

James McGregor Burns (1978) suggests that transformational leadership places a strong emphasis on followers' needs, values and morals. The leader attempts to move followers to higher standards of moral responsibility and does so by engaging with followers and helping with personal struggles regarding conflicting values. Process helps raise the level of morality in both.

The concept of servant leadership began with Robert Greenleaf (1973) who proposed that leaders can operate on basic precepts, namely:

1 *Put service before self-interest* – there is a desire to help others that takes precedence over the desire to attain power and control over others even if there is no financial 'pay off', and the fact that organizations exist to provide meaningful work.

2 *Listen first to affirm others* – the leader doesn't have the answers but asks questions, and listening is the greatest gift to others.

As such, the leader affirms confidence in others and doesn't impose their own will. According to Greenleaf, servant leaders transcend their own self-interest to serve the needs of others. The fulfilment of others is their principal aim. This is a form of ethical altruism that emphasizes increased service to others, a holistic approach to work, promoting a sense of community and the sharing of power in decision making.

Joanne Ciulla's essay 'Leadership ethics: mapping the territory' (1995) offers a good platform for starting to address ethical leadership. Starting with the view that debates on the definition of leadership are founded on the notion of what researchers think identifies good leadership, Ciulla argues that the 'ultimate question is not "What is leadership?" but "What is good leadership?"' with 'good' embracing both ethics and competence.

A focus on leadership ethics may, therefore, be a critical means from which to critically expand our knowledge and thinking about leadership. The ethics focus can begin with a reflection about the paucity of research on ethics and leadership and the fragmented way in which the discussion of ethics is often presented in the literature: a 'grab bag of empirical studies'. The main point of Ciulla's article is to demonstrate how ethics is at the heart of leadership and she does this by firstly examining, albeit briefly, the way ethics has been treated in the leadership literature. She laments not the lack of philosophic writings on ethics, but the way authors expend 'so little energy on researching ethics from any discipline'.

In arguing that authors of leadership studies expend little energy on researching ethics, Ciulla makes an important point. Any attempt to establish a platform of understanding for ethics and leadership by reviewing current thought comes up against the same barrier. Ethics is considered a critical aspect of leadership in many current texts (Yukl, 2002; Northouse, 2003) yet as Yukl states, 'there is considerable disagreement about the appropriate way to define and assess it'.

Ciulla bases much of her discussion on the treatment of ethics in leadership studies around a critique of Joseph Rost's book *Leadership for the Twenty-first Century* (1993) and by doing so is perhaps guilty of the same crime she accuses Rost of. She claims his 'chapter on ethics stands out because of its paucity of references [on ethics]' – her treatment of ethics in leadership is similarly sparse.

How people lead, or importantly, how people should lead has been the purpose of much of the past leadership research and what the resulting models reflect might be seen as the underlying moral commitments of the leader/follower relationship. Hence some theories (eg transformational leadership) where leaders recognize the choice of followers to follow as voluntary are more morally attractive than theories that disregard the input of followers. As Rost argues, 'the leadership process is ethical if the people in the relationship (leaders and followers) freely agree that the intended changes fairly reflect their mutual purposes'.

Ciulla (as we have seen) turns to the Hitler problem to help locate the role of ethics in understanding leadership: 'Was Hitler a leader?' Under morally unattractive definitions (the 'great man' and 'trait' theories) he was a leader, but under more morally attractive theories he wouldn't be seen as a leader, just a tyrant or head of state. The ethical question that needs to be asked here is 'Who decides what is morally attractive or not?'

This is where ethics in leadership comes in. The terms 'ethical' and 'moral' can be used interchangeably to refer to rules of proper conduct and, because they are inevitably linked to values, they can be described as referring to behaviours about which society holds certain values. Thus, the Hitler problem would be better answered through a consideration of ethical leadership.

So to the central tenet of Ciulla's conceptualizing about leadership. We shouldn't be concerned with 'the definition of leadership' but we should be asking 'what is *good* leadership?' That is, 'good' in the sense of morally good and technically good or effective. A good leader is someone who is effective and ethical. It might be fairly easy to judge if a leader is effective (aims and outcomes) but much more difficult to judge if they are ethical.

As Ciulla states, 'the trouble with existing leadership research is that few studies investigate both senses of good'. Implicit in many of the theories proposed over the years is the ethical question of whether leaders are more effective when they are morally good (a relationship focus, eg consideration for people) or when they are technically good (a task orientation). Unfortunately, research doesn't give a conclusive answer, and a key point of Ciulla's thesis is that 'when researchers are not explicit about their ethical commitments' we can never really address the issue of whether being kind and considerate of other people is essential for the effective leadership of organizations.

Common areas where ethical issues arise for business leaders (Kokemuller)

There is always a need to balance health and safety of the workforce with financial gain and control of costs. Managers are often faced with difficult decisions when their success is judged on the basis of their ability to meet financial performance targets. For example, there might be pressure on them to take risks by acting unethically and cutting corners on safety equipment and training in order to save money and reduce costs.

With the advent of rapidly-changing uses of technology, a leader is faced with the dilemma of 'is it ethical to monitor all online use of computers and in particular e-mail communication from work accounts?' The dilemma is that of balancing workers' privacy and freedom against the use of technology for legitimate business reasons.

The need to be transparent for open, honest and accurate reporting of organizational financial reports is an ethical concern, as is the need for transparency in communicating internal company messages honestly. Being caught in a lie or avoiding full disclosure of issues that might affect employees' jobs and careers often leads to disaster. However, being totally open and honest might harm business survival if competitors can access this data, so when, if ever, is it ethical to withhold information or lie?

Non-discriminatory practices concerning fairness at work such as equal pay and benefits are required under employment legislation and might be seen as morally correct. However, this type of policy can lead to higher cost of labour and ineffective use of resources, so is it ethically acceptable to pay people at different rates? Managing the need to be non-discriminatory in, for example, recruitment and promotion practice might lead to higher costs for diversity management training, costs that smaller companies might not be able to handle. So how do leaders approach such issues?

How do you resolve an ethical dilemma?

Decisions (or choices) may be based on two sorts of theories (introduced earlier) pertaining to ethics when discussing moral problems or dilemmas. The first focuses on the practical consequences of what you do: a teleological theory of ethics. It holds an action as morally right if it will produce the greatest possible balance of good over evil. The consequences of the act determine its value and actions acquire moral status from the consequences that result from actions. The second approach – a deontological theory of ethics – asks you to think about the actions you might be considering and claims that some actions are morally wrong. That is, that actions have moral value.

Teleological thinking focuses on the ethical principal of *utilitarianism* and the claim that the moral concern of actions should depend on the extent to which actions hurt or help individuals, ie the greatest good for the greatest number.

An often-cited example of the utilitarian approach concerns the case of the leader of a group of tourists visiting a cave on the coast. A pregnant woman becomes stuck in the mouth of the cave. With high tide rapidly approaching, unless she is unstuck, everyone will drown, except the woman, whose head is out of the cave. Unlikely as it sounds, someone has with them a stick of dynamite. There seems no quick way of freeing the woman without using the explosive, which will kill her. If they don't use it everyone else will drown. What should you do?

The argument is that you consider your options in terms of who will benefit by what you do. Who will be harmed? And what kind of harm and benefit are you talking about? Choose the option that produces the best mix of benefit over harm, in consideration of the long- and short-term consequences.

Deontological thinking suggests that some actions are inherently good, for example telling the truth, respecting others' rights and keeping confidences. Other actions are seen as bad, eg theft, manipulation and exploiting others.

Immanuel Kant, typifies deontological thought through his idea of the fundamental moral law: the categorical imperative. At the risk of oversimplification, this suggests a leader needs to act in such a way that you always (and at the same time) treat people as an end and never simply as a means to that end. People are entitled to freedom to control their own lives (ends) and are not to be deceived or manipulated as something the leader can use for their own purposes (means) without consent.

Your manager doesn't yet know that someone in your team has made a mistake which could prove costly and that you are working hard to correct. However, if you don't tell your boss about it, you will miss an important deadline. If you do tell your boss you will be blamed for the mistake and punished. Do you tell? And if you do, do you put the blame on your subordinate?

Here the argument is that as a leader you would consider how the possible actions stack up against basic moral principles such as being honest, respecting equality and other people's basic rights and recognizing individuals' vulnerability. You would choose the least problematic action.

Your organization procedures are very clear on how to do your job as a manager. However, you think you know a different and 'better' way that can help you improve your perceived productivity. If you use this new way of working (and don't adhere to the rules of the organization) you will improve your results. So what do you do?

Where does this leave the leader? While the idea of considering practical consequences and at the same time giving attention to the inherent moral value of actions may seem theoretically conflicting, the two perspectives give a practical basis upon which a leader may start to determine their choice in order to resolve an ethical dilemma.

Theme 4: Ethics, resilience and sustainability

In this final theme we will look at some of the relationships between ethics, resilience and sustainability. To us organizational resilience refers to any primary, secondary or tertiary organizations with the ability to recover from difficult business conditions quickly or endure a difficult business environment.

We feel that sustainability refers to any primary, secondary and tertiary organization that is resilient and that balances all of the various organizational issues needed to survive over a longer term. These include:

- employing as many talented people as the organization can afford;
- using the minimum natural resources needed without affecting any products' fitness for purpose;
- trying to reach new customers without losing existing ones.

Through time, experience and research we have identified some of the ethical factors that can lead to resilience and sustainability. While there are others, we have concluded that there are at least six critical factors to this occurring and wish to share them with you. These factors are:

- The organizational culture is one that:
  - does not encourage blame; nor
  - promotes punishment for no reason; and
  - is one where mistakes are viewed as an opportunity to learn.
- Ethical behaviours from leaders and managers.
- Ethical supplier relationships.
- Ethical customer relationships.
- Ethical working time factors.
- Ethical environmental management.

Organizational culture

A by-product of being human, arguably, is the propensity to make mistakes. Mistakes happen in our home and elsewhere in our personal life. Because we do not stop being human at work, perhaps we all need to accept that mistakes will happen there too. To look at the nature of a mistake and how it might impact on an organization, it might help to begin with a view or definition of the term. The Online Oxford Dictionary defines a mistake as 'an act or judgement that is misguided or wrong'. So, for example, a person in work who as a one-off (or rarely) acts irresponsibly through a lack of knowledge, experience, understanding or skills may be misguided and therefore be making a mistake. But if, after a mistake was pointed out, an opportunity to learn was offered and taken, yet that mistake was repeated, we now see a deliberate personal choice taken which in no way can be thought of as a mistake. By repeating mistakes the overall risk of harm (both to stakeholders and the organization) is increased. By increasing risk the likelihood of damage increases, which in turn can impact upon the general ability of the organization to be resilient. However, practices like this may be something the organizational culture endorses, even encourages. This can be a far more dangerous situation because while a single person might wreak havoc, culture reaches across the whole of the organization and a culture that reduces effective risk management arguably cannot be thought of as one that seeks resilience and sustainability.

In terms of what we often see, mistakes often create feelings of guilt, disappointment, anger and frustration. In organizations where low ethical behaviours can be found (ie there is little real ethical activity or it is 'token') these feelings are often replaced with acts of self-preservation. Let's now explore a sequence of events that might happen when the organizational culture is one where attitudes and behaviours towards mistakes may not be too ethical. We can also infer how this may impact upon individual and organizational resilience.

1 *Someone makes a mistake.*

   The mistake may be minor or serious – either way people may feel embarrassed, which can affect their performance and ability to 'bounce back'. Even if the mistake is genuine (an unrepeated act, little if any harm occurred and the person who made the mistake acted in good faith), if no opportunity to learn and develop exists, the likelihood is that further mistakes will occur which may be punished in some way.

2 *Any punishment that follows can generate anger, lower levels of trust and generate fear, especially if punishment is highly disproportionate.*

   Fear might lead to people covering up other mistakes (even minor ones) and even lead to interpersonal and inter-team rivalry and hostility. A hostile working environment might affect communication.

Using the Osgood-Schramm model of communication (Bhatnagar and Bhatnagar, 2012) we may see a reduction in the frequency of message transmissions, a lack of content in the message, bias from the sender, bias from the receiver of the message, misperception of message intonation, a reduced resolve to accurately re-code a message and reduced frequency of communication feedback.

It seems reasonable therefore to suggest that communication bottlenecks will emerge which may impact upon supplier, customer and other stakeholder relationships. Bottlenecks of communication therefore may reduce the ability to interpret and respond swiftly to information, perhaps a core requirement in a resilient organization.

3 *Talent becomes suppressed.*
People who can help the organization eliminate or clear bottlenecks, whether they are informational, operational or due to some other reason, can become de-motivated, especially when levels of trust are low. A culture where blame is the order of the day can create the attitude of 'why should I help – if I make a mistake I will only get punished?'

4 *At the earliest opportunity people might seek alternative employment.*
Those able to and who are frustrated or who may be fearful of the organizational culture might look for somewhere else to work at the earliest opportunity. They might even spend organizational resources seeking alternate employment opportunities. In a different organization, where the organizational culture is more in line with their own values, they will take with them essential experience and knowledge that may be in short supply. An environment where not only people are happier, able to make genuine mistakes without any retribution and where career advancement opportunities exist might increase the new organization's competitive advantage.

The organization left behind, because of any reputation as an unethical employer they may have, needs to replace the talent it lost. This may prove difficult and time consuming, averting efforts probably better used elsewhere and can be very costly. All of this reduces any competitive advantage they had through their people, reducing the organization's ability to be resilient.

5 *Those left behind may be forced to or feel they have to take on board the roles and responsibilities of those leaving.*

For a short period of time, taking on board other people's workloads may work. But if the organization chooses not to recruit for a few months (a common practice aimed at reducing the total salary bill) people can become fatigued, commitment can significantly reduce and apathy can encroach. Despite any mental toughness, there comes a point when it just is not possible:

● to work harder;

● to be more personally resilient;

● to help the organization become more resilient as a whole; and

● to become or remain sustainable.

All of this might be avoided simply through taking an ethical stance of 'no blame and no punishment' when a mistake occurs.

Ethical behaviours from leaders and managers

If you looked at personal resilience and were asked to write down a list of essential behaviours and attributes that resilient leaders and managers need to use, what would you include? When we have asked people this very question, we come across these examples on a regular basis:

● engaging well with others from all walks of life, without causing offence;

● communicating well;

● demonstrating trust in other people;

● not coercing or bullying people in order to ensure targets are met;

● not chastising people in front of others or when it is not otherwise appropriate (eg they have done no wrong);

● act with integrity: honestly, fairly and with benevolence.

As these can also be described as ethical behaviours, could we propose 'act ethically and you can become resilient'? There is some recent research carried out by the Institute of Leadership and Management (2013) along with Business in the Community that might support this view. In their report over 60 per cent of those interviewed said they had been asked to do something against their own personal values. Close to 20 per cent were asked to break specific industry regulations and nearly 10 per cent were asked in some way to break the law.

While this gives us some solid evidence of which unethical practices people are faced with, page 2 of the report provides much-needed impact data – showing what happens as a result of unethical activity, namely:

> One in ten managers (10 per cent) say they have left their jobs as a result of being asked to do something at work that made them feel uncomfortable.

If you are an HR manager, board member or other senior manager please ask yourself these two questions:

1 Could your organization function and become or continue to be resilient if 10 per cent of your first line, middle and senior personnel left?

2 Do you have contingency arrangements in case they all leave at once?

Very few organizations in our experience can exist with a 10 per cent loss in senior staff for over six months. In addition, only a handful of organizations have a contingency plan that covers such an eventuality. Hopefully this shows just some of the relationships that exist between ethical behaviour, organizational culture and resilience.

Ethical supplier relationships

One of the key essentials, in our experience, when building and maintaining resilience and sustainability is to have an ethical supply chain. Without this we feel no organization will ever achieve resilience. Large and global corporations, in particular, buy and sell to the global marketplace. Many outsource work or organizations located in developing countries as the cost of labour there is often lower and the need to comply with legislation can be cheaper. Some argue that without doing this you, your friends and others may have difficulty in affording goods.

Building an effective supply chain can take a long time and global brands often scout for future outsource partners all around the world, an outsource partner being an organization that provides goods, services or finished products to a global brand. While outsourcing overseas might be financially advantageous, a set of dilemmas exist that have the propensity to have a long-lasting and more far-reaching effect than we may have previously covered. These particular dilemmas may be emotive in nature, be difficult to resolve and be resource intensive. One of the most often seen dilemmas relates to outsource partners using child labour. Many people, especially here in the West, are opposed in principle to child labour. According to the United Nations Convention on the Rights of the Child (UNCRC), a child is defined as any boy or girl under the age of 18. According to the United Nations International Children's Emergency Fund (UNICEF), all United Nations member states except for the United States and Somalia have approved the Convention. It came into force here in the United Kingdom in 1991 and says all children have:

- the right to a childhood (including protection from harm);
- the right to be educated (including all girls and boys completing primary school);
- the right to be healthy (including having clean water, nutritious food and medical care);
- the right to be treated fairly (including changing laws and practices that are unfair on children);
- the right to be heard (including considering children's views).

So providing that children are protected, have access to education and so on, it can be proposed that child labour per se is lawful and 'not wrong', ie it is ethical. Where, arguably, it becomes 'wrong' (unethical) is when the caveats (in brackets above) are not adhered to.

It can become problematical for organizations when these caveats are breached. Media reach from interested individuals as well as relatively small enterprises can be extensive through using cloud-based video-sharing websites. If international media corporations pick up on this activity, large global players who outsource may be faced with a barrage of well-meaning complaints through social media channels. The resources needed to acknowledge interest and deal with what might be called negative publicity has spawned a new industry all in itself. Cloud-based web platforms such as Engagor, Radian 6 and others enable Twitter messages that refer to a specific company name or issue to be identified and replied to quickly. Some people may say the intention is to draw negative comments away from the public arena to a more personal arena, thus mitigating any public relations difficulties.

Apart from any negative effects on public relations resulting from using child labour, organizations may also be faced with:

- reduced sales;
- damaged relationships with strategic partners who either have ethical values or do not want any association with an organization associated with unethical activities;
- stopped or delayed investment from those investment houses with strong ethical policies.

If you were at the helm of a large organization, what do you feel would be a reasonable response if you found out an overseas supplier employed child labour? One response is outlined in an article written by Malcolm Moore in 2010. In this article Moore states:

> At least eleven 15-year-old children were discovered to be working last year in three factories which supply Apple.

Apple of course being the giant corporation based in California in the United States. Moore makes no assertion that children were harmed or at risk from harm and goes on to say that 'Apple have (subsequently) said child workers are now no longer being used, or are no longer underage'. As the head of a large organization, you may feel this is possibly an appropriate response from Apple. So which ethical dilemmas are obvious and which ones are not?

First, in this case, an obvious one is how the culture of China is different from that of the United States. In China child labour is common, especially in rural areas, in fact it can be said to be the norm. Therefore what, if any, right does a US (or any other Western) culture have to say 'the Chinese culture, in respect of using child labour, is wrong'? Save the Children looked at children's own views on the effects of work – not specifically in China, but possibly reflective of Chinese children's views. This gives us a balanced and unique insight into those affected by ethical dilemmas and subsequent decisions. Positive effects that were given by children included learning about responsibility and money, learning how to support their family, learning to communicate with other people and being helped to behave with assurance. Negative effects included: they could start liking money too much and not go to school, they may fall under the influence of bad people and self-esteem can be damaged. What we see is that children are able to recognize danger but also see benefits from work.

Perhaps what this really indicates, from a business ethics and UNCRC perspective, is that outsource partners might need a mixture of support from Western global brands (eg the provision of local schools and heath care) and monitoring (to ensure the previously mentioned caveats are not breached). But what might seem a straightforward solution to a dilemma (how can we continue outsourcing and protect children?) can be riddled with other ethical dilemmas. So anything that is provided must be well thought through.

For example, take an American company who sets up a local school in India and resources it with American teachers, using American learning standards, American learning materials and high-tech learning tools. English is the taught language medium. An Indian child may have a good command of English. But shouldn't the learning meet the needs of Indian individuals, Indian society and the Indian nation as a whole? This means providing access to Indian qualifications and learning about Indian society, along with mathematics, the world we live in and so on. How can this occur when American methods are employed? However well intentioned, the risk of imposing American societal norms and attitudes exists. Is this ethical?

Three issues have recently been highlighted. First, in the face of unethical practice, what right does another culture have to enforce its culture on another? Second, when some action is needed by a global brand, what might seem a straightforward and right thing to do might create other ethical problems. The third issue we wish to highlight is that of indirectly penalizing individuals for a problem not of their creation. Most people would say that it is right when a child labour problem occurs to fully investigate it and take appropriate action. But what if, in the supplier agreement, a contractual clause means all payments to the supply partner are suspended 'pending investigation'? This can seriously affect the cash flow of that outsource partner.

What if the supplier genuinely cannot then afford to pay employees their wages? They and their families will suffer if there is no other work or no welfare system exists. In addition to that, the suppliers to the supplier partner will have no work – meaning poverty may significantly worsen. What this serves to remind us is that any unethical action the supply partner takes can have serious repercussions for the wider business and social communities. What it also forces us to consider is if (as a global purchaser) you sought another local supplier in order to mitigate any effect upon the supply of your goods: there may be no one there. They may have liquidated from you suspending payments to what was your main partner. Also, those who may still be able to supply you may be very wary to contract with you in case the same thing happened to them. This clearly affects an organization's ability to be resilient.

Ethical customer relationships

It can take a long time to build a strong, resilient organization and brand. But this can be almost destroyed in a relatively short time if the organization starts to behave unethically in the eyes of its actual and potential customers. Common examples of how organizations can act unethically to customers include:

- enticing customers with adverts that they know contain misleading information;
- adverts that some might find offensive;

- offering discounts to some people in one geographical location but not others;
- harassing customers to purchase warranty policies that are of little or no value.

When building a brand, an organization wants customers to be able to 'trust' what the brand and products can do for them. That trust can easily be broken, not only as outlined in the four points above but also by how an organization deals or doesn't deal with concerns and complaints. Some of the unethical behaviours sometimes seen include:

- not actually listening to customers;
- being quick to dismiss their concerns;
- being offensive or rude to the customer.

As we mentioned earlier, everyone can make a mistake – that could be call handlers, salespeople, technical support, credit controllers, others within the organization and of course the customer. A customer, for example, might not have asked the right questions of a salesperson and bought the wrong product. But by treating the customer with respect, genuinely listening to their views and offering a reasonable way forward and not blaming anyone (which are all ethical behaviours) you achieve three things.

1 You increase the probability that customer trust can be retained.
2 Customers will possibly continue to buy from you.
3 Customers might tell their friends and work colleagues what great service they received.

We hope this is encouraging you to ask 'the ethical behaviours here are not being rude, being honest and acting with integrity, aren't they?' To which the answer is 'yes' – all three of them. Ethical customer relationships cannot exist, in our experience, without all three being present. But there is one factor not yet mentioned and that is that relationship building is a two-way process, the pace of which cannot be dictated by one party. By doing all of this, the possibility of customer dissatisfaction is reduced which helps to maintain your revenue streams. If your organization doesn't have a steady revenue stream, can it be resilient?

Ethical working time factors

Since 2008, many organizations have raced to pare down costs incurred from salaries, resulting in very high job losses, with some industries being affected more than others. Here in the United Kingdom around 180,000 people were made redundant between August and October 2008, 228,000 between September and November 2008 and 263,000 between October and December 2008 (Office for National Statistics, 2013). For the same three periods, vacancies reduced from 556,000, to 520,000 to 489,000. Like most other countries the United Kingdom entered a deep recession.

While the economic situation might now be improving, many organizations have continued to operate with a reduced workforce. These organizations often rely on people taking paid overtime or taking work home with them, finishing it in their own time for no financial payment. There is evidence that working long hours damages health and we propose that not only is this unethical, but it can reduce personal resilience and with that organizational resilience and also the ability to be sustainable.

For example, Van der Hulst (2003) found after reviewing the works of several health researchers around the world that long working hours were associated with cardiovascular disease, diabetes and immunology changes. Immunology changes can, in some circumstances, lead to a reduced ability to fight cancer cells. In addition to this, an article published by the NHS (2012) showed that of over 2,000 people surveyed, 66 of them had experienced a major depressive episode (MDE). This is equivalent to a rate of just over 3 per cent. The researchers then looked at the relationship between the actual length of time someone worked and compared this to the possibility of an MDE occurring. They found that people working between 11 to 12 hours a day were 2.52 times more likely to experience at least one MDE than colleagues working 7 to 8 hours a day.

So reducing employee numbers, leading to long working hours, clearly can affect both the physical and mental health of people. If people become unwell they may need long-term leave to recover, which places an added burden on a resource-stretched healthcare service as well as on the family and friends of the person who has become ill. This can lead to placing more work pressures on those left behind or insufficient human resources for the organization to function, even when times are not tough.

Ethical environmental management

One of the biggest ethical issues that must be addressed, particularly to ensure the organization is sustainable, is our attitude and behaviour towards this planet. As a result of carbon dioxide emissions, use of chlorofluorocarbons (CFCs), glacial melt and other factors, land and sea temperatures are rising. This will, in less than 10 years' time, impact upon our ability to grow food and from that the price of food will increase. Employers could end up being forced to give high pay rises just to ensure their workforce is able to live. Practices such as over-fishing could result in fishing fleets being almost permanently tied up and people being out of work as stocks attempt to recover. This could increase the total welfare payment bill and may result in increasing business taxation, which may affect the ability to be resilient.

Continued over-use of fossil fuels will increase carbon dioxide emissions; and from that will result an increase in acid rain. This will affect the ability to grow wood and other vegetation, leaving farming and sea-based industries at risk of closure. It also means that the environmental clean-up costs will increase.

Organizations can take small but high-impact steps now to slow down the pace of these harmful changes, perhaps even giving us time to develop technologies to help address a key environmental ethical dilemma (and also a key business ethical dilemma). That is how to balance our need for energy against what the planet can sustainably provide.

One of these small steps could be to use video conferencing to reduce the need for travelling to meetings. To show the value of doing this, in 2012 a large organization with two sites, one site in London and the other in the West Midlands, asked us to help them look into this very issue. Every month a team meeting was held, one month in London, the next month in the West Midlands. By using a videoconference solution (such as Citrix Online Partnership) travel costs were eliminated completely. Downtime (travelling to and from meetings) was eliminated too. In total, when adding travel costs and staff downtime costs together, the financial saving for this one meeting before including the cost of the videoconference was £800. On top of this, somewhere in the region of 1,000 travel miles did not need to be driven (5 cars at 200 miles each), reducing carbon dioxide emissions. If more organizations did this, just imagine the energy and other costs an organization could save, helping to improve its profits and contributing to greater resilience.

There are many other ways organizations can be more environmentally effective, but there is little doubt that the ethics of environmentalism plus the other five ethical factors referred to in this theme can help organizations gain a long-term competitive edge. It is this long-term competitive edge that we argue contributes to resilience and sustainability.

Conclusions

We have seen that a dilemma can be thought of as a hard-to-resolve but important issue that every leader and manager faces in the workplace.

Ethical dilemmas are often hard to resolve and often involve life-affecting choices, making decision making tough. It is likely that ethical dilemmas often arise because of a perceived need for action thought to be in the best 'short-term' economic interests of an organization. This can create a conflict in individuals who feel their values and ethical practices may be better than that of the organization. We drew upon research by the Institute of Leadership and Management in support of this. For most managers, ethics is likely to be seen as common sense, not requiring any formal engagement with ethical theories. We however argue this is not the case because resolving an ethical dilemma might be said to involve four key things:

1 Being able to understand what people actually mean when they talk about a problem relating to ethics.

2 Knowing all the various things that may trigger certain behavioural patterns.

3 Being able to objectively work out what people actually did (that caused any unethical actions).

4 Working out how it really impacted upon people, society and the organization.

Without knowing and understanding how things happen and why, managers will never be able to fully manage an ethical dilemma or problem. This knowledge and appreciation includes engaging with ethical theory, the real benefit of which might be that managers and leaders are stronger in their beliefs about ethical practice, helping them to make more informed 'hard' business decisions.

A key focus for sustainable business in current times is the need for organizations to be seen as socially responsible. By thinking, engaging with and reflecting on the nature and practice of ethics, our contention is that managers will be able to better balance all the factors needed for long-term survival.

We outlined a small framework of essential ethical factors in the last theme that we proposed must exist for any organization to be resilient and when resilience has been achieved, to maintain resilience. These factors also help to achieve sustainability. Perhaps you could compare the content with your organization's ethical performance and improve?

In closing, a brief note on the future. There are great strides being taken by many organizations to improve their ethical performance and they must be commended. There are also supportive organizations that can help people learn about ethics which we propose enhances personal resilience and through that contributes to organizational resilience. We feel the biggest future business threat is environmental and mankind's attitude has made things worse. In our view, environmental ethics must take centre stage.

References

Bhatnagar, N and Bhatnagar, M (2012) *Effective Communication and Soft Skills: Strategies for success*, Dorling Kindersley, India

Bowie, R and Frye, J (2008) *AQA Religious Studies: Ethics*, Nelson Thornes, London

Burns, J M (1978) *Leadership*, Harper & Row, New York

Ciulla, J B (1995) Leadership ethics: Mapping the territory, *Business Ethics Quarterly*, 5(1) pp 5–28

Ciulla, J B (2003) *The Ethics of Leadership*, Thompson/Wadsworth, Belmont, CA

Copp, D ed (2007) *The Oxford Dictionary of Ethical Theory*, Oxford University Press, Oxford

dalla Costa, J (1998) *The Ethical Imperative: Why moral leadership is good business*, Basic Books

Engagor [accessed 26 March 2013] Home page [Online] https://engagor.com

Greenleaf, R (1973). *The Servant as Leader*, John Wiley, Chicester

Heifetz, R A (1994) *Leadership Without Easy Answers*, Harvard University Press, Boston

Institute of Leadership and Management (2013) *Added values: The importance of ethical leadership* [Online] http://bit.ly/19MKuuJ

Jackson, R (2013) Can you bank ethically in Britain? *Money Wise* [Online] http://www.moneywise.co.uk/banking-saving/current-accounts/can-you-bank-ethically-britain

Kimmel, A J (1988) *Ethics and Values in Applied Social Research*, Sage, London

Kokemuller, N [accessed 26 March 2014] *Small Business Chronicle* [Online] http://smallbusiness.chron.com/common-types-ethical-issues-within-organizations-15238.html

Learning for Business [accessed 26 March 2014] LFB: Citrix Online Partnership [Online] http://bit.ly/103itcX

Moore, M (2010) Apple admits using child labour, *The Telegraph* [Online] http://www.telegraph.co.uk/technology/apple/7330986/Apple-admits-using-child-labour.html

NHS (2012) Working long hours 'linked to depression', January 26 2012, *NHS News* [Online] http://www.nhs.uk/news/2012/01January/Pages/overtime-work-hours-depression.aspx

Northouse, P (2003) *Leadership 3rd ed*, Sage, Thousand Oaks

Nursing and Midwives Council (2008) The code: Standards of conduct, performance and ethics for nurses and midwives, *Nursing and Midwives*

Council [Online] http://www.nmc-uk.org/Publications/Standards/The-code/ Introduction

ONS (2013) Labour Market Statistics, December 2013, Statistical Bulletin, Office for National Statistics [Online] http://www.ons.gov.uk/ons/dcp171778_338181. pdf

Rachels, J and Rachels, S (2009) *The Elements of Moral Philosophy*, McGraw-Hill, New York

Rost, J C (1993) *Leadership for the Twenty-first Century*, Praeger, Westport, CT

Sander-Staudt, M [accessed 22 May 2014] Care ethics, *Internet Encyclopaedia of Philosophy* [Online] http://www.iep.utm.edu/care-eth/

Salesforce Marketing Cloud [accessed 26 March 2013] Radian 6 [Online] http:// www.salesforcemarketingcloud.com/

Save the Children [accessed 26 March 2014] *Position on Children and Work* [Online] http://resourcecentre.savethechildren.se/sites/default/files/ documents/3227.pdf

The Online Oxford Dictionary [Online] http://www.oxforddictionaries.com/ definition/english/mistake

UNICEF UK [accessed 26 March 2014] UN Convention on the Rights of the Child [Online] http://www.unicef.org.uk/crc?gclid=CJqKvK-VprwCFZHJtAod-G AAaA&sissr=1

Van der Hulst, M (2003) Long work hours and health, *Scandinavian Journal of Work, Environment & Health*, **29**(3) pp 171–188

Yukl, G (2002) *Leadership in Organizations 5th ed.*, Prentice Hall, Upper Saddle River

Big data, big business
Insight, influence and the IT revolution – an illustration

ANDREW CUTHBERT

*T*his chapter is not intended to be a comprehensive examination of the impact of IT on the world of the future. As shown elsewhere in the book, there is a bewildering variety of changes occurring and dealing with these requires individuals and organizations to understand what leadership must look like in the future, building on trust, authenticity and integrity and, most importantly, developing a positive type of resilience.

For many, if not most, when you speak about change they immediately default to imagining it is all about IT. This is not surprising. Most see it every day and can see how it changes their lives. However, most have only a cursory awareness of the implications of new technology.

This chapter is included because looking at the challenges of the 21st century must include IT. We can't ignore it… but how best to include it? This chapter looks at one (tiny) slice of that area of change but takes the opportunity to explore it in a way that hopefully provokes thinking and shows the reader how to see the layers of meaning that sit behind that slice.

Within the next ten years or so the business world is likely to be completely transformed. We don't know the precise speed of change: external factors and the visions of individuals and organizations will determine that. Nor do we know exactly what the outcomes themselves will look like. But that they will happen is not in doubt. More importantly, change is not just inevitable, it's largely predictable too – if, as Daniel Kahneman expounds in *Thinking, Fast and Slow* (2011), we take time to look for the signs.

In the world of IT, a great example of this pending transformation is in the drive for big data, which will cause major shifts in the economic, social and commercial arenas.

As an analyst, I know that the complex patterns present in data don't just provide insights within a single vertical or field. Those insights have the potential to extend and extend, like ripples on a pool.

Here is an example with a socioeconomic aspect. Research carried out by Geraint Griffiths (2007), Chair of the Schoolvision initiative, has shown that eye conditions not picked up in current school eye exams can affect a young person's ability to read. This in turn can affect that person's self-confidence, academic outcomes and future career focus. In this cascade scenario, we see a young person growing up with self-limited horizons, perhaps becoming involved in anti-social behaviour, substance abuse, criminality, even prison. In short, a life wasted and an economic cost to bear at every misstep.

From the specifics of this example we can see an argument for both more robust eye-testing in schools and more robust training for opticians on the eye conditions in question. Moreover, the low cost of this, coupled with the potentially far-reaching significance of correcting the condition for the child in question help make this data valuable – indeed essential.

However, it can be a lifetime's work to bring about the kind of step-change Griffiths' research calls for. So, how do we move from this cumulative, incremental process to scalable, meaningful innovation that offers real commercial impact?

Technology – and specifically information technology – provides some answers. It is of course changing many aspects of the way we now live and work. People entering the job market today are doing so with very different expectations from those only a generation ago. This has implications for the way that organizations work with, manage and lead their most important resource: their people.

In science we see progress driven by new methods of data capture, analysis and synthesis, sharing and processing. Yet psychometrics, which has vast opportunities for cross-vertical influence, remains almost wholly untapped. This sleeping giant can bring new, rich data streams into play, enabling much more effective decision-making, corporate planning, market understanding and systems delivery. In other words, harnessing the power of the Information Age.

Big data and the fifth 'V'

Many data scientists speak of the famous 'four Vs': volume, velocity, variety and variability. However, it is becoming increasingly obvious that there exists a fifth variable: vertical. Traditionally, big data has been a tool for corporate sales forces to cross-analyse concepts within businesses and, at most, within a given vertical. The true potential of big data is that it has the potential for a company, or indeed sector, to hold influence and form an advantage over a range of other areas.

As an obvious example, if we teach those in our education system preventative ways of improving health then, as a direct and simultaneous result, we hypothetically will have fewer accidents. In the same way, if we create a job process that requires individuals to be able to read or write, then the motivation and need of an individual in the education system to learn these skills would increase.

This fifth V, the connection between verticals, can be seen as critical to understanding how data can really bring about benefit and deliver great opportunity for business – not least because it is currently a widely uncontested market space.

From insight to influence: Steve Jobs v Silicon Valley

In the early part of Steve Jobs' career, he made a number of key insights, and one that was to prove crucial in terms of influence: market size. Unlike his partner Steve Wozniak, Jobs perceived market size as critical. He had the vision to take the computer out of its hitherto technical environment and bring it into the home. And that changed everything.

In an interview (Morrow, 1995) while at NeXT Computing (which he founded after his first departure from Apple), Jobs spoke about the market issue. His fellow geeks at the Homebrew Computer Club in Silicon Valley saw the personal computer – the hardware – as something solely for people like them. Jobs, however, knew that the future was not in the hands of programmers but of consumers.

This understanding led to the first commercially-viable software products for home use. The early spreadsheets emerged for business and home use, along with the first games. New, sector-defining and design-led devices such as the iMac, iPod, iPhone and iPad (and their competitors) began to arrive and kept arriving. A new market evolved and kept evolving.

Several factors helped Apple to outcompete others: its much-celebrated design ethos, its brilliant marketing – but also its data strategy. The way its devices stored, shared and connected data in a consumer-friendly way was so innovative, intuitive and resonant that it flung open wide the doors. For example, the interactive, touch-sensitive iPad, used in conjunction with social media, has become a device for engagement. Rather than a non-committed consumer using a PC once a month, the iPad user will interact with the device often for many hours a day – accessing, storing, sharing and delivering valuable data.

The economics of data: An example and a comparison

The App Store concept, delivered first via the iPhone, was a commercial revolution like no other. With a captive audience on devices, apps became the revenue model of personalization and customization.

Consider then this scenario drawn from the applied use of psychometrics.

Imagine that a person with an interest in changing perceptions of the field and with friends of a similar age sets up a small business. The business looks at a single application – for the sake of argument, based on the personality trait of creative thinking. Let's also say that by happy accident they deploy their software on the App Store and get picked up to be distributed globally, hence amassing the profiles of 10,000,000 participants. And let's then say that a certain big data firm is willing to pay handsomely for each record. Since the users who signed up are an interesting market to them, as is the data held, the organization's potential to grow and make money expands.

Furthermore, the company now spends 90 per cent of its time doing what it does best. It also has created something with a higher barrier to entry and essentially a more sophisticated product. Conversely, at a business level there are fewer staff and therefore lower-risk investment costs. Consequently, the company has a vastly higher value.

Compare this with a traditional business model. Here, the business does not have many cross-vertical peers from which to gain expertise, so becomes restricted to thinking that originates only from its own sector. It therefore misses market opportunities for growth – opportunities the experienced organization could no doubt be much better placed to fill with more passion, wisdom and enthusiasm than its younger, more agile competitor.

A SWOT at a business level might be such as set out in Table 10.1.

TABLE 10.1 Simulation of a SWOT at business level

Company trait	Traditional organization	App-centric organization
Agility	Low	High
Risk	Not mitigated	Mitigated
Staff size	High	Low
Purpose	Academic validity	Commercial validity
Test cost	Charged	Free
Data volume	Low	High
Data export	Secure API	App export
Value origin	Examination	Data
Value proposition	Low	High
Vertical	Single	Cross

There is of course another angle, namely that when organizations grow, their opportunity frameworks change. At a larger size, it becomes clearer that the true value is in owning more of the data so that you can analyse what will be more sophisticated patterns.

This takes us into the realm of social media, the value of these networks and the opportunities they offer us to create unique, niche-value propositions that are both highly beneficial to the end-user and of real commercial interest.

Social networks, social change

Just as Steve Jobs had done, Facebook's Mark Zuckerberg brought some fundamentally new principles to the space. Relationship status was one of these. Facebook evolved in its early form to enable users to share statuses automatically. As it grew, it offered 'friends' the ability to see a 'wall', which would list updates from other connected users. As an example, if I as a user had had a bad day, my friend could post and tell me it would get better. A kind of online therapy therefore became a factor in the early growth of the concept. Relationship status was significant, as when it was changed, others were informed and could now see the impact on a friend whom they possibly didn't meet every day but with whom they could connect every day.

Today, the site's commercial value is enhanced by advertisements – themselves driven by another key innovation: the 'like'. This single idea may have spawned as great a revolution in IT as Einstein's $E = mc^2$ did for physics. To break the like concept down a little, we can understand that the interests we have are things about which we will wish to receive updates. Therefore, to like something and derive an ongoing social connection with it, or to friend someone and again receive regular updates on their circumstances, these things are fundamental within society. However, and significantly, they are innovations in IT.

This new vertical has now transcended traditional communication and, for those who understand it, evolved it to a better place socially and economically.

To frame this, we need to look at how fundamentally our communication methodologies have changed. In the past, for most people an update was a one-to-one event. When we got back from a trip, we rang those closest to us to say we got home safely. This was the nature of communication in real life: family first, wider circle second. The evolution of the social network may have profoundly changed that balance. Updates can now be posted one-to-many, instantly making an individual's wider network more closely aware of their personality and blurring traditional social boundaries on many levels, from work and home to family and friends. Indeed, it is even possible that the traditional family unit is no longer the individual's support network and that this role has shifted to linked online collectives.

So where is the opportunity for business? It is in the fact that due to regulations and terms and conditions around personal information, Facebook does not have an audit trail of certain data streams. As an example, when I like or unlike a page, there is no record of this, simply a record of what I actually like today. At the time of writing, the patterns held within the detail are not recorded – but, crucially, they could be exploited and analysed through well-constructed applications led by psychometricians.

When Facebook first came along, the technical infrastructure was in place to allow for the global distribution that rapidly followed. The consequences of this are still emerging. We can, however, deduce many implications of social organization around the family, work, commerce, society at large, how people engage with each other and perhaps a new area: the permanent online record.

Creating a new God?

A key recent shift in the development of the web has been undoubtedly the ease in which we can now create content. This has, I believe, radically changed how we see our own lives. In our 'Celebrity Age', an individual's life can be turned into spectacle by the creation of data which can be easily followed by others – initially individual fans and then companies as the commercial opportunities expand.

Those opportunities can truly be huge. If we know a photograph, location or an age we can create new commercial opportunities in everything from dating and relationships to job prospecting.

I have argued extensively elsewhere that the identification of social patterns could in a way bring powers perceived to be akin to a god-like influence, allowing individuals to analyse and influence culture, society, game-playing and buying behaviours. And, ultimately, delivering a framework of meaning and significance.

In this way it is likely that as data sources grow and come together, so too will the organizations that can control and analyse. Just like our genetics, our social patterns will shape the future of our world. Our social patterns deliver a greater impact than any other intervention on our lifestyle and life outcomes.

To use one example, there are certain social expectations associated with those who live in underprivileged areas of the community. These stereotypes include, among others, a high level of smoking, recreational drug-taking, participation in anti-social activities – all of which, the actuarial tables tell us, can lead to a shorter lifespan. While our individual genetic code is highly influential on our individual prospects, these external factors hold a high importance – in other words, relating to the old nature versus nurture debate.

Whichever god you believe in, 'He' works in mysterious ways. Likewise those with the all-seeing, all-knowing ability to discern social patterns in sophisticated data – data that is beyond the analytical capacity of the vast majority of our population.

The user profile: Unlocking economic potential

As the web has evolved, software developers have created tools in order to define target markets. This has fed a hunger for a deeper understanding of the user. The profile has become increasingly comprehensive. However, fundamentally, until the social revolution it had not tipped the balance of being more beneficial than offline information.

Now users are beginning to spend more time maintaining profiles and reviewing friends' profiles than browsing commercial sites – and critically, the detail is now being recorded and gathered. The profile has become rich in data, telling us an individual's age, marital status and social relationships, but also consumption patterns, interests, passions and preferences.

If today's user has a huge data profile, tomorrow's will be greater still, fuelled by a lifetime of video and images as well as personal comment on social events, effectively tracking entire life stages.

The place of psychometrics in this vast collage is to help define the profile properly and to provide insight into behaviour. The benefit of this goes beyond direct use in individual profiles to general market behaviour – it enables previously unimaginable levels of sophistication in data-driven decision-making and decision-influencing.

Through personality profiling we can identify expertise and potential, determine whether an individual has confidence, is committed, is open to challenge, is resilient, tenacious, creative, committed, driven – all of which can help us piece together how in control of their situation they feel they are. Are they future leaders, innovators, delegators? This matters because successful leadership can help steer a business through difficult and changing markets, strengthening and growing potential and profitability. Getting it wrong can lead to missed opportunities, even decline.

Furthermore, while different business growth models exist, they tend to share a common premise: the primary factor responsible for driving business growth and company value is customer loyalty. Big data can help organizations to learn more about their customers and therefore formulate better strategies to accelerate business growth.

It is a scalable approach too, from the start-up business to the multinational and macro-economic level. Increasingly, data profiling will in the future begin to show growing patterns of influence. If, for example, we know that perhaps an increase in average confidence increases GDP, then measuring changes in confidence can actually help us guide economies.

Making the connections: Analyst as consumer

So why will the transformation mentioned at the start of this essay begin to happen over the next ten years? In short, the answer is: interconnectedness. Whether technophobe or technophile, a psychometrician will, through necessity, use a mobile device, computer or tablet every day. The new experiences present to the analyst as a consumer bring forward new ideas on using technologies for data capture, data processing, and data analysis.

As big data becomes even bigger and more connected through the evolution of devices, software and networks, it is the analyst's job to protect the citizen and the consumer. We can do this through monitoring and commenting on data patterns and on how certain personality types react to different types of intervention and different types of advertising. As patterns become more sophisticated, so may our data-driven decision making. For example, it is easy to imagine a world whereby the 'watershed' may expand from its original purpose of protecting children from inappropriate TV content into blocking content for certain personality types and sensitivities.

For this degree of change to occur, legal structures will need to continue to evolve in line with business growth and our outlook on how data links together will need to become more sophisticated. Psychometricians have a huge contribution to make in this area, one that will grow based on increased testing and more sophisticated analytical tools. It is absolutely critical that psychometrics expands its influence if big data is to be used ethically as well as economically. Data-driven decision making reduces commercial risk for large organizations, yet fundamentally reduces the illusion of choice for the public. This is something that social scientists must ensure is properly monitored and regulated into the future.

For business, a real step-change can happen when what is necessary meets what is possible. That is where we stand now, at the confluence of two essential, connected and complementary factors.

Finally: Hunting the new Yukon

The consequences of this 'big data' explosion are multiple and complex, but the real outcome of this revolution will be that in years to come we won't regard 'big data' as invasive. Through time we will come to accept that our everyday choices being tracked, tagged and captured is an everyday reality.

However, we won't view this process in terms of a 1984 'Big Brother' intrusion, rather it will be viewed as offering us new solutions to the key issues in our lives, from health to career, love to personal fulfilment.

Make no mistake, as far as big data is concerned the Rubicon has been crossed and it is no longer a question of if, but when, the process will be considered the norm throughout our society. As data transfer speeds increase and devices which help shape the way we see the world become more ubiquitous as technology evolves, we will be providing information on every facet of our lives.

So what are the consequences of ultra-personalization likely to be? A more savvy and demanding consumer is a given, but its impact will also be felt by the entrepreneurs so keen to embrace it: imagine a better educated and self-interested work force – even in some of the most labour-intensive industries this may result in employees who are more difficult to manage, therefore advances will be needed in terms of HR protocols and processes.

It will be even more essential for managers to routinely identify and analyse key staff personality traits, performance strengths and weaknesses based on hard metrics, once traditionally the reserve of academic and highly-qualified assessors.

In essence, managers will need to focus on:

● the individual's ability and mindset;

● the individual's motivation and suitability for the role; and

● the specific training required to maximize individual productivity.

It is not difficult to see how a concept like mental toughness and the ability to measure it at a fine level can be extremely important. This will be true of other personality-based traits too.

While companies will continue to have their own focus, dynamics and culture, one universal need will become the norm: the need to exploit 'big data' to enable personalized training. Organizations that recognize and embrace this new reality will thrive. Those that don't will struggle to compete in an increasingly competitive environment. Essentially, future CEOs will need to be as skilled in psychology as they are in business if they are to maintain effective efficient working environments.

So what then of the immediate future? To get an indication, it is often helpful to see what the smart money is doing. And where technology investment funds are concerned, a shift is taking place away from social media itself towards what underpins it: big data.

Investors are realizing that the information gathered up by social media – Facebook, Tumblr, Twitter and the like – is demographic, behavioural, harvestable gold. And like the prospectors of old, they are making for a new Yukon, the bourgeoning Quantified Self (QS) sector. Initially concerned primarily with life-logging (eg health, diet and exercise apps) the sector is increasingly embracing cutting-edge, almost sci-fi territories such as cataloguing memories and dreams. And data delivers that.

The future may not yet have been written, but it is certainly currently being drafted. It will always be so.

And as for the final picture, Darwin was right. In nature, as in business, it isn't the strongest who survive and prosper. It is those who adapt best to changing circumstances.

In other words, those with the know-how – and the means to use it.

References

Griffiths, G (2007) *In the Hot Seat* [Online, accessed 2 April 2014] http://www.ukoptometry.co.uk/geraint-griffiths-in-the-hot-seat/

Kahneman, D (2011) *Thinking, Fast and Slow*, Penguin, London

Morrow, D (1995) Steve Jobs interview: One-on-one in 1995, *Computerworld.com* [Online] http://tinyurl.com/43yyj3o

Conclusions

DOUG STRYCHARCZYK AND CHARLES ELVIN

I t was not originally intended that this book should have a conclusion. The objective was for it to be thought provoking, which must mean that each reader can draw their own conclusions.

But writing this book and working with the contributing authors has been one of the most powerful learning experiences we have experienced. As ever the challenges have been most illuminating.

We have some conclusions that we briefly set out below.

Our original hypothesis about change is correct. It is, and will be, more dramatic and more fundamental than we have ever known and the general prognosis is that there will be lots more to come – and at an accelerating rate.

The law of unintended consequences is complicating the picture further. As we write in February 2014, the United Kingdom is experiencing its worst floods for a long time. One part of the United Kingdom, Somerset, has hundreds of square miles under water. It is an important agricultural area but is suffering devastation and loss of animal life. One of the reasons for flooding is that it had been decided to stop dredging the waterways. Why? Because a case had been made to protect endangered species whose numbers were dropping as a result of regular dredging.

The law of unintended consequences means that change will often be very unpredictable. The best and most important thing we can do is to learn to deal with it.

It does matter what type of change is happening. To respond positively you need to understand it. But there is also a consensus that irrespective of the type of change there are two fundamental responses needed from organizations if they are to be consistently successful in the future:

- *Evolve leadership style and leadership effectiveness.* The old truths remain. Twentieth-century models are still relevant and useful but the emphasis probably needs to shift from achieving performance as a result of the efforts of a few to achieving performance by engaging with all stakeholders – and some of those stakeholders will be transient. This is where trust and perhaps integrity will come to the fore.

We think that harnessing the creativity of the workforce will also be more and more important.

- *Developing a form of mental toughness.* Not just resilience, which it embraces, but the elements that mental toughness adds to that notion. Especially the preparedness to see challenge and change as an opportunity. To see that it is risk-laden but that this isn't a bad thing. Failure is not terminal – it is simply part of the way life will be.

As we noted at the beginning of the book, there is a Darwinian picture emerging. The organizations that survive will not necessarily be the biggest or strongest. They will, as ever, in all probability, be the most adaptable.

INDEX

(italics indicate a figure or table in the text)

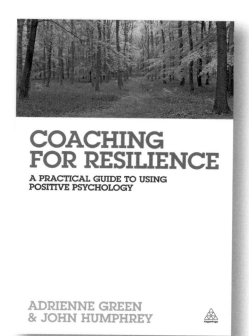